FIVE CENTURIES OF ENGLISH VERSE

IMPRESSIONS

BY

WILLIAM STEBBING

HON. FELLOW OF WORCESTER COLLEGE, OXFORD
AUTHOR OF 'SIR WALTER RALEGH: A BIOGRAPHY'
'TRUTHS OR TRUISMS', PARTS I AND II

IN TWO VOLUMES
VOL. I: CHAUCER TO BURNS

REVISED EDITION
OF
'THE POETS: CHAUCER TO TENNYSON
IMPRESSIONS'

HENRY FROWDE
OXFORD UNIVERSITY PRESS
LONDON, EDINBURGH, GLASGOW
NEW YORK, TORONTO, MELBOURNE, BOMBAY

1913

BY THE SAME AUTHOR

THREE ESSAYS: Posthumous Fame, Toleration, and Brilliant Failures. Cr. 8vo. 6*d*. net.

TRUTHS OR TRUISMS (Part I). 8vo. 4*s*. net; also on Oxford India paper, 6*s*. net.

CONTENTS: The Dead Hand—Necessary Nuisances—How to Quarrel—Counsels of Perfection—Eccentrics—Great—Freedom—Doing Without—Clerical Errors—Courtesy—Self-deception—The Marriage Lottery—A New Law of Libel—Temper—De Jure *v*. De Facto—The Elder Sister—How to Make the Most of Life—Memory—August 29, 1905—Putting the Brain into Commission—Through Whose Glasses?—Cupboards—Insincerities—Popularity.

TRUTHS OR TRUISMS (Part II). 8vo. 4*s*. net; also on Oxford India paper, 6*s*. net.

CONTENTS: Vices we could spare—Our great Prose Poem—Pauperizing—Dinner-table Talk—Concerning War—Atoms—'With one Consent they made Excuse'—The Shadow of Crime—June 22, 1911—Readable—Sophists—Sensations—'Even as this Publican!'—Pleasure in Art—Cruelty—The Ideal Newspaper—'Les grands Hommes Méconnus'—Why-How-and Whom?—'It is more Blessed to Give than to Receive'—Shakespeare's Brother-Dramatists—Inconceivably Incompatible—Man Anticipated—A new Circulating Library.

VOL. I

TABLE OF CONTENTS

	PAGES
INTRODUCTORY	5–8
GEOFFREY CHAUCER	9–21
SIR PHILIP SIDNEY	22–31
EDMUND SPENSER	32–41
WILLIAM SHAKESPEARE	42–55
BEN JONSON	56–64
JOHN FLETCHER	65–70
FRANCIS BEAUMONT	70–72
JOHN DONNE	73–82
GEORGE HERBERT	83–92
RICHARD CRASHAW	93–101
HENRY VAUGHAN	102–112
JOHN MILTON	113–127
WILLIAM BROWNE	128–135
ROBERT HERRICK	136–148
SAMUEL BUTLER	149–154
EDMUND WALLER	155–162
SIR JOHN SUCKLING	163–172
RICHARD LOVELACE	173–180
ABRAHAM COWLEY	181–192
SIR JOHN DENHAM	193–195
ANDREW MARVELL	196–205
JOHN DRYDEN	206–220

CONTENTS

	PAGES
MATTHEW PRIOR	221–227
JONATHAN SWIFT	228–232
ALEXANDER POPE	233–245
JOHN GAY	246–252
EDWARD YOUNG	253–259
JAMES THOMSON	260–268
THOMAS GRAY	269–277
WILLIAM COLLINS	278–285
MARK AKENSIDE	286–292
OLIVER GOLDSMITH	293–300
CHARLES CHURCHILL	301–305
WILLIAM COWPER	306–315
JAMES BEATTIE	316–322
THOMAS CHATTERTON	323–337
GEORGE CRABBE	338–349
WILLIAM BLAKE	350–361
SAMUEL ROGERS	362–370
THOMAS CAMPBELL	371–381
ROBERT BURNS	382–396
INDEX OF FIRST WORDS	397–416

FIVE CENTURIES OF ENGLISH VERSE

CHAUCER—TENNYSON

I MAY be asked how I can have dared to sit in judgement on five centuries of English verse. My answer is that the following pages contain reports rather of my trial before the poets than of them before me. I have sat at their feet ; and they have required me to say how I have understood them ; what I have learnt from them. So long and intimately I have talked with them, from boyhood till the eventide of life, that somehow I felt bound to render them an account of the lessons they have taught me. I thought I should like, while I could, to tell them and myself results of our companionship. To them I owe the best of my education. Whatever intelligence I possess has been fed, refined, and illuminated by them. Hereafter it will not, I trust, be deemed that I have ill repaid my debt to my benefactors by the present attempt to trace and define their magic. Most of them, early and late, have been my old familiar friends and confidants. Pleasant, gracious, fragrant memories exhaled from scores of volumes as I successively took them from their shelves to refresh my acquaintance. If the souls enshrined therein look to the intention, I do not fear that they will resent my audacity at calling the roll.

Each of the company as he passed before me has so entirely occupied my attention that I have seldom been tempted to draw comparisons. No student of poetry can avoid observing that certain writers tower above the rest. I am not speaking of particular poems. A poem may be great by virtue of the prominence of some special quality: sublimity, as Paradise Lost; passion, as the Cenci; holiness, as The Retreat; weirdness, as The Raven; tenderness, as My Mother's Picture; intensity, as The Tiger; atmosphere, as The Eve of St. Agnes; perfection of workmanship, as Shakespeare's Sonnets. The greatness I mean is a property of men as poets. It belongs to the authors of some of the pieces I have instanced, if not to all. I had begun indeed with a plan for confining my survey to some nineteen. Finally, while occasionally I have disregarded exact chronology, and have grouped authors with reference to analogies in literary character, I decided to abandon altogether assessments of comparative merit. All are peers if endued with the true poetic spirit, in whatever quantity. The Great themselves will have more justice done them, standing among their contemporaries, than in an unconnected gathering of luminaries torn from their native orbits.

My apprehension at first was that I might allow myself to contrast, marshal, even to measure out space with regard to rank in the hierarchy. Of such invidious distinctions I had a superstitious dread. I need not have been anxious. Genius beheld in the midst of its own proper and natural circumstances is invested with a halo too bright to permit a gaze once directed upon it to wander elsewhere, till a fresh name has been duly called. The proportion of room occupied in my pages has no positive relation to my estimate of merit; much or little has been requisitioned mainly according to the more or less of difficulty in gauging character and quality.

To one charge I must plead guilty. I confess, but with a sincere sense that I had no alternative. It is true that often in my quotations I have made omissions. My apology is twofold. In the first place, the laws of space forbade quotation in full. In the second, the purpose for which I quoted permitted, and even encouraged, curtailment. My motive in quoting at all was to explain my admiration of a writer or his work; to try to prove the inspiration. When, as of necessity frequently, the inspiration has ceased, the reason for taking up space otherwise required ended too. At the same time I hope to be believed when I declare that abridging was always a grief to me, and a violence to my instinct of propriety. I have constantly felt that I had to stand in a penitent's white sheet after perpetrating such an act, though I had no option but to repeat the offence.

If the effect have ever been to set a poet or his verse in too favourable a light, I accept rebuke so entirely without pain that I exult as at the performance of a good deed. Should, by some mischance, the freedoms taken by me have had the opposite consequence of marring a fine touch, I unfeignedly lament. It has been my object throughout to look for achievement, not for failure; to dwell on beauties, rather than on flaws. Did I suspect that I had been unfair to the least of the seventy-two, whether by omission, or by commission, I should be most unhappy. I have consistently inclined to regard high-, not low-water mark. My single endeavour has been to make clear to myself, if possible, the presence of inspiration. That is the quality I have sought, and endeavoured with all my power to bring to light. I have rejoiced in it when found. For the most part I have gone on my way in silence, when I have not succeeded in discovering it, or have come upon the traces of it faded or tarnished. If I have indicated poets, or poems, where it is wanting, my object has been to concentrate regard upon those it glorifies. Where I have been unable to agree with a favourable contemporary view, I have differed with hesitation and doubt as to my own. Only in two or three instances have I presumed to condemn altogether.

In general, my surmise is that I am more likely to be held guilty of exaggerated admiration than of censorious severity. I expose myself to the charge almost deliberately, and by no means unwillingly. Let anybody commune with, live with, genuine poetry; I defy him to refrain from eulogy, which to others not under the spell will seem fantastic. Inspiration acts upon poets like laughing gas. It has a peculiarity of its own, that mere sympathy communicates the delirium. Perhaps I am rather vain of the liability to a passion of enthusiasm, and invite participation.

GEOFFREY CHAUCER
1340 ?—1400

ALL springtide. Spring in the suddenness of its succession to winter. Frost and nipping winds at one moment, and, the next, fresh leafage and bright flowers. And the fragrance! Nothing in the history of literature precisely matches the phenomenon. Mightier Dante himself, incomparable among moderns till Shakespeare, was not so astoundingly meteoric. His advent was accompanied by a chorus of singers almost as admirable in form, though not in matter. As poetry attended, so it survived, him. Similarly with Shakespeare himself. He had forerunners, rivals, and followers. Geoffrey Chaucer stands alone; for ancient Gower cannot be named in the same breath; he was old before he was young. No teachers existed in this island for 'old famous Chaucer',

> in whose gentle spright
> The pure well-head of poesie did dwell;

the 'loadstarre of our language'; of 'excellencie and wonderful skill in making', as witness Spenser, Lydgate, Kirke. No series of disciples handed on the torch.

The mere mass of his writings is vast; and they were the diversions of an ambassador, soldier, and captive, Controller, perhaps architect, of royal palaces, and a busy courtier, husband of a maid of honour to Queen Philippa—the sister of Catherine Swinford. In addition to the Canterbury Tales and many minor pieces, he produced the Romaunt of the Rose, Troilus and Cressida, The Court of Love, Booke of the Dutchesse, House of Fame, Dream, and Legend of Good Women. It is verse by wholesale, though no excess of food for the imagination to last a people a century and a half, with no better than Skelton's chopped straw till very near the end to replenish the manger. A large amount is chaff for us, both stories and sentiments ; not for the fourteenth century, which knew neither Plutarch, nor much of Greek and Roman mythology. The versions of Seneca's moralities and Cato's are weariness to the bones. But there is metal worth delving for amid the prolixities. What wealth of fancy, for example, in the House of Fame ! that

>   feminyne creature,
> That never formed by nature
> Nas swich another thing y-seye.[1]

What a store of history, so far as it was accessible to his age, there ; in the Legend of Good Women ; everywhere !

Then, the Tales. Considered severally a proportion of them too may be set down as tedious. As a whole, all, and not least the good Parson's exhaustive sermon, are appropriate, almost necessary, for the presentation of a complete social picture. There is coarseness among them, often humorous, often witty, as in the Wife of Bath's ; oftener unmixed grossness, still characteristic, and needing no apology to the poet's contemporaries, though he himself humbly asks : 'May Crist for his grete merey foryeve me the sinne of many a song and many a lecherous lay.'[2]

But take others, the Squire's ' wondrous tale half told ' of Camball and of Algarsife, the Franklin's of Aurelius Arviragus and Dorigene, above all, the Knight's of Palamon and Arcite, and the Clerke's of Griselda the Patient, the Martyr. They require no extenuation in the face of the twentieth century, any more than in that of their own. The fluctuations of the mortal love-duel at Athens above all are a masterpiece of poetic art.

The subsidiary characters are allowed their due shares of importance; for example, the royal allies of the two principals; Palamon's—

> Ligurge him-self, the grete king of Trace;
> Blak was his berd, and manly was his face.
> The cercles of his eyen in his heed,
> They gloweden bitwixe yelow and reed;
> And lyk a griffon loked he aboute,
> With kempe heres on his browes stoute.
> And as the gyse was in his contree,
> Ful hye up-on a char of gold stood he.
> A wrethe of gold arm-greet, of huge wighte,
> Upon his heed, set ful of stones brighte.
> Aboute his char ther wenten whyte alaunts,
> Twenty and mo, as grete as any steer,
> To hunten at the leoun or the deer.
> An hundred lordes hadde he in his route
> Armed ful wel, with hertes sterne and stoute.[3]

and Arcite's:

> The grete Emetreus, the king of Inde,
> Cam ryding lyk the god of armes, Mars.
> His cote-armure was of cloth of Tars,
> Couched with perles whyte and rounde and grete.
> His sadel was of brend gold newe y-bete;
> A mantelet upon his shuldre hanginge
> Bret-ful of rubies rede, as fyr sparklinge.
> His nose was heigh, his eyen bright citryn,
> His lippes rounde, his colour was sangwyn,
> And as a leoun he his loking caste.
> Of fyve and twenty yeer his age I caste.
> His berd was wel bigonne for to springe;
> His voys was as a trompe thunderinge.
> An hundred lordes hadde he with him there,
> Al armed, sauf hir heddes, in al hir gere.
> Aboute this king ther ran on every part
> Ful many a tame leoun and lepart.[4]

But the rivals occupy, as is fitting, the forefront of the scene; and above even them shines the lady of their love and strife. On a bright May morning dawns upon us:

> Emelye, that fairer was to sene
> Than is the lilie upon his stalke grene,
> And fressher than the May with floures newe—
> For with the rose colour stroof hir hewe,
> I noot which was the fairer of hem two—
> Er it were day, as was hir wone to do,
> She was arisen, and al redy dight;
> For May wol have no slogardye a-night.
> The sesoun priketh every gentil herte,
> And maketh him out of his sleep to sterte,
> And seith, 'Arys, and do thyn observaunce.'
> This maked Emelye have remembraunce
> To doon honour to May, and for to ryse.
> Y-clothed was she fresh, for to devyse;
> Hir yelow heer was broyded in a tresse,
> Bihinde hir bak, a yerde long, I gesse.[5]

It is in full accordance with chivalrous romance that finally she allows herself to be the prize, passed from hand to hand, of the deadly tournament. Not a stain rests on her maidenly dignity. She knew each knight to be a right worthy bridegroom and lord.

Only second to Palamon and Arcite is the Clerk's Tale. Admirable for the literary art is the remorselessness of the touches of red-hot iron applied to Griselda's spirit, without defacement of it, or of her womanly self-respect—with never the absence from readers of a sense of suppressed tears in the narrator as he tortures her; of an eagerness in themselves to make the most of any hint of 'routhe and pitee' in the diseased soul of the suspicious, barbarous Marquis himself, notwithstanding that he was

> ful faste imagining
> If by his wyves chere he mighte see,
> Or by hir word aperceyve that she
> Were channged; but he never hir conde finde
> But ever in oon y-lyke sad and kinde.

'Kind', but 'sad'. Yet with none of the anger against fate of her peasant father, or of her husband's people whom she had made to love her. When she is driven forth, naked except for her smock, to return to her humble cottage :

> The folk hir folwe wepinge in hir weye,
> And fortune ay they cursen as they goon ;
> But she fro weping kepte hir yën dreye,
> Ne in this tyme word ne spak she noon.
> Hir fader, that this tyding herde annoon,
> Curseth the day and tyme that nature
> Shoop him to been a lyves creature.
> Agayns his doghter hastilich goth he,
> For he by noyse of folk knew hir cominge,
> And with hir olde cote, as it mighte be,
> He covered hir, ful sorwefully wepinge.[6]

If any are inclined to accompany the poor old villager in cursing as well as tears, I am afraid it is of no use for me to pray them not to extend their wrath to the poet, who is careful to explain the moral of the story to be, not so much excessive wifely humility, as

> that every wight, in his degree,
> Sholde be constant in adversitee;

with a warning, not without humour, to a modern husband to

> putte he nat his wyf in greet assay.
> This world is nat so strong, it is no nay,
> As it hath been in olde tymes yore.[7]

For myself I must confess to having always wondered how long after the Satanic ordeal—whatever is alleged of 'many a yere', and 'rest'—Petrarch and Chaucer meant the victim's worn heart-chords to keep from snapping in revolt at the ironic splendours of her restored palace !

Pathos, mirth, subtlety, and learning, alternating or together, pervade the Tales. They have the dewy freshness of meadows and woods. Birds sing in them. It is Fairyland, into which now and again a Bottom has wandered. In the Prologues, at the postern gates as well as in the grand portal, a panorama is exhibited in miniature of the now English people, and its awaking life. I do not know where else in poetry so complete, so animated a kinematograph of the classes constituting a nationality is to be found. They are all there with their distinctive gradations of character as finely delineated as if Shakespeare had been the limner. If souls transmigrate, his indeed might have lived before in Chaucer.

All the portraits are delightful; the knight:

>That fro the tyme that he first bigan
>To ryden out, he loved chivalrye,
>Trouthe and honour, fredom and curteisye.
>Ful worthy was he in his lordes werre,
>And therto hadde he (riden no man ferre)
>As wel in Cristendom as hethenesse,
>And ever honoured for his worthinesse.
>And evermore he hadde a sovereyn prys.
>And though that he were worthy, he was wys,
>And of his port as meke as is a mayde.
>He never yet no vileinye ne sayde
>In al his lyf, un-to no maner wight.
>He was a verray parfit gentil knight; [8]

the Prioress,

>ful simple and coy;
>Hir gretteste ooth was but by sëynt Loy;
>And she was cleped madame Eglentyne.
>Ful wel she song the service divyne,
>Entuned in hir nose ful semely;
>And Frensh she spak ful faire and fetisly,
>After the scole of Stratford atte Bowe,
>For Frensh of Paris was to hir unknowe.

> She was so charitable and so pitous,
> She wolde wepe, if that she sawe a mous
> Caught in a trappe, if it were deed or bledde.
> Of smale houndes had she, that she fedde
> With rosted flesh, or milk and wastel-breed.
> But sore weep she if oon of hem were deed,
> Or if men smoot it with a yerde smerte :
> And al was conscience and tendre herte.[9]

the Monk :

> A manly man, to been an abbot able.
> Ful many a deyntee hors hadde he in stable :
> And, whan he rood, men mighte his brydel here
> Ginglen in a whistling wind as clere,
> And eek as bloude as dooth the chapel-belle
> Ther as this lord was keper of the celle ;[10]

the young Squire, of dames, as well as of his father, to whom he was a ' lowly, servisable ' son ; the Wife of Bath ; the

> Sergeant of the Lawe, war and wys ;

the prosperous Franklin :

> Wel loved he by the morwe a sop in wyn ;

a Clerk of Oxenforde, as lean as his horse, on a diet chiefly of logic ; the Miller ; the Sompnour ; and many other representatives of English Plantagenet life, especially the ecclesiastical, with, to crown the whole :

> A good man was ther of religioun,
> And was a povre Persoun of a toun ;
> But riche he was of holy thoght and werk.
> He was also a lerned man, a clerk,
> That Cristes gospel trewely wolde preche ;
> His parisshens devoutly wolde he teche.
> Benigne he was, and wonder diligent,
> And in adversitee ful pacient ;
> And swich he was y-preved ofte sythes.
> Ful looth were him to cursen for his tythes,

But rather wolde he yeven, out of doute,
Un-to his povre parisshens aboute
Of his offring, and eek of his substaunce.
He coude in litel thing han suffisaunce.
Wyd was his parisshe, and houses fer a-sonder,
But he ne lafte nat, for reyn ne thonder,
In siknes nor in meschief, to visyte
The ferreste in his parisshe, muche and lyte,
Up-on his feet, and in his hand a staf.
This noble ensample to his sheep he yaf,
That first he wroghte, and afterward he taughte;
Out of the gospel he tho wordes caughte;
And this figure he added eek ther-to,
That if gold ruste, what shal iren do?
For if a preest be foul, on whom we truste,
No wonder is a lewed man to ruste;
Wel oghte a preest ensample for to yive,
By his clennesse, how that his sheep shold live.
He sette nat his benefice to hyre,
And leet his sheep encombred in the myre,
And ran to London, un-to seynt Poules,
To seken him a chaunterie for soules,
Or with a bretherhed to been withholde;
But dwelte at hoom, and kepte wel his folde,
So that the wolf ne made it nat miscarie;
He was a shepherde and no mercenarie.
And though he holy were, and vertuous,
He was to sinful man nat despitous,
Ne of his speche daungerous ne digne,
But in his teching discreet and benigne.
To drawen folk to heven by fairnesse;
By good ensample, was his bisinesse:
But it were any persone obstinat,
What-so he were, of heigh or lowe estat,
Him wolde he snibben sharply for the nones.
A bettre preest, I trowe that nowher noon is.
He wayted after no pompe and reverence,
Ne maked him a spyced conscience,
But Cristes lore, and his apostles twelve,
He taughte, and first he folwed it him-selve;

as did also his brother, a Plowman :

> God loved he best with al his hole herte
> At alle tymes, thogh him gamed or smerte,
> And thanne his neighebour right as him-selve.
> He wolde thresshe, and ther-to dyke and delve,
> For Cristes sake, for every povre wight,
> Withouten hyre, if it lay in his might.[11]

Admiration is not to be sought for Chaucer by way of alms, with a kind of compassionate indulgence for him as phenomenal for his period. For work like the Prologue, the Knight's and Clerk's Tales, enthusiasm is a right. If I speak of the writing rather than always of the writer, it is that I prefer to economize miracles. Such creations, not leaves and blossoms alone, but ripe fruit also, would have been impossibilities had they not been maturing beneath the surface. They issued from no wilderness. The soil was of courtly manners, of chivalrous, high-bred sentiment. Norman exclusiveness, in crumbling into Saxon mother-earth, had carried thither dignity and grace. Though English literature hitherto had reckoned for little, French was accessible to Englishmen. The language itself was daily being embroidered with French diction and its larger ideas. Besides, there was always Italy. Dante had just been. Petrarch and Boccaceio were. Every hungry Italian prelate, every wandering friar, every returned noble, pilgrim, and merchant was an evangelist of the new gospel of letters. Centuries were to pass before writers, of whatever race, were ashamed to borrow plots and thoughts. Chaucer, as he tells us everywhere, drank deep of the open fountains, and gloried in his draughts from them.

We cannot tell what he would have been without them. He returned them, as he slaked his thirst, with happier results than King Midas, into virgin gold. His merit, in their transmutation, in his borrowings of ideas and tone from a half-French Court, in his acceptance of foreign enrichments of his native tongue, is large enough for his admirers to be content to extol him, not for making his tools, but for his use of them. There he wrought miracles indeed. He found the nation divided by a barrier of two spoken languages. Operating from an English heart and brain for English ears, he compelled the whole to understand one tongue. English verse cannot be said to have really existed before him. He composed poems which through succeeding centuries never ceased to be read and loved. The rhythm he planted struck root so deeply that it has never lost its hold on the national ear. Dryden and Pope tried to improve upon it. Read their monotonously measured heroics, in their so-called translations, before or after the original, in its natural changefulness, and judge which is the more musical. I am almost tempted to add, which is the more intelligible.

Whatever the amount of his debts to continental literature, one constituent of his work Petrarch, Boccaccio, Dante, with the entire bounteous French tongue thrown in, could not have supplied. He contributed himself; his own spacious nature. That is visible throughout story, learning, diction, and thought. It animates and transforms the whole. His curiosity was devouring. He must have read whatever in contemporary or classical literature was for the period available. Through his reading he endeavoured to live back into the past. It may be admitted that he made at times a strange medley of his knowledge. Greek and Roman gods and goddesses ply, as it were, for reverence and worship along with the mysteries of the Christian Faith. Legend, history, and mythology, Caesar and Aeneas, Ovid and Titus Livius, are used as of equal authority for the reconstruction of antiquity. The results may sometimes be grotesque ; they compose a fabric in which at any rate Chaucer, with his public, felt at home ; even enraptured and on wings :

> On bokes for to rede I me delyte,
> And in myn herte have hem in reverence ;
> And to hem yeve swich lust and swich credence,
> That ther is wel unethe game noon
> That from my bokes make me to goon.

Only one other joy takes precedence of his homage to them. It is

> in the joly tyme of May ;
> Whan that I here the smale foules singe,
> And that the floures ginne for to springe.

Then

> Farwel my studie, as lasting that sesoun ![12]

In that sweet month he feels like the birds. They

> that han left hir song,
> Whyl they han suffred cold so strong
> In wedres grille, and derk to sighte,
> Ben in May, for the sonne brighte,
> So glade, that they shewe in singing,
> That in hir herte is swich lyking,
> That they mote singen and be light.
> Hard is his herte that loveth nought
> In May, whan al this mirth is wrought ;
> Whan he may on these braunches here
> The smale briddes singen clere
> Hir blisful swete song pitous.[13]

He loves all Nature's works, great and small, and, best among them, the simple and humble :

> Of alle the floures in the mede,
> Than love I most these floures whyte and rede,
> Swiche as men callen daysies in our toun.
> To hem have I so greet affeccioun,

> As I seyde erst, whan comen is the May,
> That in my bed ther daweth me no day
> That I nam up, and walking in the mede
> To seen this flour agein the sonne sprede,
> Whan hit upryseth erly by the morwe;
> That blisful sighte softneth al my sorwe.[14]

A gale of fresh, dewy fragrance from green grass and lowly flowers breathes over the inspirations he has borrowed from the great of Italy, and naturalizes the whole on English soil.

Spirit and thought are equally delightful. The singer is so manifestly, so piquantly, gay. His glad surprise at finding the numbers come infects his audience. A bystander cannot help rejoicing with him. Yet Black Death had been devastating the cities. Wars of royal ambition had been watering foreign fields with the blood of thousands. Excessive taxation had driven labourers and farmers into armed sedition. Religion and conscience had their profound upheavals. The poet, among his divers moods, preserved unsullied that of a sweet equanimity. He ceased not, at due seasons, to write, and even laugh, though his heart had ached. A keen satirist who hated all mockery, he had a smile for individual prioresses and friars, even for sompnours and pardoners, while he lashed the system by which they fattened. The courage of the courtier, who could thus defy the Church a short generation before it burnt Cobham at the stake must have been undaunted How he could honour and love ministers of that Church who were Christians also, we can gather from his adorable picture of a ' poure Persone of the toun '.

Altogether English poetry could want no nobler progenitor than Geoffrey Chaucer. How he shines in the light of his own halo against a curtain of darkness behind, and a darkness almost blacker to come!

The Complete Works of Geoffrey Chaucer, edited by the Rev. W. W. Skeat, Litt.D. Seven vols. Oxford: Clarendon Press, 1894.

[1] The Hous of Fame, vv. 1365-7.
[2] The Persones Tale, § 104, 1085.
[3] The Knightes Tale, vv. 2129-54.
[4] Ibid. 2156-86.
[5] Ibid. 1035-55.
[6] The Clerkes Tale. Tercia pars, vv. 598-602, and Quinta pars, vv. 897-903 and 911-14.
[7] Ibid., Pars sexta, vv. 1145-6 and 1138-40.
[8] Prologue, vv. 44-50 and 67-72.
[9] Ibid., vv. 119-26 and 143-50.   [10] Ibid., vv. 167-72.
[11] Ibid., vv. 477-528, and 533-5.
[12] Legend of Good Women, Prologue, vv. 30-9.
[13] Romaunt of the Rose, vv. 70-89.
[14] Legend of Good Women, Prologue, vv. 41-50.

SIR PHILIP SIDNEY
1554—1586

EVEN for poets it is an honour for the English Bayard to be reckoned of their fraternity. He himself never denied his vocation, though, after the manner of the age, he apologized for 'having, I know not by what mischance, in these my not old years and idlest times, slipped into the title of a poet'.[1] His own period enthusiastically acknowledged his poetic merits. By the ordinary modern reader, while his name for chivalrous virtues and accomplishments has become a proverb, he is not regarded as a poet at all.

The indiscriminateness of the neglect is the more surprising for the character of the fugitive pieces, which he scattered among his friends and associates, never heeding whether they died, or lived, and under whatever name. They are commonly of the bright and joyous character which might have been expected to echo long. Take for instance :

    O faire ! O sweete ! when I do look on thee,
      In whome all joyes so well agree,
    Heart and soul do sing in me,
      Just accord all musicke makes ;
    In thee just accord excelleth,
    Where each part in such peace dwelleth,
      One of other beautie takes,
    Since, then, truth to all mindes telleth
      That in thee liues harmonie,
    Hart and soule do sing in me.[2]

I should have supposed that the address to Love even was too airy, too unsubstantial, for the heavy foot of Time to overtake and crush it :

> Ah, poore Love, whi dost thou live,
>   Thus to see thy service lost ?
> Ife she will no comforte geve,
>   Make an end, yeald up the goaste ;
> That she may at lengthe aprove
>   That she hardlye long beleved,
> That the hart will die for love
>   That is not in tyme relieved.
> Ohe that ever I was borne,
>   Service so to be refused,
> Faythfull love to be foreborne !
>   Never love was so abused.[3]

The mere sauciness ought to have guaranteed against superannuation the repeated entreaties to the cross-grained babe to sleep, and let its mother keep her tryst, not, I am afraid, with the infant's father. So too with the mocking at a faint-hearted lover :

> Doth she chide thee ? 'Tis to show it
>   That thy coldness makes her do it ;
> Is she silent ? is she mute ?
>   Silence fully 'grants thy sute ;
> Doth she pout, and leave the room ?
>   Then she goes to bid thee come ;
> Is she sick ? why then be sure
>   She invites thee to the cure ;
> Doth she cross thy sute with No ?
>   Tush, she loves to hear thee woo ;
> Doth she call the faith of man
>   In question ? nay, 'uds-foot, she love thee than ;
> He that after ten denialls
>   Dares attempt no farther tryals,
> Hath no warrant to acquire
>   The dainties of his chaste desire.[4]

Later generations have not in any case had the curiosity to ransack hospitals of literary foundlings, on the chance of identifying the dainty creatures of his imagination. They knew, and had tired, of the subtlety and intricate thoughtfulness of the poems he acknowledged. The neglect has for centuries been a waste of precious matter; for he never wrote without striving to put into his work the best of himself according to his prevailing mood and subject. When his pen and they really suited each other, the result is exquisite in its own sort. The Arcadia, amid a mass of preposterous affectation, often breaks into loveliness. How charmingly, for instance, a shepherd's suspicion of sorcery becomes a tribute of adoration to the fascination of the sorceress :

> When I see her, my sinewes shake for feare,
> And yet, deare soule, I know she hurteth none ;
> Amid my flocke with woe my voice I teare,
> And, but bewitch'd, who to his flocke would mone ?
> Her chery lips, milke hands, and golden haire
> I still doe see, though I be still alone.[5]

Lovers twain, the one incapable of surviving the other, could not have been mourned more fittingly :

> His being was in her alone ;
> And he not being, she was none.
> They joy'd one joy, one grief they griev'd ;
> One love they lov'd, one life they liv'd.
> The hand was one, one was the sword
> That did his death, her, death afford.
> As all the rest, so now the stone
> That tombes the two is justly one.[6]

Zelmane's extraordinarily detailed inventory of Philoclea's charms in some hundred and fifty verses, ends with the prettiest analysis of the fair one's hand :

> Of my first love the fatall band,
> Where whitenesse doth for ever sit ;
> Nature herselfe enameld it ;

For there with strange compact doth lie
Warme snow, moist pearle, soft ivorie;
There fall those saphir-coloured brookes,
Which conduit-like with curious crookes
Sweet ilands make in that sweet land.
As for the fingers of the hand,
The bloudy shafts of Cupid's warre,
With amatists they headed are.

  Thus hath each part his beautie's part;
But how the graces doe impart
To all her limmes a speciall grace,
Becomming every time and place,
Which doth even beautie beautifie,
And most bewitch the wretched eye :—
How all this is but a faire inne
Of fairer guests, which dwell therein :—
Of whose high praise and praisefull blisse
Goodnesse the penne, heaven paper is;
The inke immortall fame doth lend :—
As I began so must I end :
  No tongue can her perfections tell,
  In whose each part all tongues may dwell.[7]

But Astrophel and Stella is the production by which Sidney may most adequately claim in these times to be judged as a poet; and there by its main constituents. In the ten songs interspersed the wooer is delightfully ingenious in arriving by as many different roads at one same conclusion :

This small wind, which so sweete is,
See how it the leaves doth kisse;
Each tree in his best attiring,
Sense of love to love inspiring.

Love makes earth the water drink,
Love to earth makes water sinke;
And, if dumbe things be so witty,
Shall a heavenly grace want pitty ?[8]

It was into its Sonnets, however, that he threw his full strength. Of the whole hundred and eight it is no exaggeration to say that they will stand comparison, if not with an incomparable dozen, with the rest of Shakespeare's. The famous thirty-first, with a little less wit, and a little more feeling, would be perfect :

> With how sad steps, O Moone, thou clim'st the skies !
> How silently, and with how wanne a face !
> What, may it be that even in heav'nly place
> That busie archer his sharpe arrowes tries !
> Sure, if that long-with-love-acquainted eyes
> Can judge of love, thou feel'st a lover's case,
> I reade it in thy lookes ; thy languisht grace,
> To me, that feele the like, thy state discries.
> Then, e'en of fellowship, O Moone, tell me,
> Is constant love deem'd there but want of wit ?
> Are beauties there as proud as here they be ?
> Do they above love to be lov'd, and yet
> Those lovers scorne whom that love doth possesse ?
> Doe they call vertue there ungratefulnesse ?[9]

In another the personal element captivates :

> Having this day my horse, my hand, my launce
> Guided so well that I obtained the prize,
> Both by the judgment of the English eyes
> And of some sent from that sweet enemy Fraunce ;
> Horsemen my skill in horsemanship advaunce,
> Towne folkes my strength ; a daintier judge applies
> His praise to sleight which from good use doth rise ;
> Some luckie wits impute it but to chance ;
> Others, because of both sides I doe take
> My blood from them who did excell in this,
> Thinke Nature me a man-at-armes did make.
> How farre they shot awrie ! the true cause is,
> Stella lookt on, and from her heav'nly face
> Sent forth the beames which made so faire my race.[10]

His heart, habitually humble and abashed in Stella's

SIR PHILIP SIDNEY 27

presence, is speedily intoxicated with the sweetness of a sudden taste of audacity:

> My Starre, because a sugred kisse
> In sport I suckt while she asleepe did lye,
> Doth lowre, nay chide, nay threat for only this!
> Sweet, it was saucie Love, not humble I.
> But no 'scuse serves; she makes her wrath appeare
> In Beautie's throne: see now, who dares come neare
> Those scarlet judges, threat'ning bloudie paine.
> O heav'nly foole, thy most kisse-worthy face
> Anger invests with such a lovely grace,
> That Anger's selfe I needs must kisse againe.[11]

A stray ringlet at once shames the Mistress and enraptures her Servant:

> O happie Thames, that didst my Stella beare!
> I saw thee with full many a smiling line
> Upon thy cheerefull face, Joye's livery weare,
> While those faire planets on thy streames did shine.
> The boate for joy could not to daunce forbear,
> While wanton winds, with beauties so divine
> Ravisht, staid not, till in her golden haire
> They did themselves, O sweetest prison, twine.
> And faine those Aeol's youth there would their stay
> Have made, but forst by Nature still to flie,
> First did with puffing kisse those lockes display!
> She, so disheuld, blusht: from window I
> With sight thereof cride out, 'O faire disgrace,
> Let Honor's selfe to thee grant highest place.'[12]

And then, suddenly, in the midst of the amorous frolic, figuring as a mere tag to the trifling, starts up now and again a big thought:

> Cease, eager Muse; peace, pen; for my sake stay;
> I give you here my hand for truth of this,—
> Wise silence is best musicke unto blisse.[13]

In that capacious province of English verse occupied by

28 FIVE CENTURIES OF ENGLISH VERSE

the Sonnet, it would be hard to discover more than one or two series to place by the side of Astrophel and Stella's. Single surpassing specimens, I am aware, could be cited; among them, that by Sidney himself in the collection known as Sidera :

> Oft have I musde, but now at length I finde
>   Why those that die, men say they do depart:
> Depart ! a word so gentle to my minde,
>   Weakely did seeme to paint Death's ougly dart.
> But now the starres, with their strange course, do binde
>   Me one to leave, with whom I leave my heart ;
> I heare a cryc of spirits fainte and blinde
>   That parting thus, my chiefest part I part.
> Part of my life, the loathèd part to me,
>   Lives to impart my wearie clay some breath;
> But that good part wherein all comforts be,
>   Now dead, doth show departure is a death ;
> Yea, worse than death ; death parts both woe and joy,
> From joy I part, still living in annoy.[14]

But few clusters vie with the other. There we have miniature painting of a consummate kind ; delicate tracery of all conceivable emotions of the persons in the given circumstances principally concerned—the friend, the lover, the mistress, all, that is, but the husband. The colours, mixed more, it is true, with brain than heart, still are of real passion for the time being, evoked by an effort of will. Doubtless, the entire shining structure is a palace of ice, a mirage in the desert. At all events it is extraordinarily artistic and symmetrical. Given the latitude of speech and feeling in the period, it is moral also. Sidney in a dissolute age was no libertine. None in his own time believed that he cherished designs against the honour of Essex's sister, his own once promised bride, now the neglected wife of a titled clown. The generous purpose of the poems may well have been to console, exalt the victim, by representing her with all her charms as bravely faithful to vows her husband had not kept; as resisting triumphantly temptation, however noble, ardent, and dear the tempter.

The present inability of Sidney's verse to attract readers is not flattering to modern taste, in view of the intrinsic merits. The failure is not astonishing when the change in the literary standpoint is considered. Modern poetry labours to turn the stream of its especial subject into the channel of common human nature. It was Browning's object as much as Tennyson's. It is the only receipt in literature for evading superannuation. From Sidney to Waller, the aim of courtly verse was to individualize emotions equally with manners. The theme was enclosed in a private pool, where every incident of its being, and growth, could not fail to be remarked. When it is in itself worthy, and the observer has sympathy and soul to analyse its properties, it proves to be still a pearl of price. In default of the rightful combination, much in Sidney, something in a greater genius, everything in a pile of more ordinary Elizabethan and Jacobean verse, appears to be nothing but a collection of ingenious grotesques. Elizabethan love-poetry, in its beauties and its paradoxes, is paralleled by the sacred poetry of the following generation. With a fit infusion of sensibility and passion both sorts become delightfully extraordinary. Without the addition they are extraordinary without the delightfulness.

Fashion is as omnipotent, except for an occasional rebel, in literature as in social habits and customs. In the golden days of Elizabeth, and a generation or two later, it decreed that poetry, other than dramatic, should be the diversion and the privilege of a few, of scholars and society. Shakespeare himself, in his character of poet, obeyed the edict.

Had he been born noble and wealthy, with no compulsion to be intelligible to a multitude, he possibly might have preferred throughout the honours of a sonneteer to the immortality of the creator of Macbeth, Lear, Othello, Hamlet. Sidney, a courtier, admired, beloved, a poet born, was free to choose. Though he selects for praise, as 'excellently done', Troilus and Cressida—not the Canterbury Tales, he had studied Chaucer. He panegyrizes him, notwithstanding 'great wants fit to be forgiven in so reverend antiquity'![15] While 'confessing his own barbarousness', he says he 'never heard the old song of Percy and Douglas, that he found not his heart moved more than with a trumpet'.[16] Yet he could not oppose fashion's ordinance on the legitimate purpose and aspiration of sonnet and song. He was content to set himself as poet the task of hymning his mistress's eyebrow. The applause most valued in his period, his lady's and the Court's, he won. He has paid for it by having become in popular opinion antiquated. Whether he had it in him to be a singer for all time, as is his illustrious contemporary in the lyrics of the Plays, none can decide. That contemporary himself did not essay to be at once musical and spontaneous, unless with a people's drama for a vehicle to carry and excuse poetry not à la mode. We can only wish that Sidney had tried.

The poetic school which was Sidney's died a natural death more than two centuries ago. Alike in Italy, France, Spain, and England, it originated in a world of less diffused intellectual atmosphere and friction than ours; in a world where the wheels turned more slowly round; in a more contracted circle of possible appreciation, but where any was tenfold more intense for the narrowness. The self-dedicated poet had no ambition for his own Muse to 'move as with a trumpet'. He was not solicitous to be recited in the highways. Rather he desired that fair ladies and cavaliers should debate his graceful conundrums in the asylums of their own breasts—or, better, whisper them to each other in boudoirs. Modern revivals are make-believes. No heart-strings have been ravelled into knots. There is no mistress. The intent is, not to enchant a few, but to puzzle and amaze the many. The pieces are mere metrical exercises, ghosts of a dead past, barren of all sincerity. For the moment, in the brief intervals of repose from tournaments, war, the ambushes of statecraft, and Court intrigues, Sidney was sincere enough. In a sense he was even natural; the sworn antagonist of Euphuism, that reductio ad absurdum of the type of literature which was his own. Never was there a keener instinct for grace, beauty, heroism. Before we condemn Astrophel and Stella—perhaps, the Arcadia itself—for faults equally apparent throughout undramatic Elizabethan verse, let us seek a match for Sidney's—since Chaucer—as a whole in intrinsic merits at the actual date of its production, and we shall fail.

The Complete Poems of Sir Philip Sidney, ed. Rev. A. B. Grosart (Early English Poets). Three vols. Chatto & Windus, 1877.

[1] Defence of Poesy, p. 4. Miscellaneous works, ed. W. Gray, 1820.
[2] Verses, To the Tune of a Spanish Song (Pansies from Penshurst and Wilton), viii, st. 2.
[3] Love, v (Ibid.).   [4] Wooing-stuff, vi.
[5] The Countess of Pembroke's Arcadia, Lamon's Song, x, vv 459-64.
[6] Ibid., Epitaph on Argalus and Parthenia, 41.
[7] Ibid., Zelmane, of Philoclea, xvii, vv. 122-46.
[8] Astrophel and Stella, Song viii, stanzas 15-16.
[9] Ibid. 31.   [10] Ibid. 41.
[11] Ibid. 73.   [12] Ibid. 103.
[13] Ibid. 70.   [14] A Farewell (Sidera), v.
[15] Defence of Poesy, ibid. 53.   [16] Ibid. 34.

EDMUND SPENSER
1553—1599

'Linked sweetness long drawn out'; that is the popular judgement on Spenser. Yet, by established literary edict, still unrevoked, the foundation stones of modern English poetry are Shakespeare, Spenser, and Milton. Milton keeps his place. Shakespeare has deepened, widened, his. Spenser, recognized as a classic, is become a dowager of the British Parnassus; honoured, and unread. Not one in a thousand readers takes his volumes from the shelf. At the same time, all would be ashamed to avow ignorance of them.

His verse has ceased to give pleasure, unless to the poetically-minded—in these days a diminishing class. For the educated Englishman in general the Epithalamion is high-flown; the Faerie Queene is interminable. He had the vice, for our hurried times unpardonable, of prolixity. Continually he offends readers by appearing to put no faith in their ability to supply details. In reality he could not bear not to picture the whole scene to himself, not to see the

> Bright Scolopendraes arm'd with silver scales,
> Mighty Monoceros with immeasured tayles.[1]

While he prays for sympathy in his labours:

> O! what an endlesse worke have I in hand![2]

his public is wishing he had spared much of his pains in compassion for its own. Macaulay's profane blessing on the shipwreck, negligence, or conflagration, which saved literature from a supplement to the existing seventy-two or eighty cantos of as many more, has often been echoed with interest.

Few of his admirers can deny that his immortal work would have been the better for less copiousness in language, for less facility in versification. His heavenly gift of fancy itself, as onwards it

> far'd as dauncing in delight,

might have been yet diviner had it known an occasional pause. Frequently it is hard to see the wood for the trees. In his Irish solitude his pure mind was haunted by visions more voluptuous than tempted the hermit of the Thebaid. He piled up Ossas on Pelions of gorgeous palaces only fit to be tenanted by fairest damsels

> rich attir'd
> With golden hands and silver feete beside.

Perilous adventure jostles adventure, carcasses, generally to be raised to life, are heaped on carcasses, horror on horror, heroism on heroism, until the brain reels bewildered. Moreover, the suspicion of allegory troubles the interest of the story; the archaic language also; besides that, borrowing archaisms, he is never frankly archaic. Worst of all, or withal, we miss in the professed disciple of Chaucer the open-air, the nature, the directness, of the Master.

There the root is of the explanation of the present coldness towards perhaps the most poetical of British poets. While the same cause existed always, for sufficient reasons it did not operate equally of old. For his own, and several generations to follow, which never learnt to read Shakespeare, he was the fountain of romance. Every deed of terror, self-sacrifice, conceived by minstrels, forged by monkish chroniclers, he idealized, and embalmed in honeyed verse. Imagination, the reader's as well as the writer's, wandered about a limitless, enchanted forest-Paradise, or beckoned and wantoned through vistas, hardly less lovely, of

Hell. A pageant dazzling in the framework, splendidly fantastic in the incidents! To his immediate contemporaries, as to himself, it was half real. His friends were ever prepared to scour the Spanish Main for spoil. Hundreds of glorious failures were pining, writhing, in dungeons of the Inquisition. A legion was fighting for the pure Faith in the Netherlands. Spaniards were raiding Galway. Wild Irishry furnished a permanent background. We see in his View of the Present State of Ireland, how he would have dealt with it, have clenched a mail hand, and in no velvet glove.[3] Actual dangers and guerdons were not altogether unlike, outside the Christian symbolism, to those encountered and won by the Red Cross knight, by Sir Guyon, Britomartis, Cambel, Artegall, Sir Calidore. Gloriana's champions were as fierce in spirit, pillaged and massacred giants and Paynim as ruthlessly, as Elizabeth's buccaneers despoiled and butchered Dons and Desmonds. Creatures of Spenser's brain and his royal Mistress's favour held identical commissions to enter in and possess the gate of Antichrist.

The great poem satisfied other instincts and cravings in the century of civil discord which succeeded. It inspired the twelve-year-old genius of Cowley. In hundreds of manor houses and parsonages its many pages must have afforded a blissful asylum from the babel of opposing creeds and party strifes. It was a welcome relief, during the Commonwealth, to sour Puritanism, and the Blatant Beast, and, at the Restoration, to the sensual allurements of Archimago. During the interregnum, for poetry, of the Georgian Era, that long Dunciad, it was still heard protesting, and not in vain. The deadliest blow against popular favour for Spenser was struck, less by national insensibility, than by the growing friction of life. His poetry could not have been born amid prosaic modern turmoil, competition of ambitions, topics, and interests. For appreciation it wants mental leisure, and some approach to a monopoly of it. When now, by accident, or in shame, a volume is opened, it is galloped through, prodigy of knight-errantry after prodigy. The varying lights and shades are all confused and blurred. Work like Spenser's ought to be read lovingly, as Ralegh, or as Wordsworth, faithful to him in age as in youth, would have read him. Such minutes of a day are, if any, given to him now as can be stolen from a month's supply of new literature which would have sufficed once for a reign.

None of us, however, who would derive true profit from poetry can afford to be blind to the light of so particular a star in the poetic firmament as Spenser. He reigns over a kingdom of his own. Whatever theme he touches bears the impress of his peculiar genius; and many themes were touched by him. Love he traces through all its manifold phases. Like all the poets of his time he worships at the shrine; but always with purity:

> Fayre is my Love, when her fayre golden haires
> With the loose wynd ye waving chance to marke;
> Fayre when the rose in her red cheekes appeares;
> Or in her eyes the fyre of love does sparke.
> Fayre, when her breast, lyke a rich laden barke,
> With pretious merchandise she forth doth lay;
> Fayre, when that cloud of pryde, which oft doth dark
> Her goodly light, with smiles she drives away.
> But fayrest she, when so she doth display
> The gate with pearles and rubyes richly dight,
> Throgh which her words so wise do make their way
> To beare the message of her gentle spright.
>   The rest be works of Natures wonderment;
>   But this the worke of harts astonishment.[4]

Even in an Epithalamion, a class of composition in which

the most decorous fancy was apt to run wild, his joyousness is never riotous :

> Wake now, my Love, awake ; for it is time ;
> The rosy Morne long since left Tithons bed,
> All ready to her silver coche to clyme ;
> And Phoebus 'gins to shew his glorious hed.
> Hark ! how the cheerefull birds do chaunt their laies,
> And caroll of Loves praise.
> The merry Larke hir mattins sings aloft ;
> The Thrush replyes ; the Mavis descant playes ;
> The Ouzell shrills ; the Ruddock warbles soft ;
> So goodly all agree, with sweet consent,
> To this dayes merriment.
> Ah ! my deere Love, why doe ye sleep thus long,
> When meeter were that ye should now awake,
> T' awayt the comming of your joyous Make,
> And hearken to the birds love-learned song,
> The deawy leaves among !
> For they of joy and pleasance to you sing,
> That all the woods them answer, and theyr eccho ring.[5]

Beauty he passionately admired ; beauty apparent to the senses—cheeks, lily white and rose red—hair, like golden wire—eyes, sparkling stars—

> Comming to kisse her lyps—such grace I found—
> Me seemd, I smelt a gardin of sweet flowres,
> That dainty odours from them threw around,
> For damzells fit to decke their lovers bowres.[6]

It was his mistress from whom they breathed ; and he revelled in them ; yet delighting in all such transient charms chiefly as emblems of the inner lamp, immortally fair. It,

> from whose celestiall ray
> That light proccedes, which kindleth lovers fire,
> Shall never be extinguisht nor decay ;
> But when the vitall spirits doe expyre,
> Unto her native planet shall retyre ;

> For it is heavenly borne and cannot die,
> Being a parcell of the purest skie.
> For when the soule, the which derived was,
> At first, out of that great immortall Spright,
> By whom all live to love, whilome did pas
> Doun from the top of purest heavens hight
> To be embodied here, it then took light
> And lively spirits from that fayrest starre
> Which lights the world forth from his firie carre.[7]

So habitual indeed was it for him to seek the celestial in the earthly that, when we pass from the hymn in honour of Beauty visible to human sight, to hymns of heavenly love and heavenly beauty, we are not conscious of any essential change in the spirit of the treatment. Similarly we have no sense of heterogeneousness or abruptness, when a record

> Of my love's conquest, peerlesse beauties prise,[8]

elbows the grand Easter psalm:

> Most glorious Lord of lyfe! that, on this day,
> Didst make thy triumph over death and sin:
> And, having harrowd hell, didst bring away
> Captivity thence captive, us to win:
> This joyous day, dear Lord, with joy begin;
> And grant that we, for whom thou diddest dy,
> Being with thy deare blood clene washt from sin,
> May live for ever in felicity!
> And that thy love we weighing worthily,
> May likewise love thee for the same againe;
> And for thy sake, that all lyke deare didst buy,
> With love may one another entertayne:
> So let us love, deare Love, lyke as we ought;
> Love is the lesson which the Lord us taught.[9]

No poet has ever held a more exalted view of the dignity of his vocation. He proved it by his constant tendency to lift his subject, whatever it might be, from the dust to the stars. His poems, one and all, testify to a vast expenditure of care and thought. They require as much from their readers, and affection also. In truth it is sheer waste of mental effort to get him up for the purposes of polite conversation, or even as if to satisfy a Civil Service Examiner. He must—in any of his work—be read for delight in the harmony of diction and spirit; in the Faerie Queene also for that enjoyment, if possible, of the romance, which a child might still take, apart from the archaisms. I used, when a boy, to be told that Sir Frederick Thesiger, a powerful advocate, and afterwards Lord Chancellor, would every morning attune his mind to forensic oratory by committing to memory one or two of Spenser's stanzas. That is the proper temper; and the poet will reward it.

Every poem he penned is a treasure house of imagery and of language. To understand the flexibility of English, its aptness for the expression of myriad turns of thought and feeling, all, but especially poets, should study him. Another distinctive feature of his Muse is the evenness, the pervading sweetness. Take your chance anywhere in the labyrinth of dulcet verse, redolent of more than Italian daintiness; and you will light upon none false. Not that, for sympathetic readers, there is a sense of stagnation. They are plodding through a thick undergrowth of strange deeds; suddenly a lark mounts through the stages of air, and is trilling overhead. Now and again an exquisite idea, scene, phrase, stands out; a gust of melody; oftener in the shorter poems than in the Faerie Queene, though occasionally there too. For instance, we pluck a flower like this in the garden of Acrasia:

> Thy joyous birdes shrouded in chearefull shade,
> Their notes unto the voice attempered sweet;
> Th' angelicall soft trembling voyces made
> To th' instruments divine respondence meet;

> The silver-sounding instruments did meet
> With the base murmurs of the waters fall;
> The waters fall with difference discreet,
> Now soft, now loud, unto the wind did call;
> The gentle warbling wind low answered to all.[10]

Absolute music! And it is not as if here and there some solitary islet of beauty emerged. A numerous company like to it are rising everywhere just above a flood of all but equal mellifluousness. Coral rocks with palm trees on them are seen for a moment, then disappear in the haze of an ever-rolling ocean, to be succeeded by others as lovely.

Doubtless, as I have intimated, the strain, not of the harmony alone, but also of the fortitude, grace, and goodness, unrelieved by the pressure, equally exacting, of treachery, rapacity, and lust, goes far towards explaining the languor in the study of Spenser. In poetry, as in life, it is dangerous to overtax endurance. The poet much before the close of most of his honeyed lays has exhausted the receptibility of average minds. The effect upon the relation of many of us to himself personally is altogether different. The flood of unmixed essence of fancy which scares from attempts to breast it, offers a fascinating spectacle in the person of the master floating easily over the expanse. By a remarkable fate the forlorn, noble figure of the writer attracts almost in proportion as the writings chill. We prize immeasurably references in them to himself; to the silver-streaming Thames he loved, and the banks which

> his river hemmes,
> Painted all with variable flowers,
> And all the meades adorned with dainty gemmes,
> Fit to decke maydens bowres;[11]

to

> merry London, my most kyndly nurse,
> That to me gave this life's first native course,

　　　　　Though from another place I take my name,
　　　　　An house of auncient fame ; [12]
to Ouse, which
　　　　　　　　doth by Huntingdon and Cambridge flit,
　　　　　My mother Cambridge, whom as with a crowne
　　　　　He doth adorne, and is adorned of it
　　　　　With many a gentle Muse and many a learned Wit ; [13]
to Ralegh's visit to him in
　　　　　　　　the cooly shade
　　　　　Of the greene alders by the Mullaes shore,[14]
with its result, the manifestation to the world of The Faerie Queene—an epoch in literature.

And to the friendship, as well of Sidney's mother, as of himself :
　　　　　Most gentle spirite breathed from above,
　　　　　Out of the bosom of the Makers blis,
　　　　　In whom all bountie and all vertuous love
　　　　　Appeared in all their native propertis,
　　　　　And did enrich that noble breast of his
　　　　　With treasure passing all this worldës worth
　　　　　Worthie of heaven it selfe, which brought it forth.[15]

Any rays thus shed upon his life and companionships are as welcome as they are delightful ; but they are rare ; and few trustworthy contemporary traditions and reminiscences exist to supplement them. His was not a temperament to gather about him a court of admirers who would have chronicled his words, and handed down the honour in which he was, or deserved to be, held. Even for an avowal of the vast poetical enterprise on which he had embarked, his confidence had to be forced by an accomplished stormer of hearts like ' the Shepheard of the Ocean ', who,
　　　　　Whether allured with my pipes delight,
　　　　　Or thither led by chaunce, I know not right,
　　　　　Provoked me to plaie some pleasant fit,
　　　　　And found himselfe full greatly pleased at it.[16]

Heart and spirit he instinctively kept for his verse ; and for admittance to his privacy we must go thither. In that wide and flowery region he wandered without fear or shy restraint. Fancy there opened its gates to him freely and largely ; and he trod its precincts as a master. We view him in it as he would, we may be sure, have most desired to be seen—as he most really was. It is a pleasant sight :—consoling, also in the lurid light of after miseries—bereavement, penury, hunger, despair—too probable in the general outline, though coloured perhaps by posthumous pity and shame. At all events, the creator of The Faerie Queene, the Epithalamion, Colin Clout, cannot but have dreamt, in numberless waking hours, a host of happy visions.

The Works of Edmund Spenser, ed. Rev. H. J. Todd, Archdeacon of Cleveland. E. Moxon, 1845.

[1] The Faerie Queene, Book II, Canto xii, st. 23.
[2] Ibid., Book IV, Canto xii, st. 1.
[3] A View of the State of Ireland (Works), p. 532.
[4] Amoretti, or Sonnets, No. 81.   [5] Epithalamion, vv. 74-91.
[6] Amoretti, or Sonnets, No. 64.
[7] An Hymne in Honour of Beautie, vv. 99-112.
[8] Amoretti, or Sonnets, No. 69.   [9] Ibid., No. 68.
[10] The Faerie Queene, Book II, Canto xii, st. 71.
[11] Prothalamion, vv. 11-15.   [12] Ibid., vv. 127-31.
[13] The Faerie Queene, Book IV, Canto xi, st. 34.
[14] Colin Clout's Come Home Againe, vv. 58-9.
[15] The Ruines of Time, vv. 281-7.
[16] Colin, &c., vv. 61-2 and 69-71

WILLIAM SHAKESPEARE
1564—1616

SHAKESPEARE, the poet of the Plays, and Shakespeare, the poet of the Sonnets, Venus and Adonis, and Lucrece—how is it possible that the two should have shared one mind!

In the dramas he is open, clear, direct, reckless with method, natural. The wondrous mixture of high and low, the variety—cloud and sunshine—the abundance of words, not one too many, the touches transmuting into gold the lead of the stories, which, after the fashion of his period, he preferred improving to inventing, the single illuminating sentences, the adorable simplicity, thought as wide as it is deep! Never was writer more impersonal, less, apparently, capable of egotism. It does not seem to have occurred to him to blot or polish. Nowhere are there serpentine writhings, and knot-tyings of wit. How, it might be thought, must the Euphuists have deplored the waste of opportunities by Hamlet, Prince of Denmark!

He is a grand moralist without affectation of austerity. Occasional coarsenesses are never in the grain. No playwright has ever framed finer or more honest models of family life. He enables us to picture to ourselves struggling human nature; common, not vulgar, and without the prosaic hardness of reality. He probes hearts, as no professed philosopher ever could. And the intelligibility of it all! Its transparent, absolute plainness to average minds—its infinite suggestiveness, its mysteries, to the metaphysician! Contemporaries found the successive tragedies and comedies entirely of their own time. For each subsequent generation they have been as unaffectedly modern. The secret has been neither mere nature, nor mere art. Mainly it has lain from age to age in a continuing collaboration between author and public. His public has been prompting him for more than three centuries, and he it. He and it have been breathing the same air, been impelled by the same emotions.

As remarkable are the Songs. Elizabethan lyrics have a trick, happily not invariable in them, of ingenuity and artifice. Shakespeare's, unless, perhaps, in Love's Labour Lost, shook themselves free. They grow without an effort out of the action, spirit, and character. Up they start, wild spring flowers, wherever we set our feet. All show a delicious naïveté, a bird-like liberty. Take as instances the Fairy's air in A Midsummer Night's Dream :

> I serve the fairy queen,
> To dew her orbs upon the green :
> The cowslips tall her pensioners be ;
> In their gold coats spots you see,
> Those be rubies, fairy favours,
> In those freckles live their savours ;
> I must go seek some dewdrops here,
> And hang a pearl in every cowslip's ear ; [1]

the praise of Silvia in Two Gentlemen of Verona :

> Who is Silvia ? What is she,
>   That all our swains commend her ?
> Holy, fair, and wise is she,
>   The heavens such grace did lend her,
> That she might admired be ; [2]

Balthasar's song in Much Ado About Nothing :

> Sigh no more, ladies, sigh no more :
>   Men were deceivers ever ;
> One foot in sea, and one on shore :
>   To one thing constant never ; [3]

that of Amiens in As You Like It:

> Under the greenwood tree,
>   Who loves to lie with me,
>   And tune his merry note
>   Unto the sweet bird's throat,
> Come hither, come hither, come hither;
>   Here shall he see
>   No enemy
>   But winter and rough weather; [4]

the boy's song, though the authorship is less certain, in Measure for Measure:

> Take, O take those lips away,
>   That so sweetly were forsworn;
> And those eyes, the break of day,
>   Lights that do mislead the morn:
> But my kisses bring again, bring again;
> Seals of love, but sealed in vain, sealed in vain; [5]

the air-music in The Tempest:

> Come unto these yellow sands,
>   And then take hands; [6]

Ariel's farewell to serfdom:

> Where the bee sucks, there suck I;
>   In a cowslip's bell I lie;
> There I couch when owls do cry;
> On the bat's back I do fly
>   After summer merrily:
> Merrily, merrily, shall I live now,
> Under the blossom that hangs on the bough; [7]

and the serenade in Cymbeline:

> Hark! hark! the lark at heaven's gate sings,
>   And Phoebus 'gins arise,
> His steeds to water at these springs
>   On chaliced flowers that lies;
> And winking Mary-buds begin
>   To ope their golden eyes;
> With everything that pretty is:
>   My lady sweet, arise;
>   Arise, arise! [8]

The grace and daintiness are wonderful. The variety would be yet more amazing were it not become to us a matter of course that each song should accord with its environings. In the whole range of English poetry nothing produces a fuller sense of the joy of life, the breadth of life, its completeness, than the whole lovely company. My trouble is that, while I labour to praise, and am sensible that I cannot enough, I feel I am a trespasser on the Plays, and, after a sort, utterly beside the mark. The songs do not ask, and indeed scarcely suffer, eulogies on their poetical perfection. Those airy lyrics are not rightly to be viewed as aught in themselves. They just are effluences, native emanations from the movement of the dramas on which they bloom, with less substance than a blossom, with no more of tangibility than the blossom's fragrance. Strictly, as I am well aware, I ought not to have been picking and choosing at all, and certainly not with a view to intrinsic beauty. Catches like,

> While greasy Joan doth keel the pot,
> Adieu, goodman drivel,
> For a quart of ale is a dish for a king,
> 'Tis merry in hall when beards wag all,

are as opportune where they occur as Ariel's carollings. The only plea I can offer in extenuation is, that, for the present purpose, my concern is with Shakespeare the Poet, not with Shakespeare the Dramatist.

While he was shedding, fast and carelessly, these double miracles, the Plays and their Songs, he must have been dreaming over his Lucrece, his Venus and Adonis, and his Sonnets. Throughout them, if especially in the Sonnets, he is recondite, introspective, demonstratively subtle, self-conscious, sensitively, sensuously, eager to call attention to his personal feelings and idiosyncrasies, scrupulous in diction. Though it seems grotesque to characterize Shakespeare as a stylist, there he is one, as much as Waller. The most delicate problems of life and society are attacked without the least fear of injurious interpretations. Each line has been studied, and is a study. Nothing has been thrown out to take its chance of sinking or swimming.

Signs abound of a very different mode of regarding thought and learning in general from the manner of the Plays. In those the possession of knowledge, universal knowledge, is as it were taken for granted. No parade of it is made. As it is wanted it is present in whatever character might be expected to be equipped with it. As the dramatist acquired it, the store turned at once into dramatic flesh and blood. History, law, romance, were simply materials ' pour servir '. A professed scholar like Milton might in good faith have regarded him as, in the Plays, wholly, ' fancy's child ', and his conversance with the world of the past and its literature as intuition rather than research. The praise of the ' native wood-notes wild ', had it referred to the Poems, so-called, would have been curiously inept. These Milton probably either had never known, or in his Puritan severity had chosen to forget. Critical discernment such as his, if directed to them, could not have failed to see everywhere the work of a student, hard, anxious brain-work, brain-lace-work. Not to compare them specially with dramatic dialogue and narrative, note a contrast as entire between their essential spirit and that even of the dramatic lyrics. An impassable abyss divides the gushes of song in the woods of Attica, Arden, Britain, Illyria, Prospero's isle of magic, Bohemia—never studied, never extravagant, never out of keeping—from the unbuskined poet's ecstasies of passionate desire, passionate friendship, and passionate despair.

The beauties of the Plays, surprising as they are, scarcely

surprise, as, in their due course, they unfold themselves; they seem inevitable. One would like to be sure that their author was aware of the prodigies issuing from him; that he felt he was conversing with spirits of the air. At all events in the Sonnets and Tales we are never in any doubt of his sense of copyright. He does not attempt to hide his pride in them, and in the pains they have cost him. He was entitled to be proud. If the poet's aim be to imagine every point of view from which a single idea can be contemplated, to view it with all possible lights and shades upon it, to intoxicate himself with it, until for him it grows to be the sun round which the celestial system revolves, then Shakespeare can have told himself that in his Poems he had succeeded. They evince a prodigality of effort and patience; and he desired they should. In the Plays he was a disembodied voice; a voice audible by any that chose to listen; ready to serve each character whose turn it was to be heard. Here he is his individual self, singing, discoursing, to an audience in any case very few, if fit.

Though no maker of music like this could bear to be without something of a public, I do not suppose that he expected or cared to shout his melodies into the common ear. In his Venus and Adonis he indulged an artist's, something also of a psychologist's, wish to explore the utmost extravagance of license conceivable in a Being uniting intense animalism with supernatural independence of shame and of self-respect. The wealth of imagery was lavished for scholars steeped in the spirit of the Renaissance, not, though something of humour may be suspected, for the popular admirers of the Merry Wives. The disappointed goddess's appeal to and against Death, with its tempest of furious figures and conceits, moves, and was meant to move, rather the intellect than the heart:

> ' Hard favour'd tyrant, ugly, meagre, lean,
> Hateful divorce of love,'—thus chides she Death,—
> ' Grim-grinning ghost, earth's worm, what dost thou mean
> To stifle beauty and to steal his breath,
>   Who when he lived, his breath and beauty set
>   Gloss on the rose, smell to the violet ?
>
> ' Hadst thou but bid beware, then he had spoke,
> And, hearing him, thy power had lost his power.
> The Destinies will curse thee for this stroke ;
> They bid thee crop a weed, thou pluck'st a flower :
>   Love's golden arrow at him should have fled,
>   And not Death's ebon dart, to strike him dead.' [9]

The Lucrece stirs finer and loftier feelings, yet springing from analogous sources. The innocent loveliness of Lucrece asleep is portrayed with exquisite art :

> Without the bed her other fair hand was,
> On the green coverlet ; whose perfect white
> Show'd like an April daisy on the grass,
> With pearly sweat, resembling dew of night.
> Her eyes, like marigolds, had sheathed their light,
>   And canopied in darkness sweetly lay,
>   Till they might open to adorn the day.[10]

The self-disgust of the caitiff himself at his hateful triumph is touched with the hand of a master. Note the grand third line :

> For now against himself he sounds this doom,
> That through the length of times he stands disgraced ;
> Besides, his soul's fair temple is defaced.[11]

His agonized victim prays that there may be devised :

>   extremes beyond extremity,
> To make him curse this cursed crimeful night.[12]

On his behalf, with a refinement of vengefulness, she even, like Kehama, demands of Time a reprieve for him from premature death :

> Let him have time to tear his curled hair,
> Let him have time against himself to rave,
> Let him have time of Time's help to despair,
> Let him have time to live a loathed slave,
> Let him have time a beggar's orts to crave,
>   And time to see one that by alms doth live
>   Disdain to him disdained scraps to give.[13]

It might seem that the poet, unlike the dramatist, too constantly enlarges, appears never to know when to stop. But here it was not enough for him to strike his blow, to have carried the action a stage on. It is a study upon which he is engaged. His fancy has to explore the wide field of a guiltless woman's torments at enforced partnership in an act of guilty lust. He has to ransack, and exhibit, the horrible petty details, the girl's shuddering belief that the loutish groom who shyly takes her order to fetch her husband from the camp, must be conscious of her fall, as he looks upon her :

> For Lucrece thought he blush'd to see her shame,[14]

The intensity of poetical introspection, the keenness of spiritual vivisection, reach their extreme point, however, in the Sonnets. Their subject, Southampton, Pembroke, or anybody else, and their precise object, as the chain of harmony sways to and fro, are immaterial to us. Probably they soon became so, if individual substance they ever had, to their artificer. He compacted them out of dreams, in a trance of all active mental powers but imagination. Ordinary readers in the later generations,

> That wear this world out to the ending doom,

on whom he prophetically counted—'eyes not yet created'—to immortalize his verse, will choose from a dozen to a score, more or fewer,[15] of the hundred and fifty-four to cherish.

They will dwell upon isolated lovelinesses, upon visions of dainty melancholy ;

> When to the sessions of sweet silent thought
> I summon up remembrance of things past,
> I sigh the lack of many a thing I sought,
> And with old woes new wail my dear time's waste.
> Then can I drown an eye unused to flow,
> For precious friends hid in death's dateless night,
> And weep afresh love's long since cancell'd woe,
> And moan the expense of many a vanish'd sight :
> Then can I grieve at grievances foregone,
> And heavily from woe to woe tell o'er
> The sad account of forebemoaned moan,
> Which I new pay as if not paid before.
>   But if the while I think on thee, dear friend,
> All losses are restored and sorrows end ; [16]

upon the spell of one absorbing love ; a summary of a whole life's dear loves :

> Thy bosom is endeared with all hearts,
> Which I by lacking have supposed dead ;
> And there reigns love, and all love's loving parts,
> And all those friends which I thought buried.
> How many a holy and obsequious tear
> Hath dear religious love stol'n from mine eye,
> As interest of the dead, which now appear
> But things removed which hidden in thee lie !
> Thou art the grave where buried love doth live,
> Hung with the trophies of my lovers gone,
> Who all their parts of me to thee did give ;
> That due of many now is thine alone :
>   Their images I loved I view in thee,
>   And thou, all they, hast all the all of me. [17]

For the wondrous play of fancy they will smile a pardon at the extravagance of idolatry which can find no parallel for such unchanging charm ;—not even in

a summer's day.
Thou art more lovely and more temperate ;
Rough winds do shake the darling buds of May,
And summer's lease hath all too short a date ;
Sometime too hot the eye of heaven shines,
And often is his gold complexion dimm'd ;
And every fair from fair sometimes declines,
By chance or nature's changing course untrimm'd ;
But thy eternal summer shall not fade,
Nor lose possession of that fair thou owest ;
Nor shall Death brag thou wander'st in his shade,
When in eternal lines to time thou growest :
  So long as men can breathe, or eyes can see,
  So long lives this, and this gives life to thee.[18]

He is the sun which a terrestrial adorer cannot expect to shine upon him without occasional clouds to intervene :

Full many a glorious morning have I seen
Flatter the mountain tops with sovereign eye,
Kissing with golden face the meadows green,
Gilding pale streams with heavenly alchemy :
Anon permit the basest clouds to ride
With ugly rack on his celestial face,
And from the forlorn world his visage hide,
Stealing unseen to west with this disgrace :
Even so my sun one early morn did shine
With all-triumphant splendour on my brow ;
But, out, alack ! he was but one hour mine,
The region cloud hath mask'd him from me now,
  Yet him for this my love no whit disdaineth ;
  Suns of the world may stain when heaven's sun staineth.[19]

He is the rose, which will die, as roses must, but be fragrant in the tomb :

O, how much more doth beauty beauteous seem,
By that sweet ornament which truth doth give !
The rose looks fair, but fairer we it deem
For that sweet odour which doth in it live.

The canker-blooms have full as deep a dye
As the perfumed tincture of the roses,
Hang on such thorns, and play as wantonly
When summer's breath their masked buds discloses:
But, for their virtue only is their show,
They live unwoo'd and unrespected fade;
Die to themselves. Sweet roses do not so:
Of their sweet deaths are sweetest odours made:
  And so of you, beauteous and lovely youth,
  When that shall fade my verse distills your truth.[20]

To the poet himself the whole were no garden from which to cull a blossom here and there; they made a single bouquet, to be enjoyed as a whole. Such it still is to his modern worshippers, who, if put to the tragic necessity of choosing, I can well believe, would, to save the Sonnets, sacrifice Lear, The Tempest, Othello. There the difference is between them and the common lover of poetry, like myself. It is the same difficulty which arises in the endeavour to form a true estimate of Sidney's analogous series. Here, as with that, it is simple justice to strive to see through the eyes of the author himself. By Shakespeare, as by Sidney, and with more inexorable consistency, the universe of fancy had been ransacked to crown his ideal of boundless friendship. There are conceits which excite a smile, and wild freaks of self-denial and forgiveness. Thus, it is rank treason to discover in the Beloved—the ever 'kind and true' because 'eternally fair'—specks on the 'sun's' disk, like apparent fickleness and cruelty; merest peccadilloes, though among them be desertion; robbery of a mistress's love; nay, positive aversion:

  Then hate me when thou wilt![21]

He had himself anticipated a charge of monotony in his verse,
    so barren of new pride,
  So far from variation or quick change.[22]

But if he is thought tedious, it is that the reader has not learnt, or does not care, to follow, step by step ; to apply the microscope to passion. Each Sonnet adds a fresh touch to elaborate tracery. The workmanship, to be appreciated, must be regarded in the spirit in which it was executed. Shakespeare was compelling his own heart to beat before him while he registered its every pulsation. The theme he had set himself was a fantasy of love, one-sided, feeding on itself, conjuring up all possible experiences of joy and suffering it could traverse. If one can be proved to be wanting, he has failed ; if none, he has triumphed.

When a great artist has undertaken difficult work, and has done it superlatively well, it is officious to attempt to criticize, or even justify, the enterprise. To try to explain the selection of the particular subject is lawful. Strange as it seems for the creator of King Lear, Macbeth, The Tempest, Hamlet, Othello, Shylock, Romeo and Juliet, A Midsummer Night's Dream, to have complained of his introduction into the career which led direct to them, without which they might never have existed, it was disgust at the Stage which probably we have in a large measure to thank for the star-shower of the Sonnets. A heart such as his must have sorely ached before it gave way to a moan like this :

> Alas, 'tis true I have gone here and there,
> And made myself a motley to the view,
> Gored mine own thoughts, sold cheap what is most dear.
> Made old offences of affections new ;
> Most true it is that I have looked on truth
> Askance and strangely ! [23]

before he could bring himself to chide bitterly with Fortune,

> The guilty goddess of my harmful deeds,
> That did not better for my life provide
> Than public means which public manners breeds.

> Thence comes it that my name receives a brand,
> And almost thence my nature is subdued
> To what it works in, like the dyer's hand;
> Pity me then and wish I were renew'd.[24]

In inditing his Sonnets, he was free at least from the slavery to public caprices, which he abhorred. He had to consult not moods of the crowd, but those of his friend, or his own. As he wove his brain into these miracles of embroidery, doubtless he felt that he

> possessed his soul before he died.

Paying no heed what became of a Hamlet and the like, he looked with assured hope to his Sonnets for immortality:

> So long as men can breathe, or eyes can see,
> So long lives this, and this gives life to thee.[25]

> Yet do thy worst, old Time; despite thy wrong,
> My love shall in my verse ever live young.[26]

> When you entombed in men's eyes shall lie,
> Your monument shall be my gentle verse,
> Which eyes not yet created shall o'er-read;
> And tongues to be your being shall rehearse,
> When all the breathers of this world are dead;
> You still shall live—such virtue hath my pen—
> Where breathe most breaths, even in the mouths of men.[27]

He deceived himself both in underrating the greatness of one part, the chief, of his life's business, and in overrating the capacity of posterity at large for comparative appreciation of the other. The Sonnets owe to the Dramas, not indeed a survival of their radiance, but an infinite expansion of its range. If 'with that key' Shakespeare 'has unlocked his heart',[28] it is that the Plays by thousands of lightning flashes had guided after-ages through the shades in which the casket was lying all but forgotten. At the same time it may be acknowledged that, if there be still room for

WILLIAM SHAKESPEARE

fresh bewilderment in the endeavour to plumb and measure the height, depth, and breadth of the powers of an eternal, inscrutable paradox, there are always the Sonnets to make darkness visible by occupying the vacant space. Students of letters, to offer a precedent for the doubled enigma, must go back as far as to Dante—and then, perhaps, in vain.

Shakespeare, ed. W. G. Clark and W. Aldis Wright. Macmillan & Co.
[1] A Midsummer Night's Dream, Act ii, Sc. 1.
[2] Two Gentlemen of Verona, Act iv, Sc. 2.
[3] Much Ado About Nothing, Act ii, Sc. 3.
[4] As You Like It, Act ii, Sc. 5.
[5] Measure for Measure, Act iv, Sc. 1.
[6] The Tempest, Act i. Sc. 2.   [7] Ibid., Act v, Sc. 1.
[8] Cymbeline, Act ii, Sc. 3.
[9] Venus and Adonis, vv. 931-7 and 943-8.
[10] The Rape of Lucrece, vv. 393-9.   [11] Ibid., vv. 717-19.
[12] Ibid., vv. 69-70.   [13] Ibid., vv. 981-7.   [14] Ibid., v. 1344.
[15] Nos. 18, 29, 30, 31, 33, 54, 55, 60, 71, 72, 73, 76, 81, 86, 87, 89-98, 99, 104, 116.
[16] No. 30.   [17] No. 31.   [18] No. 18.   [19] No. 33.
[20] No. 54.   [21] No. 90.   [22] No. 76.   [23] No. 110.
[24] No. 111.   [25] No. 18.   [26] No. 19.   [27] No. 81.
[28] Wordsworth, Miscellaneous Sonnets, Part II, No. 1.

BEN JONSON

1573 ?—1637

L'ALLEGRO owes amends to the memory of Ben Jonson for popularizing the legend that learning was his chief distinction. Like inferior contemporaries who referred to Jonson's learning, Milton limited the qualification to the drama.[1] By that he intended panegyric rather than blame. Later ages have construed the criticism as general, and read into it a charge of pedantry. Far from repelling any such insinuation, Jonson himself, it must be admitted, seems in his plays to confirm it. Yet I do not know that, applicable as it may be to him, it is not equally appropriate to others. For the most part dramatists of the period were scholars, and not shy of displaying their classical attainments. To Jonson's lyrics, at all events, it is not much more relevant than to Fletcher's, certainly not more than to Shakespeare's Venus and Adonis, or the Rape of Lucrece.

Consider them on their intrinsic merits; and it may be argued that they have equals; I think it would be hard to find their superiors. Simplicity is among their primary charms, as in the ideal woman:

> Give me a look, give me a face,
> That makes simplicity a grace;
> Robes loosely flowing, hair as free;
> Such sweet neglect more taketh me,
> Than all the adulteries of art;
> They strike mine eyes, but not my heart.[2]

The same quality rises to perfection in the Song to Celia:

Drink to me, only with thine eyes,
   And I will pledge with mine;
Or leave a kiss but in the cup,
   And I'll not look for wine.
The thirst that from the soul doth rise,
   Doth ask a drink divine;
But might I of Jove's nectar sup,
   I would not change for thine.

I sent thee late a rosy wreath,
   Not so much honouring thee,
As giving it a hope that there
   It could not wither'd be.
But thou thereon didst only breathe,
   And sent'st it back to me;
Since when it grows, and smells, I swear,
   Not of itself, but thee.[3]

Nothing here is elaborate; there is scarcely a show of ingenuity. The idea is the merest thistledown. The words might be set to an infant school for a spelling exercise. They have fallen each into its own natural, necessary place, as easily as the stones into the walls of Thebes at the bidding of Amphion's lute.

So with the eulogy of Truth:

   Truth is the trial of itself,
     And needs no other touch;
   And purer than the purest gold,
     Refine it ne'er so much.

   It is the life and light of love,
     The sun that ever shineth,
   And spirit of that special grace,
     That faith and love defineth.

   It is the warrant of the word,
     That yields a scent so sweet,
   As gives a power to faith to tread
     All falsehood under feet.[4]

It runs as limpidly as a popular hymn; only, with depths in it. The Epitaph on 'Elizabeth' would equally befit a village tombstone and a monument in Westminster Abbey:

> Underneath this stone doth lie
> As much beauty as could die;
> Which in life did harbour give
> To more virtue than doth live.[5]

Doubtless art informed the fabric; but the scaffolding is gone. It is seldom indeed that, as towards the conclusion of the otherwise spontaneous lament for the Child of Queen Elizabeth's Chapel:

> Weep with me, all ye that read
>   This little story;
> And know, for whom a tear you shed
>   Death's self is sorry,[6]

he cares in his lyrics to parade his knowledge, astronomical or mythological—'three-filled Zodiacs', and repentant 'Parcae'. Such display is exceptional. Commonly, even when he chooses to be gracefully, almost coldly, Hellenic, as in a Hymn to Diana, there is no affectation of classical tropes and phraseology:

> Queen and huntress, chaste and fair,
>   Now the sun is laid to sleep,
> Seated in thy silver chair,
>   State in wonted manner keep:
>   Hesperus entreats thy light,
>   Goddess, excellently bright.
>
> Lay thy bow of pearl apart,
>   And thy crystal shining quiver;
> Give unto the flying hart
>   Space to breathe, how short soever
>   Thou that mak'st a day of night,
>   Goddess excellently bright.[7]

The same virtue distinguishes the famous epitaph on Lady Pembroke :

> Underneath this sable herse
> Lies the subject of all verse,
> Sidney's sister, Pembroke's mother ;
> Death ! ere thou hast slain another,
> Learn'd and fair, and good as she,
> Time shall throw a dart at thee ! [8]

Jonson's authorship has been disputed on the ground, partly, of its appearance, with an added stanza, in manuscripts of William Browne's poems ; partly, of Browne's reference in his elegy on Lady Pembroke's grandson, Lord Herbert, to verses by him mourning the young lord's grand-dame. Possibly the copyist intentionally prefixed Jonson's six lines to Browne's ; and Browne's own allusion in his epitaph on Lord Herbert, still more probably, was to his undoubted elegy on the grandmother. To me the stanza, terse and masterful, breathes all over of Jonson. But he is rich enough to dispense even with it, or with any other controverted attributions in Underwoods.

I have dwelt first on the beauty of his simplicity, in answer to the popular fable of his pedantry. The feature which, more than his learning, and equally with the simple sweetness, impresses me in his verse, is the gift of thinking high thoughts while he sings. The melody flows on meanwhile ; the diction, which suited the lament for a dead child, remains as unaffected, though on a different plane, when he discourses profundities. The meaning is recondite, the language continues to be beautifully natural. View the Picture he dreams of a noble mind lodged in as fair a body :

> A mind so pure, so perfect fine,
> As 'tis not radiant, but divine ;
> And so disdaining any trier,
> 'Tis got where it can try the fire.

> Whose notions when it will express
> In speech, it is with that excess
>   Of grace, and music to the ear,
>   As what it spoke it planted there.
> The voice so sweet, the words so fair,
> As some soft chime had stroked the air,
>   And though the sound were parted thence,
>   Still left an echo in the sense.
> But that a mind so rapt, so high,
> So swift, so pure, should yet apply
>   Itself to us, and come so nigh
>   Earth's grossness; there's the how and why.
> Hath she here, upon the ground,
> Some Paradise or palace found,
>   In all the bounds of Beauty, fit
>   For her t' inhabit? There is it.
> Thrice happy house, that hast receipt
> For this so lofty form, so straight,
>   So polish'd, perfect, round, and even,
>   As it slid moulded off from heaven.
> Smooth, soft, and sweet, in all a flood
> Where it may run to any good;
>   And where it stays, it there becomes
>   A nest of odorous spice and gums.
> In action, wingèd as the wind;
> In rest like spirits left behind
>   Upon a bank, or field of flowers,
>   Begotten by the wind and showers.[9]

It is the same in the imaging of true love:

> A golden chain let down from heaven,
>   Whose links are bright and even,
> That falls like sleep on lovers;[10]

in his promise of Heaven's blessing to the honest soldier:

>   Go seek thy peace in war;
> Who falls for love of God shall rise a star;[11]

and, lastly, in the two sublime elegies—pæans rather—one on the young Marchioness of Winchester:

> Go now, her happy parents, and be sad,
> If you not understand what child you had,
> If you dare grudge at heaven, and repent
> T' have paid again a blessing was but lent;
> If you can envy your own daughter's bliss,
> And wish her state less happy than it is; [12]

the other, on the two friends, Sir Lucius Cary and Sir H. Morison:

> It is not growing like a tree
> In bulk, doth make men better be;
> Or standing long an oak, three hundred year,
> To fall a log at last, dry, bald, and sear;
> A lily of a day
> Is fairer far in May
> Although it fall and die that night;
> It was the plant and flower of light.
> In small proportions we just beauties see;
> And in short measures, life may perfect be. [13]

Really Jonson's is too big a soul to be labelled under either simplicity or art. In one, as in the other, he is a master. He is equally enchanting, whether he sue to Celia in words of one syllable, with sense, sweet sense, corresponding, or tie knots with joyous ingenuity, and exquisite rhythm. Hear him, as in an ecstasy he compares the beauties of Charis to all conceivable perfection:

> Have you seen but a bright lily grow,
>   Before rude hands have touch'd it?
> Have you mark'd but the fall of the snow
>   Before the soil hath smutch'd it?
> Have you felt the wool of the bever?
>   Or swan's down ever?
> Or have smelt o' the bud of the briar?
>   Or the nard in the fire?
> Or have tasted the bag of the bee?
> O so white! O so soft! O so sweet is she! [14]

Or as he rhapsodizes on the dead mistress's glove and

> The rosy hand that wear thee,
> Whiter than the kid that bare thee.[15]

He can be at once extravagant and excusable, in the absurdly pretty conceit of the sand in an hour-glass being the remains of a lover, who

> in his mistress' flame, playing like a fly,
> Was turned to ashes by her eye.[16]

The variety is inexhaustible. He is at home in a fencing school, with a right noble moral:

> It is the law
> Of daring not to do a wrong; 'tis true
> Valour to slight it, being done to you.[17]

Perhaps he is even too jovially inspired in a wine-cellar, Bacchus's temple, where the god makes

> Many a poet,
> Before his brain do know it.[18]

We feel him to be always certain of his effect, whatever the subject. Above all, how generous with praise, well worth having, was this man who has been accused of malevolence and mean jealousy! Good words, not merely for the dead, whom it costs nothing to praise, but for living contemporaries, fellow workers, rivals! And, among those, laudation, not of manifest inferiors alone, a Nicholas Breton, a Thomas Wright, a May, a Rutter, but of a Chapman also, a Beaumont, a Fletcher, a William Browne.

His admiration stops not with genius which he was confident he could match, probably exceed. He had the honesty of intellect, the greatness of soul, to recognize a superior. Never has Shakespeare—outshining, in spite of 'small Latin and less Greek', even 'Marlowe's mighty line '—been crowned with a worthier wreath than Jonson's to a Beloved Memory. The elegy is the sole authentic source of all we know, or need to know, of contemporary opinion on the portent. And he who does obeisance is the one man who could with any show of right have grudged it!

> Soul of the age!
> The applause! delight! the wonder of our stage!
> My Shakespeare, rise! I will not lodge thee by
> Chaucer, or Spenser, or bid Beaumont lie
> A little further off, to make thee room:
> Thou art a monument without a tomb,
> And art alive still, while thy book doth live,
> And we have wits to read, and praise to give.
> Triumph, my Britain, thou hast one to show,
> To whom all scenes of Europe homage owe.
> He was not of an age, but for all time!
> And all the Muses still were in their prime,
> When, like Apollo, he came forth to warm
> Our ears, or, like a Mercury, to charm.
> Nature herself was proud of his designs,
> And joyed to wear the dressing of his lines!
> Yet must I not give nature all; thy art,
> My gentle Shakespeare, must enjoy a part;
> For a good poet's made as well as born
> And such wert thou! [19]

Rare Ben Jonson indeed! Rough-tongued, hard-drinking, self-assertive; lavish and out-at-elbows, not ashamed to beg, to petition for conversion of official marks into market pounds; miscellaneous in his companionships, from Prince Charles at Whitehall to King James's victim, romantic Ralegh in the Tower: a fond remembrance for holy Henry Vaughan and courtly Suckling alike; a very Prince of Bohemia; a despot in his Apollo Club room, where he promulgated his laws [20] to a circle of vassals, often foes in disguise; on the lyre, most of all, a sovereign, and there, I scarcely fear to say, no man's inferior, unless his Dear Master's'. When his own and a couple of succeeding generations classed the two together, they did not go so far wrong that we cannot at least understand them. As I read, I have felt throughout, in meditating how to rank him as poet, not as dramatist, that he must sit either nowhere, or among the Greatest. Am I wrong in seating him with them?

The Works of Ben Jonson, ed. William Gifford.
[1] L'Allegro, vv. 131-2.
[2] Epicoene, or, The Silent Woman, Act i, Sc. 1.
[3] To Celia, Song 9 (The Forest). [4] Truth (Underwoods, No. 26).
[5] Epitaph on Elizabeth L. H. (Epigrams, No. 124).
[6] Epitaph on Salathiel Pavy—A Child of Queen Elizabeth's Chapel (Epigrams, No. 120).
[7] Cynthia's Revels; or, The Fountain of Self-Love, Act v, Sc. 3.
[8] Epitaph on the Countess of Pembroke (Underwoods, No. 15).
[9] The Picture of the Mind (Underwoods, Eupheme, No. 4).
[10] Epode (The Forest, No. 11).
[11] An Epitaph to a Friend, Master Colby, to persuade him to the Wars Underwoods, No. 32).
[12] Elegy on the Lady Jane Paulet, Marchioness of Winton Underwoods, No. 100).
[13] A Pindaric Ode to the immortal Memory and Friendship of that Noble Pair, Sir Lucius Cary and Sir H. Morison. Strophe (Underwoods, No. 87).
[14] A Celebration of Charis. IV. Her Triumph (Underwoods).
[15] Cynthia's Revels, Act iv, Sc. 1.
[16] The Hour-Glass (Underwoods, Miscell. Poems, No. 6).
[17] To William, Earl of Newcastle, on his Fencing (Underwoods, No. 88).
[18] Dedication of the King's New Cellar to Bacchus (Underwoods, No. 66).
[19] To the Memory of my beloved Master William Shakespeare, and what he hath left us (Underwoods, No. 12).
[20] Leges Convivales—Rules for the Tavern Academy.

FRANCIS BEAUMONT, 1584—1616

AND

JOHN FLETCHER, 1579—1625

JOHN FLETCHER, as the senior, might well claim to have his name placed first in the strange, famous partnership. The reversed order is in accordance with all we might have expected from the author of The Faithful Shepherdess. What we could have least anticipated is, perhaps, if he were to be a professional dramatist at all, that he should have fathered, whether singly, or jointly, many of the pieces attributed to the literary firm. He ought to have been read in books, not seen on the stage ; to have been poet, not playwright. As a dramatist, he was applauded by two or three generations. He might have been immortal as a poet with Herrick, possibly with Spenser and Milton.

No heights, in lyrics, were beyond the author of the delightful farewell of the Satyr to his adored type of chastity :

> Thou most virtuous and most blessed,
> Eyes of stars, and golden-tressed
> Like Apollo ! tell me, sweetest,
> What new service now is metest
> For the Satyr ? Shall I stray
> In the middle air, and stay
> The sailing rack, or nimbly take
> Hold by the moon, and gently make
> Suit to the pale queen of night
> For a beam to give thee light ?

> Shall I dive into the sea,
> And bring thee coral, making way
> Through the rising waves that fall
> In snowy fleeces ? Dearest, shall
> I catch thee wanton fawns, or flies
> Whose woven wings the summer dyes
> Of many colours ? Get´thee fruit,
> Or steal from Heaven old Orpheus' lute ?
> Holy virgin, I will dance
> Round about these woods as quick
> As the breaking light, and prick
> Down the lawns, and down the vales
> Faster than the windmill-sails.
> So I take my leave, and pray
> All the comforts of the day,
> Such as Phoebus' heat doth send
> On the earth, may still befriend
> Thee and this arbour ! [1]

of the exquisite appeals, to Death, or against Death :

> Lay a garland on my hearse
>   Of the dismal yew ;
> Maidens, willow branches bear ;
>   Say, I died true ;
> My love was false, but I was firm
>   From my hour of birth.
> Upon my buried body lie
>   Lightly, gentle earth ; [2]

and

> Weep no more, nor sigh, nor groan ;
> Sorrow calls no time that's gone :
> Violets plucked the sweetest rain
> Makes not fresh nor grow again ; [3]

or of the Passionate Lord's ecstasy over 'only melancholy', of which Il Penseroso itself shows reminiscences ;

Hence, all you vain delights,
As short as are the nights
  Wherein you spend your folly !
There 's nought in this life sweet,
If man were wise to see 't,
      But only melancholy :
      Oh, sweetest melancholy !

Welcome, folded arms, and fixed eyes,
A sigh that piercing mortifies,
A look that 's fasten'd to the ground,
A tongue chain'd up without a sound !

Fountain-heads, and pathless groves,
Places which pale passion loves !
Moonlight walks, when all the fowls
Are warmly housed, save bats, and owls !
      A midnight bell, a parting groan !
      These are the sounds we feed upon ;
Then stretch our bones in a still gloomy valley :
Nothing 's so dainty sweet as lovely melancholy.[4]

The Faithful Shepherdess is one song. There are pauses of dialogue, full of tranquil poetry, of plot, or a semblance of plot, just for rest to the singer's throat. Then out melody bursts from heath, grove, or river. English poetry has nothing to match it ; not its, in other ways, unparalleled superior, A Midsummer Night's Dream ; not Comus. From the Satyr's joyous amazement, in the first scene, at the sight of the fair vestal Clorin :

      Lowly do I bend my knee,
      In worship of thy deity ;[5]

to his vigil in the wood, where his great master, Pan,

      Entertains a lovely guest,
      Where he gives her many a rose,
      Sweeter than the breath that blows
      The leaves ;[6]

thence, to his flitting with a wounded swain in his arms.

> Through still silence of the night,
> Guided by the glow-worm's light,[7]

with the final parting from the maiden he reverently loves, the poet has transfigured the 'rude man and beast'. It is a new being that would have surprised and charmed graceless Ovid no less than self-dedicated Clorin.

Fletcher's fancy, like the god's 'flower plucked with holy hand', has a kindly magic power. From it, in turn, the rough amorous god of field and forest rises etherealized—like his satellite—into the beneficent genius of fold and cot,

> that keep'st us chaste and free
> As the young spring,[8]

with priests as gracious, good, and tuneful. Wanton, heartless, heart-breaker, Adonis-persecuting Venus he remoulds into a

> Fair sweet goddess, queen of loves,
> Soft and gentle as thy doves;[9]

the broom-man's humble wares become things of beauty to be purchased with kisses:

> For a little, little pleasure,
> Take all my whole treasure;[10]

and the beggar's rags and homespuns realize Ariel's life of bliss:

> In the world look out and see,
> Where's so happy a prince as he![11]

Even a dead landlord, revisiting his inn, bids the guests regale on his best, with no bill to follow, except for a decent funeral![12]

Whatever the theme, be it the awaking to a sense of the witchery of:

>   Beauty clear and fair,
>   Where the air
>   Rather like a perfume dwells;
>   Where the violet and the rose
>   Their blue veins in blush disclose
>   And come to honour nothing else.
>
>   Where to live near,
>   And planted there,
>   Is to live, and still live new;
>   Where to gain a favour is
>   More than light, perpetual bliss,
>   Make me live by serving you; [13]

be it a merry threat against teetotallers:

>   He that will to bed go sober
>   Falls with the leaf still in October; [14]

or the hard problem:

>   Tell me, dearest, what is love? [15]

the touch is always light and happy. Fletcher has the gift, as Shakespeare in his Songs, of spontaneity. Like Shakespeare, he is in them impersonal, though after a different fashion. Shakespeare's lyrics suggest character, whether of the singer, or of the scene they diversify. Fletcher's usually breathe neither of the particular play in which they occur, nor of the poet, but of his real period. His genius, when actually he was writing under James, is distinctly Elizabethan. His poetry partakes of the essence of that golden age, with its double front; on one side patriotism and enterprise, often heroic, often rapacious, and Renaissance romance on the other. Ralegh represented both aspects; Fletcher, in his lyrics, the second. As poet he is ever on the wing, and sings as he flies. To us it is an abrupt plunge from the pure ether of his lyrics to his mere earth, either tragedy, or comedy, An early seventeenth-century audience felt no shock at the contrast, of which probably neither it nor the author was particularly sensible.

The high poetical rank of Fletcher's songs is indisputable. Yet, unless in anthologies, they do not appear, until recent times, to have been printed apart from his and his colleague's dramas. Beaumont, while still living, was introduced to the public as a poet. As a translator he is well entitled to praise. His juvenile version of Ovid's metamorphosis of Prodromus. though selected unfortunately for modern taste, indicates an intuitive feeling for the analogy between the Elizabethan and the Augustan spirit. It explains the bygone fondness for Dan Ovid as the prince of story-tellers. The bulk of his original writing, unless we override tradition and internal evidence, and share equally between him and Fletcher the lyrics in the pieces in which he collaborated, is, but for an occasional line, such as

> Sorrow can make a verse without a muse.[16]

characterized by sheer mediocrity. It is made up for the most part of cobwebs and spluttering fireworks, with two capital exceptions.

But then, what exceptions! How could our English Helicon do without Beaumont's reminiscences of Ben Jonson's fellowship!

> What things have we seen
> Done at the Mermaid! heard words that have been
> So nimble, and so full of subtile flame,
> As if that everyone from whence they came
> Had meant to put his whole wit in a jest,

Of his dull life ; then when there hath been thrown
Wit able enough to justify the town
For three days past ; wit that might warrant be
For the whole city to talk foolishly
Till that were cancell'd ; and when that was gone,
We left an air behind us, which alone
Was able to make the two next companies
Right witty ; though but downright fools, mere wise ! [17]

How, above all, could it spare the reverie in Westminster Abbey !

> Mortality, behold, and fear,
> What a change of flesh is here !
> Think how many royal bones
> Sleep within this heap of stones ;
> Here they lie, had realms and lands,
> Who now want strength to stir their hands ;
> Where from their pulpits seal'd with dust,
> They preach, ' In greatness is no trust ! '
> Here 's an acre sown indeed
> With the richest, royal'st seed,
> That the earth did e'er suck in
> Since the first man died for sin ;
> Here the bones of birth have cried,
> ' Though gods they were, as men they died ; '
> Here are sands, ignoble things
> Dropt from the ruin'd sides of kings.
> Here 's a world of pomp and state
> Buried in dust, once dead by fate ! [18]

It is one of the many strange transformation scenes in poetical history. Suddenly, as we weary over a painful elegy on Lady Rutland, or fret at the petty whimsicalities of an amour with a dead mistress in her grass-green mantle of the grave, a veil seems to have been withdrawn, and the true man to appear—a fit companion for John Fletcher !

The Works of Beaumont and Fletcher, ed. George Darley. Two vols. E. Moxon, 1840.

[1] The Faithful Shepherdess, Act v, Sc. 5.
[2] The Maid's Tragedy, Act ii, Sc. 1.
[3] The Queen of Corinth, Act iii, Sc. 2.
[4] The Nice Valour; or, the Passionate Madman, Act iii, Sc. 3.
[5] The Faithful Shepherdess, Act i, Sc. 1.
[6] Ibid., Act iii, Sc. 1.   [7] Ibid., Act iv, Sc. 2.
[8] Ibid., Act i, Sc. 2.   [9] The Mad Lover: Act v, Sc. 1.
[10] The Loyal Subject, Act iii, Sc. 5.
[11] The Beggar's Bush, Act ii, Sc. 1.
[12] The Lovers' Progress, Act iii, Sc. 5.
[13] The Elder Brother, Act iii, Sc. 5.
[14] The Bloody Brother, Act iv, Sc. 2.
[15] The Captain, Act ii, Sc. 2.
[16] An Elegy on the Death of the Countess of Rutland.
[17] Mr. Francis Beaumont's Letter to Ben Jonson, vol. ii, p. 710.
[18] On the Tombs in Westminster Abbey.

DR. JOHN DONNE
1573—1631

A STRANGE career, a strange nature! Heir to a saving London merchant. Brought up a Roman Catholic. Comrade of Essex and Ralegh in the famous dare-devil raid upon Cadiz, and in the less fortunate Islands Voyage. Beloved of stately, charming Countesses, and other ladies many, with more of charm and less of stateliness. Shining at Courts foreign and English. Revelling at taverns with Ben Jonson and the players, as wild a wit as the wildest. A born rebel against convention, and its slave. According to Izaak Walton, by the time he was twenty, to Jonson, by twenty-five, in the front rank of poets, admirable alike for skill and for audacity. Baring his heart in its nakedness, which was 'le tout', by voice and pen to earn his circle's applause. Never, during his singing season, condescending to print, which would have brought the public renown he despised. Scattering among love ditties insolently amorous, angelic hymns, not rarely unangelically besmirched. Then—suddenly—priest, preacher, theologian, dignitary, moralist, faithful husband, —a theme, cheek by jowl with meek, profound Hooker, courtly and saintly Herbert, decorous, dexterous, and diplomatic Wotton, for the seventeenth-century chastened Boswell; his Muse sulky, because forbidden to be proterva, productive of none but an occasional, perhaps apocryphal, psalm; yet, it may be, hard tasked at times to scowl down a protesting sigh after the naughty praedecanal nights, when there were cakes and ale and aching brows, rioting, remorse, and rioting again!

The verse of his youth is a complete armoury of whatever can be said in flattery of women, and of most that can be imagined against them. The compliments he pays them are always double-edged :

>   I walk to find a true love : and I see
>   That 'tis not a mere woman, that is she,
>   But must or more or less than woman be.
>   Yet know I not which flower
>   I wish ; a six or four ;
>   For should my true-love less than woman be,
>   She were scarce anything ; and then, should she
>   Be more than woman, she would get above
>   All thought of sex, and think to move
>   My heart to study her, and not to love.
>   Both these were monsters ; since there must reside
>   Falsehood in woman, I could more abide
>   She were by art than nature falsified.[1]

By preference he is frankly abusive :

>   If thou be'est born to strange sights,
>   Things invisible go see,
>   Ride ten thousand days and nights
>   Till Age snow white hairs on thee ;
>   Thou, when thou return'st, wilt tell me
>   All strange wonders that befell thee,
>   And swear
>   No where
>   Lives a woman true and fair.[2]

In his rage against a coquette who has induced Love to implant himself with all her barbed lures and deceits in his heart, he threatens the god and her that, after executing a misanthropic will by which he gives, among other generous bequests of nothings,

>   My best civility,
>   And courtship to an University,

he will, vindictively, even perish :

> I'll undo
> The world by dying, because love dies too.
> Then all your beauties will be no more worth
> Than gold in mines, where none doth draw it forth,
> And all your graces no more use shall have
>   Than a sun-dial in a grave :
>   Thou, Love, taught'st me by making me
>   Love her who doth neglect both me and thee,
> To invent and practise this one way, to annihilate all three ![3]

Conjugal affection itself with him has more passion than respect in it :

> Stay O sweet, and do not rise ;
> The light that shines comes from thine eyes :
> The day breaks not, it is my heart,
> Because that you and I must part.
>   Stay, or else my joys will die,
>   And perish in their infancy.[4]

Ingenuity is his forte ; and in that he is transcendent. Try to unravel the web, for instance, of The Primrose, The Bracelet—Ben Jonson's favourite—with its alternate curses and blessings upon the thief of the jewel, according as, child of Hell or ' honest man ', he kept or restored it—and think how little Mrs. Donne, and other objects of the poems—perhaps, for the most part, fortunately—understood of them. His fancy coils and uncoils, as if it were a serpent, progressing all the time. Its point of honour is to say nothing as it had ever been said before; to be brilliant, almost idolatrous ; everything which a lover can be, except sweet and gentle.

Yet, within the limits, what mastery ! Readers must allow for a harshness of phraseology, which Donne seems to have cultivated, and for a rhythm which, though possessing a harmony of its own, is as uncouth. Subject to these eccentricities, they will find the appeal, for instance, to his young wife exquisite :

> Dear love, for nothing less than thee
> Would I have broke this happy dream ;
>   It was a theme
> For reason, much too strong for fantasy.
> Therefore thou waked'st me wisely ; yet
> My dream thou brokest not, but continued'st it.
> Thou art so true that thoughts of thee suffice
> To make dreams truths and fables histories ;
> Enter these arms, for since thou thought'st it best
> Not to dream all my dream, let 's act the rest.
>
> As lightning, or a taper's light,
> Thine eyes, and not thy noise, waked me ;
>   Yet I thought thee—
> For thou lovest truth—an angel at first sight ;
> But when I saw thou saw'st my heart,
> And knew'st my thoughts beyond an angel's art,
> When thou knew'st what I dreamt, when thou knew'st when
> Excess of joy would wake me, and camest then,
> I must confess it could not choose but be
> Profane to think thee anything but thee.
>
> Coming and staying show'd thee thee,
> But rising makes me doubt that now
>   Thou art not thou.
> That Love is weak where Fear's as strong as he ;
> 'Tis not all spirit pure and brave
> If mixture it of Fear, Shame, Horrour have.
> Perchance as torches, which must ready be,
> Men light and put out, so thou deal'st with me.
> Thou camest to kindle, go'st to come ; then I
> Will dream that hope again, but else would die.[5]

Here are fire and grace too, added to the marvellous sword-play of ' wit ', in its Elizabethan meaning. Remarkable, however, as it is, it has its parallels elsewhere in Donne's verse. Finer examples may be cited from other poets of poetic workmanship, art, craft, of thought, of inspiration, severally; few finer, of all in combination. In him the casuist and the poet, with an anticipation even of the preacher, were wrought into a single being. It is impossible to distinguish which is the groundwork, which the embroidery, which the master, which the servant. Thought is interlaced with thought. There are aphorisms as wise as they are epigrammatic; for instance:

> Christ's gallant humbleness.
> Be thine own palace, or the world's thy gaol.
> He that believes himself doth never lie.

Ideas knot themselves together, as if they never could be disentangled. Then in an instant the pattern unfolds itself radiantly clear, only an instant later to present a fresh bewildering maze.

No one class of the poems can claim a monopoly of this sinuous subtlety. We find it equally in the pieces entitled 'Divine'; for instance, in the explanation of the Christ-God's assumption of frail flesh:

> that so
> He might be weak enough to suffer woe.

There too it appears in union with passion and a bitter humour; as in the scoffing defiance of the King of Terrors;

> Death, be not proud, though some have called thee
> Mighty and dreadful, for thou art not so;
> For those, whom thou think'st thou dost overthrow,
> Die not, poor Death, nor yet canst thou kill me.
> From rest and sleep, which but thy picture be,
> Much pleasure, then from thee much more must flow,
> And soonest our best men with thee do go;
> Rest of their bones, and soul's delivery.
> Thou'rt slave to Fate, chance, kings, and desperate men,
> And dost with poison, war, and sickness dwell,
> And poppy, or charms can make us sleep as well,

And better than thy stroke! why swell'st thou then?
One short sleep past, we wake eternally,
And Death shall be no more; Death, thou shalt die.[6]

Yet more triumphantly book-lore, philosophy—of the prae-inductive order—bigness of brain, and passion—all his eminent gifts—united to produce the Letters, and the pieces comprised in the Anatomy of the World, and the Progress of the Soul. We can watch, as in the epistle to Lady Salisbury, an idea expanding, swelling into a solemn chant. A grander note still sounds in the Second Anniversary of the death of Elizabeth Drury. There, in a sublime vein Donne at once mocks and exalts Death:

Think thee laid on thy death-bed, loose and slack,
And think that but unbinding of a pack,
To take one precious thing, thy soul, from thence.
Think thyself parch'd with fever's violence;
Anger thine ague more, by calling it
Thy physic; chide the slackness of the fit.
Think that thou hear'st thy knell, and think no more,
But that, as bells call'd thee to church before,
So this to the triumphant church calls thee.
Think Satan's sergeants round about thee be,
And think that but for legacies they thrust.
Give one thy pride, to another give thy lust;
Give them those sins which they gave thee before,
And trust th' immaculate blood to wash thy score.
Think thy friends weeping round, and think that they
Weep but because they go not yet thy way.
Think that they close their eyes, and think in this,
That they confess much in the world amiss,
Who dare not trust a dead man's eyes with that
Which they from God and angels cover not.[7]

If for all a release, death surely was immediate bliss for one already half ethereal in life, whose

> pure and eloquent blood
> Spoke in her cheeks, and so distinctly wrought
> That one might almost say, her body thought ; [8]

one whom it was impossible fitly to praise or mourn :

> She, she is dead, she's dead ; when thou know'st this,
> Thou know'st how dry a cinder this world is ! [9]

Upwards mounts the strain, delineating an ideal maiden— as the elegist imagined the girl he had never seen—caught up to Heaven at fifteen—to its climax :

> Since His will is that to posterity
> Thou should'st for life and death a pattern be,
> And that the world should notice have of this,
> The purpose and th' authority is His.
> Thou art the proclamation ; and I am
> The trumpet, at whose voice the people came. [10]

Donne's age felt the majesty of his thought. It saw no presumptuousness in the prediction :

> I will through the wave and foam,
> And shall in sad lone ways, a lively sprite,
> Make my dark heavy poem light, and light.
> For though through many straits and lands I roam,
> I launch at Paradise, and I sail towards home ! [11]

In the Satires a different key is struck. He is neither Psalmist and eulogist, nor lover, wit, and gay courtier. No longer even is he a Sphinx propounding enigmas. He is a hammer, red-hot, exulting in searing as it crushes. Hard, unsparing, he becomes as austere a moralist then as his master Persius, and as deliberately rugged. With a fervour far exceeding the Roman's he denounces the moral cowardice of Christian gentlemen :

> Hast thou courageous fire to thaw the ice
> Of frozen North discoveries ; and thrice
> Colder than salamanders, like divine
> Children in th' oven, fires of Spain and the line,

> Whose countries limbecs to our bodies be,
> Canst thou for gain bear? and must every he
> Which cries not, 'Goddess!' to thy mistress, draw,
> Or eat thy poisonous words? Courage of straw!
> O desperate coward, wilt thou seem bold, and
> To thy foes and his, who made thee to stand
> Sentinel in his world's garrison, thus yield,
> And for forbid wars leave th' appointed field?
> Know thy foes; the foul devil, he whom thou
> Strivest to please, for hate, not love, would allow
> Thee fain his whole realm to be quit; and as
> The world's all parts wither away and pass,
> So the world's self, thy other loved foe, is
> In her decrepit wane, and thou, loving this,
> Dost love a wither'd and worn strumpet; last,
> Flesh, itself's death, and joys which flesh can taste,
> Thou lovest; and thy fair goodly soul, which doth
> Give this flesh power to taste joy, thou dost loathe.[12]

As bravely he upholds the right, the duty, of manly, not litigious, Doubt:

> Doubt wisely; in strange way,
> To stand inquiring right, is not to stray:
> To sleep, or run wrong, is. On a huge hill,
> Cragged and steep, Truth stands, and he that will
> Reach her, about must and about must go.
> And what the hill's suddenness resists, win so.
> Yet strive so, that before age, death's twilight,
> Thy soul rest, for none can work in that night.[13]

Contemporaries admired, for the novelty, Donne's experiments to test how much rhythm and rhymes will bear without breaking. They objected so little to unscrupulous coarseness, which did not confine itself to secular verse, that King James insisted upon the ordination of the author of the audacious Epithalamion on his daughter, and made him Dean of St. Paul's. Quaint quips and turns of a high-flavoured conceit delighted them, as they spiced their dishes with ambergris and scents. They regarded allusions to physiological and medical details as by no means inappropriate to mysteries of Faith. Many modern critics and students have so steeped themselves in the most brilliant of English literary eras as to find nothing distasteful in its ugly accidents of social usage. The rest of us may have been a little spoilt by the magnificent cleanliness of one transcendent writer of the period. We are tempted to forget that Epithalamia and the like did not shock Shakespeare's own admirers. But we have to do with facts; and the fact is that the ordinary lover of poetry wants to be free to dip into a volume without having to allow for rudenesses of diction or sentiment in consideration of its date. It is nothing to him as he reads, or lets read, that the singer in his hot youth, at the time he sang, was a professed wit, or preying upon the Spaniard. He does not care to pick his way through mud on the chance of happening, like a barn-door fowl of superior discernment, upon a precious stone in the midden. A habit consequently has grown up of ceasing popularly to reckon Donne as more than a contributor to selections, while, without recognizing the source, we use many of his lines and phrases as elements of the English language.

I have expressed my sorrow for the common neglect, and have endeavoured to trace the cause. The attempt and the result aggravate the regret, and for the poet as well as his work. The more I consider the excellence of that and its blemishes, the harder it remains to comprehend how the same fancy should have vented such grossness with such ethereal conceptions; how an offensive classical allusion should have been allowed to jar and mar the transfiguration declared in noble language to be wrought at Ordination by the laying-on of hands; how the same potent fancy should have employed itself, at one moment, on epistolary communications to noble Englishwomen full of lofty beauty and piety, and, at another, on letters from Sappho suggestive of all the reverse. It may readily be believed that the various obnoxious verses 'had been loosely scattered in their author's youth'; that 'in his penitential years he wished his own eyes had witnessed their funerals'.[14] Still the problem is unsolved, how they could ever have been born of him. Still posterity, which might have pardoned obscurity, but insists that literature for its daily food shall be wholesomely pure, has to share the penalty with him for licence which has lost it, in the mire, not a few heavenly anthems!

John Donne—Poems, ed. E. K. Chambers. Two vols. Lawrence & Bullen, 1896. (Also, John Donne—Poems, complete, ed. A. B. Grosart. Two vols. Fuller Worthies' Library, 1872.)

[1] The Primrose, At Montgomery Castle, vv. 8-20.
[2] A Falling Star, Song, st. 2.
[3] The Will, vv. 21-2 and 46-51.
[4] Break of Day.   [5] The Dream (Songs and Sonnets).
[6] Holy Sonnets, x (Divine Poems).
[7] An Anatomy of the World—On the Progress of the Soul—The Second Anniversary, vv. 93-112.
[8] Ibid., vv. 244-6.
[9] An Anatomy of the World—The First Anniversary, vv. 427-8.
[10] An Anatomy of the World—The Progress of the Soul—The Second Anniversary, vv. 523-8.
[11] The Progress of the Soul, Song vi, vv. 53-7.
[12] Satire III, vv. 21-42.   [13] Ibid. 77-84.
[14] Isaak Walton. Life of Dr. John Donne, p. 35. Oxford, 1824.

GEORGE HERBERT

1593—1633

THE model, the exemplar, the prince, of sacred poets. Not equal to one of his immediate successors in mystic piety, to another in enthusiasm; but knowing best what he wanted, and able to execute whatever he felt needed and ought to be accomplished by his pen. Made to lead, not follow. Sidney's peer in rank, force of brain, warmth of heart, sense of national duty, courtly fascination, romance. Endowed with a fancy as vivid as Sir Philip's for singing in ladies' bowers of a mistress's curls, enchanted groves, and purling streams refreshing a lover's wooing. Diverted thence by a more powerful strain in his nature, chivalrous after another sort, which enlisted him as the sworn soldier of his Church.

Had he remained a courtier, his own age and posterity would have lost The Temple in exchange for many dexterous songs, if only on 'a scarf or glove', on 'fictions and false hair'. He must have sung, whatever the subject. His nature, the bent of the period, and of the society to which he had belonged, being what they were, he hymned a Heavenly, very much as otherwise he would have extolled an earthly, love. Unconsciously he spun his lines:

Catching the sense at two removes.

The prevailing taste was to treat a topic for verse as the scientific chemist treats a substance he is compelling to reveal all its capabilities. Herbert is not a whit behind Sidney in the almost cruel skill and patience with which he dissects the subject of his adoration. Read, in proof,

The Reprisal, Easter Wings, The Sinner, Conscience, The Anagram, the last three lines of The Dawning, Affliction, Jesu, Love Unknown, Paradise, The Bag, Praise, Grief, The Source, The Odour, The Forerunners, The Rose. And these are but specimens!

They exhibit the extravagance, often the 'coarseness', which he stigmatizes as deforming contemporary love-ditties. In them the adorable simplicity of Gospel truths, the pure awe of Christian mysteries, are grotesquely travestied. He seems to think it enough that imagery is eccentric for it to be beautiful. He attests the sincerity of service to Heaven by the racking of fancy. Even the passion with which doubtless he started has, long before the climax, spent all motive force in its passage round the sharp curves of wit. If they stood alone, and we were unacquainted with Herbert's holy life and character, we might have been tempted to think the author something perhaps of a self-deceiver, and certainly little of a poet. Happily the faults are fashion's rather than his. A true soul shines out from the excrescences of style, and, what mainly concerns us here, an inspired singer.

Not all his artifices, fireworks of wit, themselves are to be condemned. In their season, and kept within due bounds, they add piquancy and point to pregnant thought. I could not wish away the surprise that the dead Christ should have found no warm heart to sojourn in :

> O blessed bodie ! Whither art thou thrown ?
> No lodging for thee but a cold hard stone ?
> So many hearts on earth, and yet not one
>   Receive thee ?[1]

A grand idea animates the enigma :

> Ah, my deare God ! though I am clean forgot,
> Let me not love thee, if I love thee not.[2]

It is a touching appeal of dumb creation to Man to worship the Creator that he alone owns, on behalf of all, the voice, pen, and knowledge, being the appointed 'Secretary' of God's praise.[3] We feel the pathetic sweet reality in the unreality of a literal acceptance of the entreaty not to 'grieve the Holy Spirit':

> And art thou grieved, sweet and sacred Dove,
>   When I am sowre,
>   And crosse thy love?
> Grieved for me? The God of strength and power
>   Griev'd for a worm?[4]

The conceit, again, that Man's Maker, like a fairy godmother, after forming him, proceeded to pour from a glass upon his head all earthly gifts but 'rest', in order that, if not goodness, weariness might toss him to his Father's breast,[5] is of an ingenuity indistinguishable from, and as winning as, simplicity.

He has told how, when he began to sing of celestial joys, he feared he could never be at pains sufficient to deck the lustrous sense. He sought out quaint words, trim invention, curling metaphors, blotting often that he had written, till he heard a whisper:

> There is in love a sweetnesse readie penn'd.[6]

Had he foreseen, and cared to gratify, the curiosity of posterity, by arranging his poems in order of date, he would have enabled us to judge how far they comply with the counsel. As it is, they manifestly differ in the degree of obscuration of a 'plain intention'. Though all are liable to occasional contortions of fancy, these frequently divert rather than offend. Thus, we recognize the seventeenth century, not its eccentricities, in the point of view of primaeval purity, when,

> Before that sinne turn'd flesh to stone,
> And all our lump to leaven ;
> A fervent sigh might well have blown
> Our innocent earth to Heaven ; [7]

of Redemption, as an old-world story of ill-requited seignorial magnanimity ; [8] of Humility, as a character in an Aesop's fable ; [9] of the wondrous metamorphosis of the whilom King of Terrors ; now, through the Saviour's death :

> gay and glad
> As at doom's day.
> When souls shall wear their new array,
> And all thy bones with beautie shall be clad ; [10]

of the dizzy play of transfused spirits, human and divine, in Clasping of Hands ; [11] and of Sunday, the day on which 'Heaven's gate stands ope'. yet 'a day of mirth ' :

> O Day most calm, most bright.
> The fruit of this, the next world's bud.
> Th' indorsement of supreme delight.
> Writ by a friend, and with his bloud :
> The couch of time ; cares calm and bay ;
> The week were dark but for thy light ;
> Thy torch doth show the way. [12]

Not rarely, though I know that the rust of antiquity is never wholly absent from Herbert's verse, I am reluctant to acknowledge any qualification by such an accident of its perennial, absolute music. To all time belongs a succession of lovely creations ; the picture of the soul swaying from hope to despair, and from despair to hope, according as it feels that spirit or flesh, brute or angel, or God's creature, is in the ascendant :

> take thy way ; for sure thy way is best ;
> Stretch or contract me thy poore debter :
> This is but tuning of my breast,
> To make the musick better ; [13]

the cry to the falling star to lodge in the singer's heart, and, having burnt its lusts to death, fly homewards with it to their Saviour's bright dwelling;[14] the agonized gratitude in the Dialogue, with its indignant disclaimer of a right to share in the benefits of Christ's sacrifice;[15] the perfect grace of Church-music:

>   Now I in you without a bodie move,
>   Rising and falling with your wings;
>   We both together sweetly live and love,
>   Yet say sometimes, ' God help poore Kings!'[16]

the spiritualizing of groans, ' quick and full of wings ', from a contrite heart:

>   And ever as they mount, like larks they sing:
>   The note is sad, yet music for a king;[17]

the black gloom, with one thin ray piercing through, of Mortification, man's death in life;[18] the Christmas Carol, combining the senses into one interchangeable offering of thanksgiving, till the sunshine sings, and the music shines;[19] Divine Love's lovingly impatient imperativeness to the timid guest;[20] the prayer at waking to be enabled to discover the Creator and his works by the fresh light of the new dawn:

>   Teach me thy love to know:
>   That this new light, which now I see,
>   May both the work and workman show:
>   Then by a sunne-beam I will climbe to thee;[21]

and that precious thing, the Christian's patent of nobility for menial toil:

>   Teach me, my God and King,
>   In all things thee to see,
>   And what I do in any thing,
>   To do it as for thee.
>   A servant with this clause
>   Makes drudgerie divine;
>   Who sweeps a room, as for thy laws,
>   Makes that and th' action fine.[22]

Lastly, there are Virtue, and The Flower. The first is of a quiet beauty which is curiously winning :

> Sweet day, so cool, so calm, so bright,
> The bridall of the earth and skie ;
> The dew shall weep thy fall to-night ;
>   For thou must die.
>
> Sweet rose, whose hue angrie and brave
> Bids the rash gazer wipe his eye ;
> Thy root is ever in its grave,
>   And thou must die.
>
> Sweet spring, full of sweet dayes and roses,
> A box where sweets compacted lie ;
> My musick shows ye have your closes,
>   And all must die.
>
> Only a sweet and virtuous soul,
> Like season'd timber, never gives ;
> But though the whole world turn to coal,
>   Then chiefly lives.[23]

As for The Flower, what self-abasement, what a proud soaring fancy !

> How fresh, O Lord, how sweet and clean
> Are thy returns ! ev'n as the flowers in spring ;
> To which, besides their own demean
> The late-past frosts tributes of pleasure bring.
>   Grief melts away
>   Like snow in May,
> As if there were no such cold thing.
>
> Who would have thought my shrivel'd heart
> Could have recover'd greennesse ? It was gone
> Quite underground ; as flowers depart
> To see their mother-root, when they have blown ;
>   Where they together
>   All the hard weather,
> Dead to the world keep house unknown.

These are thy wonders, Lord of Power,
Killing and quick'ning, bringing down to hell
  And up to heaven in an houre;
Making a chiming of a passing bell.
      We say amisse
      This or that is;
Thy word is all, if we could spell.

O that I once past changing were,
Fast in thy Paradise, where no flower can wither!
  Many a spring I shoot up fair,
Offring at heav'n, growing and groning thither;
      Nor doth my flower
      Want a spring-showre,
My sinnes and I joining together:

But while I grow in a straight line,
Still upwards bent, as if heav'n were mine own,
  Thy anger comes, and I decline:
What frost to that? What pole is not the zone,
      Where all things burn,
      When thou dost turn,
And the least frown of thine is shown?

And now in age I bud again,
After so many deaths I live and write;
  I once more smell the dew and rain,
And relish versing: O my onely light,
      It cannot be
      That I am he
On whom thy tempests fell all night.

These are thy wonders, Lord of love,
To make us see we are but flowers that glide:
  Which when we once can finde and prove,
Thou hast a garden for us, where to bide.
      Who would be more,
      Swelling through store,
Forfeit their Paradise by their pride.[24]

As his best, when in the mood to sing, and not singing

because the Church Calendar ordered a song, he can scarcely be excelled. Mistrust of the vanity of imagination had habituated him to check spontaneous inspiration. As soon as he gave it freedom, forth it gushed, sparkling, gracious, and grateful. The diction is at once forcible and elegant; not the less racy that it is scholarly, not the less fitted for prayer and praise that it had been the language of Universities and Courts.

He was a religious enthusiast grafted on a man of the world. I wonder whether his votaries read and meditate on the wisdom of the Church-porch.[25] What can Nicholas Ferrar, his pious literary executor, have thought of that part of the bequest? Never was there produced a more useful manual for the conduct of life. In general its maxims might have been fathered by Poor Richard. It is a storehouse of advice, not in the least fanatical, against a host of common follies; 'the third glass'; the taking of God's name in vain, which, worse than lust, wine, and avarice, with their positive, if evil, pleasures, 'gets thee nothing': living beyond one's means, especially in middle life or age; the as silly 'scraping', than which nothing is 'so wasteful'; play 'for gain, not sport', and 'striving to sit out losing hands'; much laughter—'The witty man laughs least'; fierceness in arguing—'Cunning fencers suffer heat to tire'; with many other saws as true, and as secular. Lofty and generous precepts are liberally intermixed; such as:

> Fool not; for all may have
> If they dare try, a glorious life or grave;
>
> Take starres for money; starres not to be told
> By any art;
>
> Thy friend put in thy bosome; wear his eies
> Still in thy heart, that he may see what 's there.

All worldly joyes go lesse
To the one joy of doing kindnesses.

Scorn no man's love, though of a mean degree;
Love is a present for a mightie King.

But there remains the pervading collocation of cold, worldly sagacity with the fiery zeal, the ecstatic piety, of the Churchman. It is phenomenal. A suspicion will obtrude itself, not so much that the Saint may once have been ever so little of a sinner, as that the original man of the world, of affairs, continued to underlie the preacher, the psalmist!

May he not have been happy in his early death? Had he lived, he could not but have become a Prince of the Church. Statesmanlike, learned, of noble blood, renowned, he must have found protestations, 'Nolo episcopari', flatteringly overridden. With many-sided powers such as his, he would in the end have ruled. With a rigid, one-sided conscience such as his, the Ritualism of a Laud doubled with the Puritanism of a Cotton Mather, he might, for the soul's good, have persecuted. That, in the days which followed, he would himself have suffered—for never could he have bowed or bent—matters less; but he would not have been the parish priest of Bemerton, of The Temple, the sweet, the soul-saving, singer we love.

The Temple (or The Church). By George Herbert. Facsimile Reprint of the First Edition. With Introduction by A. B. Grosart. Elliot Stock, 1876.

[1] Sepulchre.
[2] Affliction (last two lines).
[3] Providence.
[4] Grieve not the Holy Spirit
[5] The Pulley.
[6] Jordan.
[7] The Holy Communion.
[8] Redemption.
[9] Humilitie.
[10] Death.

FIVE CENTURIES OF ENGLISH VERSE

[11] Clasping of Hands.
[13] The Temper.
[15] Dialogue.
[17] Sion.
[19] Christmas.
[21] Mattens.
[23] Vertue.
[25] The Church-porch—Perirrhanterium.

[12] Sunday.
[14] The Starre.
[16] Church-Musick.
[18] Mortification.
[20] Love, p. 183.
[22] The Elixer.
[24] The Flower.

RICHARD CRASHAW

1613 ?—1649

'If the Roman Congregation which adjudicates on claims to sanctity knew its business, it would long since have beatified Richard Crashaw. Rightly did Cowley in his lovely monody hail him Poet and Saint. The pure, beautiful unworldly spirit ; as unfitted to struggle with circumstances as a nestling shaken out by a gale upon the rough earth ; who, but for the kind offices of his brother in exile and genius, might—poet, scholar, artist, musician, linguist, though he was—have, without a protesting murmur, starved to death on the stones of Paris ! Such a 'sport' as that hard age of battlings to the death among antagonisms, political, national, theological, seemed specially adapted to produce in sheer contrariety to itself. Nothing in it of combative humanity and its energies ; all soul and its yearnings. Less of the theologian, even the ecclesiastic, than Herbert, once a man of the world and affairs ; infinitely less than Donne, who never ceased to be ; but formed beyond either to exist, breathe, and sing, in an atmosphere of pure spirit ; a Christian poet-recluse.

A nature like his might have been expected to burst into hymns ; as of the Epiphany, with its crowd of fast-hurrying fancies ; and of meek abdication of all hope unless from one source, like the paraphrase of the Dies Irae. For him, though still a Protestant, nothing was alien in adoration, charmingly extravagant, of 'the Admirable' Saint Teresa's self-martyrdom. The sweetness, somewhat cloying, of the shower of fancy accompanying the gift of a prayer-book to a lady hesitating on the margin of Romanism, was natural in the pietist. When, as rarely, he actually fails, it is through undertaking subjects requiring material sublimity. Thus the Sospetto d'Herode, a poor anticipation of Milton, is, like its Italian original, a jumble of tiresome exaggeration. The picture of Satan, chained to his throne of quenchless fire, is inartistically overladen. The Devil's rage in particular, that a lowly infant, cradled in a manger, should have been chosen as his rival for the sovereignty of earth, is ridiculous. Happily Crashaw's good taste felt the inadequacy of the epic, and the version did not proceed beyond the first book.

His genius was made for suffering, not for doing; not for profound thought, but for tender feeling. There, too, and more seriously than in service to a Saint Teresa, he was liable to error from lack of a due sense of proportion. Rapt into a Paradise of pious imagination, he strays into the grotesque. In that series of lovely images, The Weeper, angels are told off to draw into their crystal vials water from the Magdalene's eyes for their Master to drink, and for 'their own wine'! So plenteous is the supply that it furnishes 'two walking baths', 'compendious oceans'. The hymn on the Circumcision, amidst a host of beauties, illustrates the same extraordinary incompetence to bridle fancy. So long, however, as the poet keeps within his own field, he redeems what in another would be bad taste with his irresistible ingenuousness, blissful resignation, dreaming abstraction, incapability of imagining wrong. Every blemish he blots by a beauty. It seems an outrage even to plead excuses for transgressions which arise out of a flood of holy aspiration after absorption of the human into the Divine.

Had he stopped with strains like the Epiphany, the Weeper, the Circumcision, the Anglican laud of Santa Teresa, he would still have been a poet to cherish. Not a sting, not one drop of venom. None even in the few secular English pieces. None hidden under the excellent diction of the many Classical. But 'bounded', one who had read in him so far might say; 'a singer with no large repertory; no unexpectedness about his delicate, graceful Muse'. Let any who so think listen, in the Hymn of the Nativity, to the shepherds' enumeration of their wonderings, during their search for the new-born king, where they should find him laid; how one had imagined

> the curl'd drops, soft and slow,
> Come hovering o'er the place's head,
> Off'ring their whitest sheets of snow
> To furnish the fair infant's bed;
> 'Forbear,' said I; 'be not too bold,
> Your fleece is white, but 'tis too cold';

while another in fancy

> saw the obsequious Seraphim
> Their rosy fleece of fire bestow,
> For well they now can spare their wings,
> Since Heaven itself lies here below;

only for both to find the Heavenly Babe nestling peacefully in the Virgin's bosom:

> No, no, your King's not yet to seek
> Where to repose His royal head;
> See, see, how soon His new-bloom'd cheek
> 'Twixt mother's breasts is gone to bed.
> 'Sweet choice,' said we, 'no way but so
> Not to lie cold, yet sleep in snow!' [1]

They may go on to the jubilant summons by Heaven to the Madonna:

> Rise up, my fair, my spotless one,
> The Winter's past, the rain is gone,
> The Spring is come, the flowers appear,
> No sweets—save thou—are wanting here; [2]

to the poet's ardent appeal to his own soul to pass the boundaries of

        One little world or two,

in the search of fitting service to The Name Above Every Name :

    Go, Soul, out of thyself, and seek for more ;
        Go, and request
    Great Nature for the key of her huge chest
    Of Heaven's, the self-involving set of spheres—
    Which dull mortality more feels than hears—
        Then rouse the nest
    Of nimble Art, and traverse round
    The airy shop of soul-appeasing sound ;
    And beat a summons in the same
        All-sovereign name,
    To warn each several kind
    And shape of sweetness, be they such
        As sigh with subtle wind
        Or answer artful touch ;
    That they convene and come away
    To wait at the love-crowned doors of that
        Illustrious day ; [3]

and still mount up to the passion of the Flaming Heart—Santa Teresa's ;

    By the full Kingdom of that final kiss
    That seized thy parting soul, and seal'd thee His ;
    By all the Heaven thou hast in Him—
    Fair sister of the Seraphim !—
    By all of Him we have in thee ;
    Leave nothing of myself in me.
    Let me so read thy life, that I
    Unto all life of mine may die ! [1]

till they arrive, lastly, at the ecstasy of Sancta Maria Dolorum, where

        Son and Mother
    Discourse alternate wounds to one another !
        Quick deaths that grow
    And gather as they come and go.

His nails write swords in Her, which soon her heart
    Pays back with more than their own smart;
Her swords, still growing with His pain,
Turn spears, and straight come home again.
    She sees her Son, her God,
    Bow with a load
    Of borrow'd sins, and swim
In woes that were not made for Him.
    Ah, hard command
    Of love! Here must She stand,
Charged to look on, and with a steadfast eye
    See her life die;
Leaving her only so much breath
As serves to keep alive her death.[5]

The eleven stanzas are an inspiration, I would almost say, incomparable in hymnology—a combination of woe and triumph, submission and sovereignty, pathos, spiritual sublimity, everything!

'Lastly', did I write? Yes; and I think it Crashaw's furthest, his highest, effort in the region of sacred song. Yet not the final, the loftiest, within his compass as mere poet. It has been so much, and so naturally, the custom to regard him as set apart for minstrelsy in the Sanctuary, that I question if many of his professed admirers often recall another work of his with which I question if even the Mater Dolorosa can vie in absolute melody. How often have the nightingale's praises been sung, and how often most worthily! Gather the whole choir into the lists, and you must award the wreath of Laureate of the grove to Crashaw. Nothing could be more masterly than the ease, the instinct with which, in the contest he has figured between a musician by the Tiber and a feathered rival, he measures a bird's untutored instinct against a lute's 'trembling murmurs', 'wild airs', combining all into a triumphant diapason.

Philomela is doomed to be vanquished in the cruel, fatal struggle—'sweet soul'—

> To measure all those wild diversities
> Of chatt'ring strings, by the small size of one
> Poor simple voice, rais'd in a natural tone.

But glorious the defeat, and death !

> Her supple breast thrills out
> Sharp airs, and staggers in a warbling doubt
> Of dallying sweetness, hovers o'er her skill,
> And folds in wav'd-notes with a trembling bill
> The pliant series of her slippery song ;
> Then starts she suddenly into a throng
> Of short thick sobs, whose thundering volleys float
> And roll themselves over her lubric throat
> In panting murmurs 'still'd out of her breast,
> That ever-bubbling spring, the sugar'd nest
> Of her delicious soul, that there does lie
> Bathing in streams of liquid melody.
> There might you hear her kindle her soft voice
> In the close murmur of a sparkling noise,
> And lay the groundwork of her hopeful song,
> Still keeping in the forward stream, so long,
> Till a sweet whirlwind, striving to get out,
> Heaves her soft bosom, wanders round about,
> And makes a pretty earthquake in her breast,
> Till the fledged notes at length forsake their nest,
> Fluttering in wanton shoals, and to the sky,
> Wing'd with their own wild echoes, pratt'ling fly.
> She opes the floodgate, and lets loose a tide
> Of streaming sweetness, which in state doth ride
> On the wav'd back of every swelling strain,
> Rising and falling in a pompous train;
> And while she thus discharges a shrill peal
> Of flashing airs, she qualifies their zeal
> With the cool epode of a graver note,
> Thus high, thus low, as if her silver throat

Would reach the brazen note of war's hoarse bird.
Her little soul is ravish'd, and so pour'd
Into loose ecstasies, that she is placed
Above herself, Music's enthusiast ! [6]

And again, lastly—a last 'lastly '—what of the Inspiration known to a whole world unknowing else of Crashaw, which any readers I have—which I myself—have been waiting to see marshalled and ranked—what of :

Whoe'er she be,
That not impossible She,
That shall command my heart and me ?

Where'er she lie,
Lock'd up from mortal eye,
In shady leaves of Destiny ;

Till that ripe Birth
Of studied Fate stand forth,
And teach her fair steps to our earth ;

Till that divine
Idea take a shrine
Of crystal flesh, through which to shine ;

Meet you her, my Wishes,
Bespeak her to my blisses,
And be ye call'd, my absent kisses.

I wish her beauty,
That owes not all its duty
To gaudy tire, or glist'ring shoe-tie ;

A face that's best
By its own beauty dress'd,
And can alone command the rest,—

A face made up
Out of no other shop
Than what Nature's white hand sets ope ;

A well-tamed heart,
For whose more noble smart
Love may be long choosing a dart ;

Life that dares send
A challenge to his end,
And when it comes say, Welcome, friend!

Sidneian showers
Of sweet discourse, whose powers
Can crown old Winter's head with flowers;

Soft silken hours,
Open suns, shady bowers;
'Bove all, nothing within that lowers;

Whate'er delight
Can make Day's forehead bright,
Or give down to the wings of Night.

I wish her store
Of worth may leave her poor
Of wishes; and I wish—no more.

Now if Time knows
That Her, whose radiant brows
Weave them a garland of my vows—

Her whose just bays
My future hopes can raise,
A trophy to her present praise,

Her that dares be
What these lines wish to see—
I seek no further—it is She.

'Tis She, and here
Lo! I unclothe and clear
My Wish's cloudy character!

May She enjoy it,
Whose merit dare apply it,
But Modesty dares still deny it.

Such Worth as this is
Shall fix my flying wishes,
And determine them to kisses.

Let her full glory,
My fancies, fly before ye,
Be ye my fictions, but—her story.[7]

A student of poetry must be cold-blooded who has not loved Her always! Loved, not a glimpse of her whole heavenly self here and there, but every lineament! Why, then, have I put off trying to fix the delightful, fleeting vision till the end? Where earlier could I have lodged the strange intruder into a body of verse, with that single, unclassable exception—notwithstanding even Music's Duel—harmonious and self-consistent? No explanation of Her birth is forthcoming; no suggestion of a kindly, blushing Waller-Cowley 'ghost' working under Crashaw's name. Only, there She is! There her portrait hangs in a frame of gay, most innocently, exquisitely, saucy wit, not unbefitting, yet somehow perplexingly unexpected, as proceeding from the shy scholar, the most spiritual, except one, of singers on the banks of England's Helicon! A surprise, a paradox, with nothing further, I suppose, to be said about it than that paradoxes and surprises are, after all, incidental to genius.

The English Poems of Richard Crashaw, ed. W. B. Turnbull. John Russell Smith, 1858.

[1] Quem Vidistis, Pastores? A Hymn of the Nativity, sung by the Shepherds.
[2] On the Glorious Assumption of Our Blessed Lady.
[3] To the Name Above Every Name, the Name of Jesus.
[4] The Flaming Heart.
[5] Sancta Maria Dolorum.
[6] Music's Duel.
[7] Wishes to his Supposed Mistress.

HENRY VAUGHAN, SILURIST
1622—1695

Two centuries of oblivion, and half one of semi-recognition! A harsh fate to have befallen as sweet and pure a singer as the whole Stuart period produced. The reception of works spread over a long poetical career was not, in Vaughan's own lifetime, enthusiastic. A few neighbours of discernment, such as 'the matchless Orinda', and the learned Dr. Thomas Powell, admired; the public was cold. He could not believe that it would be inveterately and innocently unmindful. He was convinced of the right of his art to reverence. Poets had ever—

> like the nymphs, their pleasing themes—
> Haunted the bubbling springs and gliding streams;
> And happy banks! whence such fair flow'rs have sprung,
> But happier those where they have sat and sung!
> Poets—like angels—where they once appear
> Hallow the place.

For himself, he had faith that his verse could glorify his own native Usk:

> When I am laid to rest hard by thy streams,
> And my sun sets, where first it sprang in beams,
> I'll leave behind me such a large, kind light,
> As shall redeem thee from oblivious night.[1]

He was prepared for 'entailes of povertie', the doom of song; for posthumous 'malice', even for intervals of 'neglect';[2] certainly not for two centuries of utter forgetfulness of his existence, whether for good or ill. I can myself understand that for his Cavaliers he was too grave, and too much of a Churchman for Puritans, to whom otherwise his piety should have commended him. Yet the extreme of the neglect remains to me an extraordinary phenomenon of literary history. Even since he was, as it were, discovered a generation ago, the appreciation, if ardent, has been confined to a circle comparatively narrow. His genius is still too much regarded as in the nature of a curiosity.

The cause is not to be found in the direction of his fancy to one specific, and not generally popular, class of topics. Unequal in degree of excellence, like all writers of his, perhaps of every, age, he never sinks, whatever the subject, to mediocrity. The rhythm is constantly harmonious; the diction, with a phrase now and then provincial or obsolete, is the English of one 'born to it', as, according to his twin brother Thomas he was not.[3] In secular poetry, profane, as it used foolishly to be called, in the Olor Iscanus and Thalia Rediviva, he strikes divine strings, and each often delightfully. As a translator he reproduces the spirit of the master with wonderful flexibility and intelligence. Juvenal's declamation, and, yet more, Ovid's complaints of exile lose little of their freshness in his renderings. In original verse the flame playing about his love lyrics is ever bright, though, as he justly boasts, 'only in its own innocence'.

Never, indeed, had bard less reason than he to be penitent for 'every publish'd vanity'.[4] Dates have to be remembered. Fida's magnanimous inventory to her Lysimachus of the young Medusa's maiden charms—a legion of witcheries —doubtless shows some seventeenth-century luxuriance. So, too, while the poet had a fine eye for physical phenomena, for a passing shower, or the daily wonder of dawn, he is not to be blamed for regarding external nature as a dependency of humanity. In his view, a star shone upon our earth, not by the law of its own being, but from inquisitiveness about the doings of Man. Similarly, in Stuart days, he must not be set down as a reformed rake for a tender retrospect of his youth's ' merry mad mirth ' of full cups at the Globe Tavern, of ' royall, witty sacke ', endowing the soul with ' brighter suns ', and ' dreams poeticall '.[5] His very real humour was no overflow from an inner reservoir of coarseness, any more than it hid spite at destiny for overdoing the internal equipment of poets, and ' beggaring ' them ' outwardly '. The grimness—seldom far removed from the gaiety—occasionally deepening into horror, as in the Charnel-house [6]—issued from no remorse, we may be sure, at the recollection of ancient excesses.

Such as it is, the secular verse is indisputably virtuous, and has, in addition, much positive charm. I could not, however, claim for Henry Vaughan in its right any distinct place among English poets. He might have been fitfully remembered as are Habington, Denham, Davenant, or possibly, he might, without a serious imputation upon national intelligence, not have been. His true line he found in sacred poetry. This dedication of his Muse had in it nothing revolutionary. It is far less astonishing than for Donne to have re-awaked in Izaak Walton's Hagiology. A very serious self must always have existed inside the author of the Charnel-house. Whatever the exact dates of the several contents of Thalia Rediviva, the Eclipse testifies to a spirit as pious as sanctifies the Silex Scintillans:

> Thy anger I could kiss, and will;
> But O Thy grief, Thy grief, doth kill.[7]

I am disposed to be sceptical of the carousals at the Globe; to think that the reveller gazed oftener up at the starry ceiling than into the bowl. At any rate, before he was thirty he had turned his meditations, his whole heart and soul, entirely Heavenwards. The Silex Scintillans has its variety, its diversities, like the mundane poems. The symbolism and tortuousness of wit, habitual to seventeenth-century hymnology, will now and again irritate, as in The Proffer, instead of elevating. Frequently, even in some of the noblest pieces, a beautiful opening is lost in a tedious and strained conclusion. Though he never needs, as some, to scourge his natural piety, to blow it into a white heat, from doubt of its spontaneity, we often feel that he is on his guard against being too much of a poet, against the use of religious fervour as an incentive to imagination. But when he leaves his love, gratitude, and awe to their proper province of emotions craving expression, and his poet's instinct to its rightful liberty as voice to express and interpret, I feel inclined to indulge in praise which I know must sound hyperbolical.

A warm glow of faith in a higher world, both of past and future, far from dulling, quickens, his imagination. It awakens him to previsions anticipating Wordsworth's:

> Nine months Thy hands are fashioning us,
>   And many years—alas!
> Ere we can lisp, or ought discuss
>   Concerning Thee, must pass:
> Yet have I known Thy slightest things,
>   A feather, or a shell,
> A stick, or rod, which some chance brings
>   The best of us excel.
> Dull, wretched worms! that would not keep
>   Within our first fair bed,
> But out of Paradise must creep
>   For ev'ry foot to tread![8]

Beings from above are ever communing with him on the wooded banks of Usk:

My God, when I walk in those groves
  And leaves, Thy Spirit doth still fan,
I see in each shade that there grows
  An angel talking with a man.[9]

Unearthly music arouses for him the dead forest-King, wasting 'all senseless, cold, and dark':

And yet—as if some deep hate and dissent
  Bred in thy growth betwixt high winds and thee,
Were still alive—thou dost great storms resent
  Before they come, and know'st how near they be.[10]

He is glad with the bird, who pardons the tempest, and is grateful for the sunshine:

Hither thou com'st; the busy wind all night
Blew through thy lodging, where thy own warm wing
Thy pillow was. Many a sullen storm,
For which coarse man seems much the fitter born,
    Rain'd on thy bed
    And harmless head.

And now as fresh and cheerful as the light,
Thy little heart in early hymns doth sing
Unto that Providence, Whose unseen arm
Curb'd them, and cloth'd thee well and warm.
  All things that be praise Him; and had
  Their lesson taught them when first made.

For each enclosèd spirit is a star
  Enlight'ning his own little sphere,
Whose light, though fetch'd and borrowèd from far,
  Both mornings makes and evenings there.[11]

With all creation he rejoices in the Dawn; but it is the majesty of Night which awes and comforts him:

Dear Night! this world's defeat;
The stop to busy fools; care's check and curb;
The day of spirits; my soul's calm retreat
  Which none disturb!
Christ's progress, and His prayer-time;
The hours to which high Heaven doth chime.

God's silent, searching flight;
When my Lord's head is fill'd with dew, and all
His locks are wet with the clear drops of night;
   His still, soft call;
  His knocking time; the soul's dumb watch,
When spirits their fair kindred catch.

Were all my loud, evil days
Calm and unhaunted as is thy dark tent,
Whose peace but by some angel's wing or voice
   Is seldom rent;
  Then I in Heaven all the long year
Would keep and never wander here.

But living where the sun
Doth all things wake, and where all mix and tire
Themselves and others, I consent and run
   To ev'ry mire;
  And by this world's ill-guiding light,
Err more than I can do by night.

There is in God—some say—
A deep, but dazzling darkness; as men here
Say it is late and dusky, because they
   See not all clear.
  O for that Night! where I in Him
Might live invisible and dim! [12]

All *Silex Scintillans* is a treasure-house of long-buried jewels. About several, from the instant of their extrication out of the tomb in which the whole fair sisterhood lay hidden, there has never been a question. The appealing, profound affectionateness of *The Retreat* was recognized at once:

   Happy those early days, when I
   Shin'd in my angel infancy!
   Before I understood this place
   Appointed for my second race,
   Or taught my soul to fancy ought
   But a white celestial thought;
   When yet I had not walked above
   A mile or two from my first love,

And looking back—at that short space—
Could see a glimpse of His bright face;
When on some gilded cloud or flow'r,
My gazing soul would dwell an hour,
And in those weaker glories spy
Some shadows of eternity;
Before I taught my tongue to wound
My conscience with a sinful sound,
Or had the black art to dispense
A sev'ral sin to ev'ry sense,
But felt through all this fleshly dress
Bright shoots of everlastingness.

O how I long to travel back,
And tread again that ancient track!
That I might once more reach that plain,
Where first I left my glorious train;
From whence th' enlighten'd spirit sees
That shady City of palm-trees.
But ah! my soul with too much stay
Is drunk, and staggers in the way!
Some men a forward motion love,
But I by backward steps would move;
And when this dust falls to the urn,
In that state I came, return.[13]

Never in a Hymn has the adorable simplicity of Peace been surpassed:

My soul, there is a country
  Far beyond the stars
Where stands a wingèd sentry
  All skilful in the wars:
There above noise and danger,
  Sweet Peace sits crown'd with smiles,
And One born in a manger
  Commands the beauteous files.
He is thy gracious Friend,
  And—O my soul awake!—
Did in pure love descend,
  To die here for thy sake.

If thou canst get but thither,
 There grows the flower of Peace.
The Rose that cannot wither,
 Thy fortress, and thy ease.

Leave then thy foolish ranges;
 For none can thee secure,
But One, who never changes,
 Thy God, thy life, thy cure.[11]

If ever poet were inspired, Henry Vaughan must have been he, when he breathed, rather than penned, Beyond the Veil:

They are all gone into the world of light!
 And I alone sit ling'ring here;
Their very memory is fair and bright,
 And my sad thoughts doth clear.

It glows and glitters in my cloudy breast,
 Like stars upon some gloomy grove,
Or those faint beams in which this hill is dress'd,
 After the sun's remove.

I see them walking in an air of glory,
 Whose light doth trample on my days:
My days, which are at best but dull and hoary,
 Mere glimmering and decays.

O holy Hope! and high Humility,
 High as the heavens above!
These are your walks, and you have show'd them me,
 To kindle my cold love.

Dear, beauteous Death! the jewel of the just,
 Shining nowhere but in the dark;
What mysteries do lie beyond thy dust,
 Could man outlook that mark!

He that hath found some fledg'd bird's nest, may know
 At first sight, if the bird be flown;
But what fair dell or grove he sings in now,
 That is to him unknown.

And yet, as angels in some brighter dreams
  Call to the soul when man doth sleep,
So some strange thoughts transcend our wonted themes,
  And into glory peep.

If a star were confin'd into a tomb,
  Her captive flames must needs burn there;
But when the hand that lock'd her up gives room,
  She'll shine through all the sphere.

O Father of eternal life, and all
  Created glories under Thee!
Resume Thy spirit from this world of thrall
  Into true liberty.

Either disperse these mists, which blot and fill
  My perspective still as they pass;
Or else remove me hence unto that hill
  Where I shall need no glass.[15]

Never did devotional verse fuse, like Henry Vaughan's, as here, and in **Jesus Weeping**, subtlety into sweetness:

Thou so full of pity art—
Pity which overflows Thy heart!—
That, though the cure of all man's harm
Is nothing to Thy glorious Arm,
Yet canst not Thou that free cure do,
But Thou must sorrow for him too,
  Then farewell joys! for while I live,
My business here shall be to grieve:
A grief that shall outshine all joys
For mirth and life, yet without noise;
A grief whose silent dew shall breed
Lilies and myrrh, where the curs'd seed
Did sometimes rule; a grief so bright
'Twill make the land of darkness light,
And while too many sadly roam,
Shall send me—swanlike—singing home.[16]

Not rarely it is as if he had schemed to hide his meaning;

but search, and you will always discover tenderness at the root, as in this:

> I walk'd the other day, to spend my hour,
>   Into a field,
> Where I sometimes had seen the soil to yield
>   A gallant flow'r;
> But Winter now had ruffled all the bow'r,
>   And curious store
> I knew there heretofore.
> Then taking up what I could nearest spy,
>   I digg'd about
> That place where I had seen him to grow out;
>   And by and by
> I saw the warm recluse alone to lie,
>   Where fresh and green
> He liv'd of us unseen.[17]

Supply the rest out of your own inner consciousness; and then look into the text to see whether you have answered the riddle.

Research has brought to light little about Vaughan's career in the world. He had seen much of it, as his poems indicate. It recollected little of him. In youth he had lived with the wits, but not been of them. From early middle age to grey hairs he practised medicine. Of his scientific skill we have no record. That he healed affliction often by contact with his soul we may be certain; as, too, that, while the physician questioned nature, it was, as for St. Francis, to find God in all. No regular theologian, a mystic rather, he yet had developed for himself as elaborate a Church as Laud, without a mitred persecutor to work it. A Cavalier, as pure as if of King Arthur's Table in its prime, he had assisted at battles, though doubtless to save, not take, life. Not the less did he suffer, with his brother, for the cause they deemed the right. When at length it triumphed, the children of the Saint and Martyr failed to remember the faithful minstrel's losses and perils, even his most pathetic tears on the grave of their dead sister :

A rosebud born in snow ! [18]

He never reminded them. A long existence, eventful without events tabulated and dated, though not without friends, if few, ended in apparent penury and obscurity, by 'Isca's loved arbours'.

Where first it sprang in beams ;— sure—
though the sun be far—
Doing the works of day, to rise a star ! [19]

A beautiful soul ! Not unhappy in that, without a biographer to imprison petty details in clay, his verse is his life.

The Poems of Henry Vaughan, Silurist, ed. E. K. Chambers, with Introduction by H. C. Beeching. Two vols. (The Muses' Library.) Lawrence & Bullen, 1896.

[1] To the River Isca (Olor Iscanus).
[2] To I. Morgan (Thalia Rediviva).
[3] Remains of Thomas Vaughan, Anthroposophia Theomagica (Grosart's ed. of Vaughan—Fuller Worthies' Library, vol. i, p. 298).
[4] Dedication to Jesus Christ (Silex Scintillans, part i).
[5] A Rhapsodis.
[6] The Charnel-house (Olor Iscanus).
[7] The Eclipse (Thalia Rediviva).
[8] Thou that know'st for whom I mourn (Silex Scintillans).
[9] Religion (Silex, &c.).
[10] The Timber (Silex, &c.).
[11] The Bird (Silex, &c.).
[12] The Night (Silex, &c.).
[13] The Retreat (Silex, &c.).
[14] Peace (Silex, &c.).
[15] They are all gone, &c. (Silex, &c.).
[16] Jesus Weeping (Silex, &c.).
[17] I Walk'd the Other Day, to Spend My Hour (or Hidden) (Silex, &c.).
[18] An Epitaph upon the Lady Elizabeth, Second Daughter to His Late Majesty (Olor Iscanus)
[19] Rules and Lessons (Silex, &c.).

JOHN MILTON
1608—1674

A GIANT! How he towers in letters above his age, though it was that of Dryden, Cowley, Bunyan! A born poet, if ever poet was born, but a greater poet had he been a lesser man. His superiority is not in imagination, in style, and in learning alone; it is first of all in the man, his will, his character, his sword and spear of a brain. For his place in the eternal kingdom of poetry he had to contend with the temptations to him of his period. He was put to his option for or against the Muse in a crisis of conflicts of intellect, religion, ethics. Wars were being waged, less with foreign foes than between classes, and inside human breasts, with weapons he could brandish among the strongest and bravest. Happily free thought in politics, theology, morals, and the dialectic trophies of Tetrachordon, Areopagitica, divorce tracts, Eikonoklastes, if they intercepted many a Christmas Carol, Lycidas, and Comus, did not dry up the fountain. But if they left us the Poet, they quenched the Elizabethan in him.

Whatever the gain in other directions, it is impossible not to deplore that loss. Between his twenty-fourth year and his thirtieth he had enriched literature with works, which have, of their kind, no superiors in the language. The imagery of L'Allegro and Il Penseroso, and their cadences, contain inexhaustible beauties. It is difficult to see or recall anything fair and ideal in English life which a line from one or another of them does not exquisitely illustrate and develop. They charm for that they say, and, infinitely more, for all they suggest. Between them they make a succession of lovely vignettes, alternating with and supplementing, sometimes by way of contrast, one another:

>The lark begins his flight,
>And, singing, startles the dull night,
>From his watch-tower in the skies,
>Till the dappled dawn doth rise.

Then,

>the ploughman, near at hand,
>Whistles o'er the furrowed land,
>And the milk-maid singeth blithe,
>And the mower whets his scythe,
>And every shepherd tells his tale
>Under the hawthorn in the dale.

The day is done at last with its open-air toils, and its open-air joys; and night descends, with its rest for day's toilers:

>To bed they creep,
>By whispering winds soon lulled asleep.

But for us, the listeners to the lay, its truest interest now begins; for it is of himself that the poet proceeds to sing; of the treasures of his fancy, the visions of his youth:

>Towered cities please us then,
>And the busy hum of men,
>Where throngs of knights and barons bold,
>In weeds of peace, high triumphs hold,
>With store of ladies, whose bright eyes
>Rain influence, and judge the prize
>Of wit or arms, while both contend
>To win her grace whom all commend.
>Such sights as youthful poets dream
>On summer eves by haunted stream.
>Then to the well-trod stage anon
>If Jonson's learned sock be on,
>Or sweetest Shakespeare, Fancy's child,
>Warble his native wood-notes wild.
>And ever against eating cares
>Lap me in soft Lydian airs.

Married to immortal verse,
Such as the meeting soul may pierce,
In notes with many a winding bout
Of linked sweetness long drawn out
With wanton heed and giddy cunning,
The melting voice through mazes running,
Untwisting all the chains that tie
The hidden soul of harmony.[1]

Or he may incline to woo mute silence and

Him that yon soars on golden wing,
Guiding the fiery-wheelèd throne,
The Cherub Contemplation.

In such a mood,

Oft, on a plat of rising ground,
I hear the far-off curfew sound
Over some wide-watered shore,
Swinging slow with sullen roar.

. . . . . .

Or let my lamp at midnight hour
Be seen in some high lonely tower,
Where I may oft outwatch the Bear,
With thrice-great Hermes, or unsphere
The spirit of Plato, to unfold
What worlds or what vast regions hold
The immortal mind that hath forsook
Her mansion in this fleshly nook:
And of those demons that are found
In fire, air, flood, or underground,
Whose power hath a true consent
With planet or with element.
Sometime let gorgeous Tragedy
In sceptred pall come sweeping by,
Presenting Thebes, or Pelops' line,
Or the tale of Troy divine,
Or what—though rare—of later age
Ennobled hath the buskined stage.

. . . .

H 2

But let my due feet never fail
To walk the studious cloister's pale,
And love the high embowèd roof,
With antique pillars massy-proof,
And storied windows richly dight,
Casting a dim religious light.
There let the pealing organ blow,
To the full-voiced quire below,
In service high and anthems clear,
As may with sweetness, through mine ear,
Dissolve me into ecstasies,
And bring all Heaven before mine eyes.
And may at last my weary age
Find out the peaceful hermitage,
The hairy gown and mossy cell,
Where I may sit and rightly spell
Of every star that heaven doth shew,
And every herb that sips the dew,
Till old experience do attain
To something like prophetic strain.[2]

Happy dreams of a poet's life; and doomed never to be realized!

Fletcher might have fathered the Song on May Morning:
Now the bright morning-star, Day's harbinger,
Comes dancing from the east, and leads with her
The flowery May, who from her green lap throws
The yellow cowslip, and the pale primrose.
Hail bounteous May, that dost inspire
Mirth, and youth, and warm desire!
Woods and groves are of thy dressing
Hill and dale doth boast thy blessing.
Thus we salute thee with our early song,
And welcome thee, and wish thee long:[3]

and any or all in Arcades:
O'er the smooth enamelled green,
Where no print of step hath been,
Follow me, as I sing
And touch the warbled string;

> Under the shady roof
> Of branching elm star-proof
>   Follow me.
> I will bring you where she sits,
> Clad in splendour as befits
>   Her deity.
> Such a rural Queen
> All Arcadia hath not seen.[4]

As for Comus, Sir Henry Wotton did well to testify that he knew no English parallel to the Doric delicacy, 'ipsa mollities', of its songs and odes.[5] No lyrist, Greek or British, could have surpassed the elegance of :

> Sabrina fair,
>   Listen where thou art sitting
> Under the glassy, cool, translucent wave,
>   In twisted braids of lilies knitting
> The loose train of thy amber-dropping hair;
>   Listen for dear honour's sake,
>   Goddess of the silver lake,
>   Listen and save![6]

or of the gracious Spirit's farewell :

> To the ocean now I fly,
> And those happy climes that lie
> Where day never shuts his eye,
> Up in the broad fields of the sky.
> There I suck the liquid air,
> All amidst the gardens fair
> Of Hesperus, and his daughters three
> That sing about the golden tree.
> Along the crisped shades and bowers
> Revels the spruce and jocund Spring;
> The Graces and the rosy bosomed Hours
> Thither all their bounties bring.
> There eternal Summer dwells,
> And west winds with musky wing
> About the cedarn alleys fling
> Nard and cassia's balmy smells.

> But now my task is smoothly done :
> I can fly, or I can run
> Quickly to the green earth's end,
> Where the bowed welkin slow doth bend,
> And from thence can soar as soon
> To the corners of the moon,
> Mortals, that would follow me,
> Love Virtue ; she alone is free.
> She can teach ye how to climb
> Higher than the sphery chime ;
> Or, if Virtue feeble were,
> Heaven itself would stoop to her.[7]

'Doric delicacy', in truth ! Only the eulogy need not have been confined to 'odes and songs'. The whole masque, though as many-hued as a rainbow, is one dainty lyric.

In the Ode on the Nativity, fine as are its orthodox sublimities, we can save our admiration of such features for later inspirations where they naturally abound. The noticeable features of its special Miltonic phase are the lyric finish ; the note of pity for exiled Paganism from the recent denizen of the Arcadia of Cam :

> The lonely mountains o'er,
> And the resounding shore,
> A voice of weeping heard and loud lament ;
> From the haunted spring and dale
> Edged with poplar pale,
> The parting Genius is with sighing sent ;
> With flower-inwoven tresses torn
> The Nymphs in twilight shade of tangled thickets mourn.[8]

The grace, the tenderness, are similarly the qualities in Lycidas which we may be forgiven for valuing above the passion of its polemical rhetoric :

> For we were nursed upon the self-same hill,
> Fed the same flock, by fountain, shade, and rill ;
> Together both, ere the high lawns appeared,
> Under the opening eyelids of the Morn,

JOHN MILTON

> We drove a-field, and both together heard
> What time the grey-fly winds her sultry horn,
> Battening our flocks with the fresh dews of night,
> Oft till the star that rose at evening bright
> Toward heaven's descent had sloped his westering wheel.
> Meanwhile the rural ditties were not mute:
> Tempered to the oaten flute,
> Rough Satyrs danced, and Fawns with cloven heel
> From the glad sound would not be absent long;
> And old Damoetas loved to hear our song.
>
>   But oh! the heavy change, now thou art gone,
> Now thou art gone and never must return!
> Thee, Shepherd, thee the woods and desert caves,
> With wild thyme and the gadding vine o'ergrown,
> And all their echoes, mourn.
> The willows, and the hazel copses green,
> Shall now no more be seen
> Fanning their joyous leaves to thy soft lays.
> As killing as the canker to the rose,
> Or taint-worm to the weanling herds that graze,
> Or frost to flowers, that their gay wardrobe wear
> When first the white-thorn blows;
> Such, Lycidas, thy loss to shepherd's ear.[9]

And yet again, from this same happy period, there is a surpassing sonnet—one in the narrow list of those capable of being simply enjoyed without a troubling thought of the art and the labour:

> O Nightingale, that on yon bloomy spray
>   Warblest at eve, when all the woods are still,
>   Thou with fresh hope the lover's heart dost fill,
> While the jolly hours lead on propitious May.
> Thy liquid notes that close the eye of day,
>   First heard before the shallow cuckoo's bill,
>   Portend success in love. O, if Jove's will
> Hath linked that amorous power to thy soft lay,
> Now timely sing, ere the rude bird of hate
>   Foretell my hopeless doom, in some grove nigh;

> As thou from year to year hast sung too late
> For my relief, yet hadst no reason why.
> Whether the Muse or Love call thee his mate,
> Both them I serve, and of their train am I.[10]

Yes; a supreme charm of the entire delightful wreath of early blossoms is that the never-absent art, even the learning, are reconciled with perennial freshness, with a seeming spontaneity. Each is at once old, and young— in a word, Elizabethan. As we read, we never think of the singer, only of the song.

With such gifts, such achievements, a career might have been supposed to be decided. A most worthy, a delightful vocation! To wander through enchanted gardens, with a lofty moral spell against any Armida, to dream lovely dreams of Fairyland and Chivalry! Another Spenser was apparently in the making, with a stronger grasp of reality, a more masculine control of fancy and words. Alas! King Arthur's destined laureate came back from Italy, to find himself in the eddies of a flood of party warfare soon to swell into a whirlpool. His was neither an intellect, nor a character to hold aloof in a turmoil of elements he felt himself able to breast. No half measures were possible. There was no longer an atmosphere which a creator of successors to Comus and the Arcades could have breathed, unless he had, like Henry Vaughan, and then but incompletely, made a Thebaid of his own nature. No plaints of the lyric Muse, no popular flatteries would, we may be sure, have turned aside the future fiery pamphleteer, the crusher of Salmasius, the Cromwellian Latin Secretary, from the strife of politics. But, in fact, counter temptations were not offered. In 1645 he had been induced to print a modest edition of his poems. The demand for it appears to have been of the slightest. The master poet of the age was allowed to hang up his harp for fifteen years without a protest. It may be said it was his own choice ; that he preferred to wrangle in the press with antagonists foreign and domestic. At any rate he was given no proof that his countrymen would have preferred for him to sing.

When he resumed his lyre by his own impulse—still through no popular requisition—he strung it anew, and to a new key. He was no longer the bard of L'Allegro and Il Penseroso. That being might for him have never existed. The germ of austerity had always been there. Occasionally it had effervesced into unexpected bitterness in the lighthearted days, as amidst the tears of affection for Lycidas. It, and even something of the analogous solemnity in the mere rhythm of the future, are discoverable in the earlier verse. They mark the odes, on the Circumcision, at a solemn Music, the Passion, and Time. Youth, hope, and enthusiasm originally had gaily repressed them, or led them, dancing, in their train. Learning and ardent piety had equally then been present, and blissfully had ministered to the soul of music. Now they survived, while their masters, playfellows rather, were departed, dead, and all but forgotten.

Had the poet never risen from his trance of many years, had he died in his sleep along with the bright impulses of his youth, the inspirers of Comus, Lycidas, and the rest, none could have wondered. The surprise is that he awoke fully inspired still, but as if with no remembrance that he had ever been inspired before. He had been a student of nature and of men. Of the one he had rejoiced to note every trait, every mood. He had read as sympathetically the hearts of men ; and they were free to read his. Now he was shut out from daylight ; and he had lost faith in humankind. Booklore was his compensation for both.

His thirst for it had always been eager. For the present and the future it was his single loophole into the world outside. Fortunately for himself, in youth, in early manhood, in the heat of battle single-handed against half Europe, he had ransacked divers folio-packed libraries. He had studied, devoured, not, like Shakespeare, to use, but to know. His brain stored the whole. When poetry once more lit its lamp within to brighten the dark days of defeat and persecution, the flame pierced through a pile of learning, under which, in its variety, a Bentley might have staggered. It was entirely compatible with the statuesque proportions, and the one touch of pathos, austerely suppressed, of Samson Agonistes; it neither made nor marred Paradise Regained. It rendered Paradise Lost possible.

He had not amassed his learning with any view of employing it for furniture of his poetry. Being there it served and was served by it. To borrow from the Ancients was in those days the reverse of discreditable. It is scarcely far-fetched to suspect that in characterizing Shakespeare by his 'native wood-notes wild', he hinted indulgently at a lack of solid classical information. Undoubtedly he would have been disposed more to pity than admire a writer for having to live down the defect. He himself in the elasticity of youthful fancy, with all nature open to his eyes, had not suffered from the load his memory had to carry. Fallen on evil days, and reduced to gazing on vernal bloom, and summer's rose, through the mirror of his books, he would have been a worker of miracles indeed had his later imaginings winged their way upwards purged of all the learned dust in which they were doomed to nest. That he could not wholly effect. It is little short of miraculous that he should have approached so gloriously as in his mighty epic towards disguising the inadequacy of his substitutes.

Any impatience in these days at the profuseness of the learning in Paradise Lost arises, I believe, from a deeper feeling than weariness of the mass. The adaptations of Homer and Virgil are beautiful enough to have earned their own pardon. The real offence is that the poet is constantly balking the desire of his readers to come closer to himself by interposing some Ancient Classic. No one can study the poem without a conviction of the existence in the author, somewhere beneath the lustrous metallic surface, of a personality fascinatingly emotional. Milton acts as if he were the more determined to disappoint the curiosity that it is natural and eager. That is the chief cause of offence. There are specific blemishes besides. The canvas is impracticably vast. The idea of civil war in God Almighty's Heaven is an inconceivable monstrosity. The introduction of the mutinous artillery, with the ponderous jesting of the rebels at the awkward surprise of the tumbled Angels, indicates an extraordinary want of the saving sense of humour. We are tempted throughout to feel that there is too much of Hell in Heaven, and, for Seraphs, though fallen, too little of Heaven in Hell. But all other shortcomings, literary and personal, are insignificant beside the primary one, the refusal of admittance into the singer's own mighty heart.

An insurmountable wall within, to which the dead learning itself adds only battlements and barbicans, everywhere shuts invading lovers out. Of all poets with a right to the name none has ever written with a self more inaccessible, a morgue more chilling. Readers of the lyrics could, if needs must, have rested content with them. They might have accepted them as if dropped from the sky. The melody is all-sufficing. In fact, they confide to us much as to their author's nature. In Paradise Lost there is a craving for human companionship ; and the narrator, who felt none, denies it. Even with Dante the student can walk in awed fellowship through the Inferno. He is aware of a soul shuddering, fevered, at the agonies it has created, and quakes and burns in company. Over the personality of Milton, in Heaven, in Hell, among the flowers of Eden themselves, a cloud perpetually hangs, radiant it may be, but impenetrable, humiliating.

It is a profound, an abiding disappointment. I can understand how, through it, to some, great minds too, Paradise Lost has seemed to be a failure, a brilliant failure. Of less account is the complaint that it occupied powers which might have produced a series of lovely sisters to the Arcades, L'Allegro, and Il Penseroso. This I have been tempted myself to regret. But I know that the sentiment is unreasonable. In the first place, it was a choice between something and nothing. The flowering time of ethereal lyrics was over for Milton. Moreover, a hundred, if that be an imaginable vision, like them could never have supplied the place of the single epic. Paradise Lost, with banded piety for its body-guard, was a pillar of fire keeping alive, throughout the roamings of Johnson's dilapidated Poets about their dreary desert of some hundred years, the sacred instinct of inspired verse.

With all the blurs, it is a mine of fancy, a thicket of beauties. Observe the pomp of rhythm, as various as it is majestic, its billowy ebb and flow. Where in the Prometheus, the Inferno, Macbeth, is there the superior of Satan's encounter with Death ?

> the Shape—
> If shape it might be called that shape had none
> Distinguishable in member, joint, or limb :
> Or substance might be called that shadow seemed,

For each seemed either—black it stood as Night,
Fierce as ten Furies, terrible as Hell,
And shook a dreadful dart ; what seemed his head
The likeness of a kingly crown had on.[11]

Is there a charge of deficiency in tenderness? Tenderness clothes Eve, always lovely, always heart-innocent, in her Garden. It softens the ache of exile for her and Adam :

Some natural tears they dropped, but wiped them soon ;
The world was all before them, where to choose
Their place of rest, and Providence their guide.
They, hand in hand, with wandering steps and slow,
Through Eden took their solitary way.[12]

It steeps in celestial pity—though for himself—the swanlike chant of the old man—old for a poet of his century, and of his troubles, at fifty-nine—over his perished eyesight. The lament—repeated in a sternly heroic sonnet—is rival of the moonlit rhapsody of Lorenzo and Jessica for primacy of melody in English blank verse :

Hail, holy Light ! Thee I revisit safe,
And feel thy sovran vital lamp ; but thou
Revisit'st not these eyes, that roll in vain
To find thy piercing ray, and find no dawn ;
So thick a drop serene hath quenched their orbs,
Or dim suffusion veiled. Yet not the more
Cease I to wander where the Muses haunt
Clear spring, or shady grove, or sunny hill,
Smit with the love of sacred song ; but chief
Thee, Sion, and the flowery brooks beneath,
That wash thy hallowed feet, and warbling flow,
Nightly I visit, nor sometimes forget
Those other two equalled with me in fate,
So were I equalled with them in renown,
Blind Thamyris and blind Maeonides,
And Tiresias and Phineus, prophets old
Then feed on thoughts that voluntary move
Harmonious numbers, as the wakeful bird

> Sings darkling, and in shadiest covert hid,
> Tunes her nocturnal note. Thus with the year
> Seasons return ; but not to me returns
> Day, or the sweet approach of even or morn,
> Or sight of vernal bloom, or summer's rose,
> Or flocks, or herds, or human face divine ;
> But cloud instead and ever-during dark
> Surrounds me, from the cheerful ways of men
> Cut off, and, for the book of knowledge fair,
> Presented with a universal blank
> Of Nature's works, to me expunged and rased,
> And wisdom at one entrance quite shut out.[13]

From the same deep well of pathos—if similarly self-centred—rose the tears which watered the funeral-wreath of the girl-wife, little more than bride, dead in child-birth :

> Methought I saw my late espoused saint
>   Brought to me like Alcestis from the grave,
>   Whom Jove's great son to her glad husband gave,
> Rescued from Death by force, though pale and faint.
> Mine, as whom washed from spot of child-bed taint
>   Purification in the Old Law did save,
>   And such as yet once more I trust to have
> Full sight of her in Heaven without restraint,
> Came vested all in white, pure as her mind.
>   Her face was veiled ; yet to my fancied sight
>   Love, sweetness, goodness, in her person shined
> So clear as in no face with more delight.
>   But, oh ! as to embrace me she inclined,
>   I waked, she fled, and day brought back my night.[14]

These, it is true, were involuntary sobs extorted by positive heartaches. They were not Byronic confidences exchanged with the outside world, or even with a circle of admirers. They were no appeals for condolence. Still, with their echoes in our ears, we well may mourn the more for the general rigour of self-repression. It is the secret of the failure—this a positive failure, as, notwithstanding Coleridge's admiration, it seems to me—of Paradise Regained. The Christ Milton might have painted had he given the rein to his natural instinct of Divine compassion ! As it is, the one grace, accordant with its Quaker genesis, which the composition possesses, is that of an equably calm and chill winter sunset. The poet's purity, his moral dignity, too exalted for visible emotion, were not similarly out of tune with the marvellous tale of the fall of Angels and Man. Flaws there bear testimony at all events to a Titanic consciousness of power. In it, from it, over it shines a colossal character. If it was no habit of Milton's to ask for sympathy, if he moves on a plane above vulgar admiration, as little does he condescend to seek to excite curiosity by hiding himself. Simply, his was become a hermit soul. Yet it remains one, when visible, worthy in the highest degree of contemplation. We should find it hard to name its equal for personal grandeur in English literature.

The Poetical Works of John Milton, edited by David Masson. Macmillan & Co., 1874.

[1] L'Allegro. [2] Il Penseroso. [3] Song on May Morning.
[4] Arcades, Song, ii.
[5] Letters of Wotton, ed. L. Pearsall-Smith. Two vols. Henry Frowde, Clarendon Press, 1907.
[6] Comus, Song. [7] Comus, Spirit " Epilogizes ".
[8] On the Morning of Christ's Nativity, xx.
[9] Lycidas. [10] To the Nightingale : Sonnets, i.
[11] Paradise Lost, Book II, vv. 666-73.
[12] Ibid., Book XII, vv. 645-9. [13] Ibid., Book III, vv. 21-50.
[14] On his Deceased Wife : Sonnets, xxiii.

WILLIAM BROWNE, OF TAVISTOCK

1591—1643?

THE confessed disciple of Sidney, with

>His shepherd's lay, yet equaliz'd of none,[1]

and of

>Divinest Spenser, heav'n-bred, happy Muse![2]

a master of Keats; author of poems, golden apples of the Hesperides, had he but suffered them to ripen on the bough.

Never was a more unmistakable poet so given to tantalizing admirers with the promise of beauties, which he insists upon expanding to tedium, or into caricatures. Nature equipped him for a poet, and, I can only suppose, as in some other cases, overdid her work. She supplied either an excess of facility, or too much modesty for him to understand that he was his proper self only when at his highest. What that was he probably never measured, whether for good or for ill. If the possession of a critical faculty highly developed checks inspiration, the utter want of the gift is almost equally injurious. Browne cannot have had it in any degree; or he would not continually have spoilt his choicest verse by tasteless additions. Thus, whether the earlier part of the famous epitaph on Lady Pembroke be his, or, as I think it, by Ben Jonson, he at all events went far towards marring it by the second half.[3] His tendency similarly to blur his undisputed work with his own sleeve is so habitual that the falling-off is even an argument in the doubtful instance for his authorship. This absence of the instinct when to stop, and a habit of diffuseness, are grave faults. So is a passion for extravagant conceits, as that

> A mead a wanton river dresses
> With richest collars of her turning esses;[4]

as if the stream were a Lord Chief Justice; or that the poet's pen

> blubb'ring her sable tears lets fall
> In characters right hieroglyphical.[5]

Such defects may among them account for a dearth of popularity in Browne's own time, unless for the excellent humour of Lydford Journey.[6] Certainly they explain the neglect, but very partially dissipated yet, which has since enveloped him.

If the general reading public had patience, as perhaps it cannot be expected to have, it would find that the mannerisms and fantastic phrasings, the tediousness itself, are more than balanced by intrinsic beauties. Nowhere, not even by Herrick, in English poetry since Chaucer—with the one universal Stratford-on-Avon exception to all rules—is physical nature treated with such insight as in Britannia's Pastorals. Apparent all over the surface as are the literary trickeries of the period, we feel throughout, under the Oxford scholar and the Templar, the inborn rural instinct. One is satisfied that the orchestra of dawn is described from personal experience, when

> The mounting lark, day's herald, got on wing,
> Bidding each bird choose out his bough and sing.
> The lofty treble sang the little wren;
> Robin the mean that best of all loves men;
> The nightingale the tenor, and the thrush
> The counter-tenor sweetly in a bush.[7]

With a realism which enhances the picturesqueness, Night

draws in his verse for us her gradual curtain over the landscape :

> Now great Hyperion left his golden throne
> That on the dancing waves in glory shone,
> For whose declining on the western shore
> The oriental hills black mantles wore,
> And thence apace the gentle twilight fled,
> That had from hideous caverns ushered
> All-drowsy Night, who in a car of jet
> By steeds of iron-grey, which mainly sweat
> Moist drops on all the world, drawn through the sky,
> The helps of darkness waited orderly.
> First thick clouds rose from all the liquid plains ;
> Then mists from marishes, and grounds whose veins
> Were conduit-pipes to many a crystal spring ;
> From standing pools and fens were following
> Unhealthy fogs ; each river, every rill
> Sent up their vapours to attend her will.
> These pitchy curtains drew 'twixt earth and heaven,
> And as Night's chariot through the air was driven,
> Clamour grew dumb, unheard was shepherd's song,
> And silence girt the woods ; no warbling tongue
> Talk'd to the Echo ; satyrs broke their dance,
> And all the upper world lay in a trance.
> Only the curled streams soft chidings kept ;
> And little gales that from the green leaf swept
> Dry summer's dust, in fearful whisp'rings stirr'd,
> As loath to waken any singing bird.[8]

The Devon patriot hymns as accurately as exultantly the delights and glories of his fair fatherland :

> Hail thou my native soil ! thou blessed plot
> Whose equal all the world affordeth not !
> Show me who can so many crystal rills,
> Such sweet-cloth'd valleys or aspiring hills ;
> Such wood-ground, pastures, quarries, wealthy mines ;
> Such rocks in whom the diamond fairly shines ;
> And if the earth can show the like again,
> Yet she will fail in her sea-ruling men.

> Time never can produce men to o'ertake
> The fames of Grenville, Davies, Gilbert, Drake,
> Or worthy Hawkins, or of thousands more
> That by their power made the Devonian shore
> Mock the proud Tagus.[9]

Even while the poet gives fancy the rein in imagining the glories of Oberon's fairy palace, the banquet, the music, and the revels,[10] the countryman is still observant of rural proportions.

When, quitting the 'humble styled Pastoral', he ceases to
> Tread through the valleys, dance about the streams,

he can be the equal, as lover or mourner, of the best inspired frequenters of the Mermaid or Globe. The fourteen sonnets to Caelia, his wife to be, are as full of sweetness as of grace. Take for example, the seventh:

> Fairest, when I am gone, as now the glass
> Of Time is mark'd how long I have to stay,
> Let me entreat you, ere from hence I pass,
> Perhaps from you for evermore away,
> Think that no common love hath fir'd my breast,
> Nor base desire, but virtue truly known,
> Which I may love, and wish to have possess'd,
> Were you the high'st as fair'st of anyone;
> 'Tis not your lovely eye enforcing flames,
> Nor beauteous red beneath a snowy skin,
> That so much binds me yours, or makes you fame's,
> As the pure light and beauty shrin'd within;
> Yet outward parts I must affect of duty,
> As for the smell we like the rose's beauty.[11]

Herrick's name might have been signed to the so-called Sonnet:

> For her gait, if she be walking,
>   Be she sitting I desire her
> For her state's sake, and admire her
> For her wit if she be talking.
>   Gait and state and wit approve her;
>   For which all and each I love her.

>Be she sullen, I commend her
>For a modest. Be she merry,
>For a kind one her prefer I.
>Briefly everything doth lend her
>>So much grace, and so approve her,
>>That for everything I love her.[12]

The reply to the question whom he loves might almost compete with Crashaw's 'She':

>Hearken then awhile to me;
>And if such a woman move,
>As I now shall versify:
>Be assur'd, 'tis she, or none
>>That I love, and love alone.
>Nature did her so much right,
>>As she scorns the help of Art;
>In as many virtues dight
>>As e'er yet embraced a heart.
>So much good so truly tried,
>>Some for less were deified.
>Wit she hath without desire
>>To make known how much she hath;
>And her anger flames no higher
>>Than may fitly sweeten wrath.
>Full of pity as may be,
>>Though perhaps not so to me.
>Reason masters every sense,
>>And her virtues grace her birth;
>Lovely as all excellence,
>>Modest in her most of mirth;
>Likelihood enough to prove,
>>Only worth could kindle love.
>Such she is; and if you know
>>Such a one as I have sung;
>Be she brown, or fair, or so,
>>That she be but somewhile young;
>Be assur'd, 'tis she, or none
>>That I love and love alone.[13]

Delightful as a lover, he had it in him, when he chose, to rise yet higher as a mourner, and, in a memorable case, to be to perfection both in one. The elegy on Lady Pembroke contains fine lines on himself as well as his departed patroness :

> I, hapless soul, that never knew a friend
> But to bewail his too untimely end ;
> Whose hopes, cropp'd in the bud, have never come,
> But to sit weeping on a senseless tomb,
> That hides not dust enough to count the tears,
> Which I have fruitless spent, in so few years ;
> I, that have trusted those that would have given
> For our dear Saviour and the Son of Heaven,
> Ten times the value Judas had of yore,
> Only to sell him for three pieces more,
> I that have lov'd and trusted thus in vain,
> Yet weep for thee.[14]

There is equal beauty in the lament for her grandchild, Lord Herbert :

> All that sweetness, all that youth,
> All that virtue, all that truth
> Can or speak, or wish, or praise,
> Was in him in his few days.
> His blood of Herbert, Sidney, Vere,
> Names great in either hemisphere,
> Need not to lend him of their fame,
> He had enough to make a name,
> And to their glories he had come
> Had Heaven but given a later tomb.[15]

But a couple of epitaphs testify to nobler capabilities still. Very near does that on Mrs. El:Y. approach in grace to Ben Jonson's on Elizabeth :

> Underneath this stone there lies
> More of beauty than are eyes,
> Or to read that she is gone,
> Or alive to gaze upon.

> She in so much fairness clad,
> To each grace a virtue had;
> All her goodness cannot be
> Cut in marble. Memory
> Would be useless, ere we tell
> In a stone her worth.—Farewell![16]

Of the four lines on the month of his young wife's death what more can I say than that for tender terseness, agony of pathos, they stand unparalleled!

> May! Be thou never graced with birds that sing,
>   Nor Flora's pride!
> In thee all flowers and roses spring,
>   Mine only died.[17]

A pool is William Browne's poetry, rather than a stream sparkling in sunshine! We may take our fill of gazing into its still mirror, and see hills reflected there,

> Gallantly crown'd with large sky-kissing trees;[18]

groves,
> where birds from heat or weather,
> Sit sweetly tuning of their notes together;[19]

or Venus ascending to Olympus,
> Along the milky way by many a star.[20]

We can listen while
> on the breast of Thames
> A heavenly bevy of sweet English dames,
> In some calm ev'ning of delightful May,
> With music give a farewell to the day;[21]

or imagine ourselves, and he, of the poet's kindly company, when,
> on Isis' banks,
> And melancholy Cherwell, near the ranks
> Of shading willows, often have we lain
> And heard the Muses and Apollo's strain
> In heavenly raptures, as the pow'rs on high
> Had there been lecturers of poesy,
> And nature's searcher, deep philosophy.[22]

It is charming; and the charm is the deeper for the

personal accent. Yet at the same time no poetry of the period produces more the impression that it is of the period, its direct effluence. A tide of early seventeenth-, even sixteenth-, century spirit floats the verse along; and not the less, but the rather, that the writer himself floats upon it also. A certain want in the mass, not in the special pieces I have quoted, confirms the feeling. We have not, as in Herrick, as we shall have in Waller, the sense of art, of an artist. The general reader requires in poetry finish, which only the artist can give. Its absence may help to explain the lack of popularity for William Browne of Tavistock. But, in compensation, no poetry of the age has more of the age's essence, and for the student tells more about it.

William Browne of Tavistock, ed. Gordon Goodwin: Introduction by A. H. Bullen. Two vols. Lawrence and Bullen, 1894.

[1] Britannia's Pastorals, Book II, Song ii, v. 248.
[2] Ibid., Book II, Song i, v. 1001.
[3] On the Countess Dowager of Pembroke (Miscell. Poems).
[4] Brit. P., Book I, Song iv, vv. 353-4.
[5] Ibid., Book I, Song v, vv. 75-6.
[6] Lydford Journey (Miscell. Poems).
[7] Brit. P., Book I, Song iii, vv. 197-202.
[8] Brit. P., Book II, Song i, vv. 771-96.
[9] Brit. P., Book II, Song iii, vv. 601-13.
[10] Brit. P., Book III, Song i, vv. 721-970.
[11] Sonnet vii (Miscell. Poems, Odes, Songs, and Sonnets).
[12] 'Sonnet' (Miscell. Poems, &c.).
[13] Brit. P., Book II, Song ii, vv. 194-222.
[14] An Elegy on the Countess Dowager of Pembroke, vv. 101-12 (Miscell. Poems).
[15] On Charles, Lord Herbert of Cardiff and Shurland.
[16] An Epitaph on Mrs. El:Y. (Miscell. Poems: Epitaphs)
[17] In Obitum. M. S. x. Maij, 1614 (Ibid.).
[18] Brit. P., Book I, Song iv, v. 580.
[19] Brit. P., Book I, Song iv, vv. 351-2.
[20] Brit. P., Book III, Song ii, v. 76.
[21] Brit. P., Book II, Song ii, vv. 231-4.
[22] Brit. P. Book III, Song i, vv. 698-704.

ROBERT HERRICK
1591—1674

A CLERIC, as were Donne, and Herbert, and Crashaw; and how joyously unlike! Nothing in him, except the poet, of the strong-willed, philosophical, remorseful, Dean to be, sensual courtier-soldier that was; of the earnest, high-bred priest of Bemerton; of the unworldly enthusiast of Cambridge. Just the cheerful, kindly, easy-going, scholarly parson, of the character pervading English literature and life, from the days of Chaucer—though hardly after his ideal—to those of Dorsetshire Barnes. At times the type may have been submerged by the passion, the emotions, of Hoopers and Lauds, Baxters, Wesleys, Newtons, Simeons, Newmans; but it has always rested safe from the theological billows above in the reposeful deeps. No hermit was our Robin Herrick, either before, or after, Orders. Pupil and correspondent of rare Ben Jonson, he remembered, with more practical appreciation doubtless than Vaughan, the lyric feasts,

> Made at the Sun,
> The Dog, the Triple Tun;
> Where we such clusters had,
> As made us nobly wild, not mad.[1]

A scholar of 'my beloved Westminster', 'a free-born Roman', that is, of 'the golden Cheapside', he ever rejoiced to fly back, whether in fact or fancy, to London, his 'home' always, and

> blest place of my nativity.[2]

Nevertheless, he was a countryman by instinct. His affection for all country pursuits, traditions, and superstitions, was extraordinarily keen. He had, too, country blood in him, with the resulting right to shelter in good old manor houses from the tempests of theology and politics. To his rural associations, together with his genial heart, and a muse as genial—incapable, each, of sourness from persecution—we owe sketches of an English Arcadia as bright, fresh, and real, as Chaucer himself could have drawn.

A merry England indeed this of Herrick's! In it King Oberon and Queen Titania still held their Court. Luxurious their feastings, ' less great than nice ', on the pith of sugared rush, mandrake's ears, and

> The broke heart of a nightingale
> O'creome in music ; [3]

with, to quench royal thirst,

> A pure seed-pearl of infant dew,
> Brought and besweeten'd in a blue
> And pregnant violet.[4]

And if Oberon has his junketings, why not Corydon his? If only sweet Phyllis, or, if she be not at hand, as sweet Anthea, or, in lack of both—for life is fleeting—Amarillis, or Corinna,

> fresh and green as Flora,

will consent to attend him to the Wake, to ' feast, as others do ', on

> Tarts and custards, creams and cakes ;

or to the garlanded May-pole, ere

> All love, all liking, all delight
> Lies drown'd with us in endless night.[5]

Never was there a more companionable poet. Whatever the apparent theme, it is sure speedily to resolve itself into the question :

> Where may I find my shepherdess ? [6]

Seemingly it is easily answered ; so ubiquitous is She ; so eager is the wooer ; so well disposed, like Suckling's and like Sheridan's, to discover fascination in the most diverse feminine types. Cupid's pretty cheating wiles [7] scarcely were needed to entrap him. We see the favourite of the hour hiding within every garden.[8] Nature instructs its ministers to be on the watch to guide her to the evening tryst :

> Her eyes the glow-worm lend thee.
> The shooting stars attend thee ;
>   And the elves also
>   Whose little eyes glow
> Like the sparks of fire befriend thee.[9]

Corydon, or Robin, waxes rapturous over the fair one's dress, the thread about the wrist, the ribbon round the waist, the sheen, the undulations, of the silken frock ; the studied negligence of her attire :

> A sweet disorder in the dress
> Kindles in clothes a wantonness :
> A lawn about the shoulders thrown
> Into a fine distraction :
> And erring lace, which here and there
> Enthralls the crimson stomacher :
> A cuff neglectful, and thereby
> Ribbons to flow confusedly :
> A winning wave, deserving note,
> In the tempestuous petticoat :
> A careless shoestring, in whose tie
> I see a wild civility :
> Do more bewitch me than when art
> Is too precise in every part.[10]

Or the object of his worship may be yet more personal :

> Some asked me where the rubies grew,
>   And nothing I did say :
> But with my finger pointed to
>   The lips of Julia.

Some ask'd how pearls did grow, and where:
  Then spoke I to my girl,
To part her lips, and show'd them there
  The quarrelets of Pearl.[11]

It may be that
  a ringlet of her hair
Caught my poor soul, as in a snare;[12]

or that her lips—the same that had erewhile pardonably beguiled a honey-bee to an intoxicating, and misunderstood, sip [13]—were taken by him to the fruit market:

  Cherry-ripe, ripe, ripe, I cry,
  Full and fair ones; come and buy.
  If so be you ask me where
  They do grow, I answer: There,
  Where my Julia's lips do smile;
  There's the land, or cherry-isle,
  Whose plantations fully show
  All the year where cherries grow.[14]

Or the witchery is in a voice which strikes mute,[15] or in pretty feet, which

  Like snails did creep
    A little out, and then,
  As if they played at Bo-peep,
    Did soon draw in again.[16]

Only—lovers and beloved, all, are warned:

  Gather ye rose-buds, while ye may:
    Old Time is still a-flying;
  And this same flow'r that smiles to-day
    To-morrow will be dying.[17]

By nature Herrick was an Aeolian Harp. I am tempted, on reading his masterpieces, to believe that, according as the wind of circumstance had played thus or thus on his fancy, he might have written L'Allegro and Il Penseroso, A Midsummer Night's Dream, a Romeo and Juliet, a Faithful

Shepherdess. Nothing could have come strange to him. Question his pathos; and he replies with an appeal to his brother suddenly reported to be dying:

> Life of my life, take not so soon thy flight,
> But stay the time till we have bade good night,
> Thou hast both wind and tide with thee; thy way
> As soon dispatched is by the night as day.
> Let us not then so rudely henceforth go
> Till we have wept, kiss'd, sigh'd, shook hands, or so.
> Pay we our vows and go; yet when we part,
> Then, even then I will bequeath my heart
> Into thy loving hands; for I'll keep none
> To warm my breast, when thou, my pulse, art gone.
> No here I'll last, and walk—a harmless shade—
> About this urn, wherein thy dust is laid,
> To guard it so, as nothing here shall be
> Heavy to hurt those sacred seeds of thee.[18]

We feel an unlimited reserve of power in all directions, though by preference he sang of love, sometimes metaphysically, as in the delightful dialectics of The Kiss;[19] oftener jocundly, and with what he admits to be sometimes 'wantonness'—'cleanly', as benevolently he qualifies it.[20]

Not always is love, however, itself mirthful:

> The sweets of love are mix'd with tears.[21]

Still less is life in general. He was cursed, or blessed, not only with an affectionate heart, but with a tender conscience. His Muse was prone to dwell with grave alarm on thoughts of his own end, and the slenderness of his preparation for meeting it. Death was one thing for an innocent child:

> Here a pretty baby lies
> Sung asleep with lullabies;
> Pray be silent, and not stir
> Th' easy earth that covers her.[22]

It wore a forbidding aspect to the world-worn poet in the

gloom which often will gather over the sunniest nature. Past midnight would come the bellman with his lantern and his light, to warn of the general Session :

> Rise, ye debtors, then, and fall
> To make payment, while I call.[23]

In his sick vigils, when to his trembling fancy :

> the passing bell doth toll,
> And the furies in a shoal
> Come to fright a parting soul,[24]

he sobs forth his half-despairing, half-protesting Litany. Vainly he endeavours to strip the open grave of its terrors, to cajole Death by gay salutes and caresses, as in the fine mephistophelic invitation to his winding-sheet :

> Come thou, who art the wine and wit
> Of all I've writ.[25]

A more lasting, more genuine, and more comforting, if not altogether satisfying, emotion, as he tosses on his bed, entreating

> The winds to blow the tedious night away,
> That I might see the cheerful peeping day,[26]

is neither of defiance, nor of hopelessness, nor yet of hopefulness, but of unquestioning resignation :

> Call, and I'll come ; say Thou the when and where.[27]

He has been glad for us ; and we owe it to him to share his grief. We need not, however, be too distressfully sorry for his sorrow. The emotional nature of Robin the Poet may probably, as he frolicked with his bevy of 'Queens of Roses', have laid up some cause of uneasiness for the Vicar of Dean Prior. But I discredit the legend of youthful excesses, and think the after-penitence poetically exaggerated. At all events, the offences doubtless were not so flagrant as to falsify his asseveration at the close of the Hesperides :

> Jocund his verse was, but his life was chaste ;

or to hinder him from leaving on record as a cardinal article of his Creed, which does not expect God to be indulgent to 'the bad' :

> I do believe the good, and I,
> Shall live with Him eternally.[28]

To a certain extent the horrors of the night-watches, like the gaieties of daylight, were all in the twenty-four hours' poetic work, and left little bitterness behind. It is difficult, and superfluous to try, to disbelieve the general current of internal testimony in the body of his verse, in age as in youth, to the prevailing serenity of the man.

He had a propensity for playing at melancholy as at joviality. Thus, he fears that the morning dew on a clump of primroses implies sorrow, and pauses—nor is ridiculous—to console :

> Why do ye weep, sweet babes ? Can tears
>   Speak grief in you,
>   Who were but born
> Just as the modest morn
> Teem'd her refreshing dew ?
> Alas ! you have not known that shower
>   That mars a flower,
>   Nor felt th' unkind
> Breath of a blasting wind.
> Nor are ye worn with years,
>   Or warp'd as we,
>   Who think it strange to see
> Such pretty flowers, like to orphans young,
> To speak by tears before ye have a tongue.[29]

With equal ease and charm he could be sad or merry. A touch, and the bright stream dances out. A Prince's birth—the future James the Second's!—has to be welcomed:

> May his pretty dukeship grow
> Like t' a rose of Jericho.
> May his soft foot, where it treads,
> Gardens thence produce and meads;
> And those meadows full be set
> With the rose and violet.[30]

A humbler babe thanks God for its simple meal; [30] and the charms of Phyllis or Julia could have extracted nothing half so sweet:

> Here, a little child, I stand,
> Heaving up my either hand;
> Cold as paddocks though they be,
> Here I lift them up to Thee,
> For a benison to fall
> On our meat, and on us all.[31]

On any and every text the easy flow, the airy glancing hither and thither! Perhaps a little too facile, too even. But how direct and clear—how straight each arrow's flight to its special mark in heart or brain! English poetry of the sixteenth and seventeenth centuries is rich, for instance, in love songs: but very rare, unless in one or two of the great Elizabethans, are Herrick's dainty crispness, delicious naïveté! What a natural stylist he! The incomparable harmony of diction! How the words, not one too many, seem to have been fated each to its particular spot and time! By an inner force, which disguises itself as merest chance, all flutter down, as irresponsible autumn leaves on a still afternoon into their ordained resting-places on the woodland moss. Such certainty too! The reader never is afraid that the poem, which started with a gallop, will stumble broken-winded before its close. In so rare a phenomenon of dullness, as the Dirge of Dorcas, one suspects that the singer is simply amusing himself with the picture of the sordid regret of the widows for kind, dead neighbour Tabitha's flesh-pots, and charity garments :

>   Ah, Dorcas, Dorcas! now adieu!
>   Thou being dead,
>   The worsted thread
>   Is cut that made us clothing.[32]

It is, at any rate, seldom indeed that his wit and humour, any more than his grief and repentance, admit of the least misapprehension. Never did poet's ordinary emotions glide more buoyantly and softly down a smoother current of melodious rhythm, laving sunnier imagery! His fixed place in the poetical hierarchy so far may not be exalted, though very honourable. I dare not say his seat must have been among the princes. I am sure it would have been securely his own. There are magnates whom we could more easily have spared than him, just as he is. He is necessary.

Praise thus qualified is, I believe, the rightful due of Herrick, as measured by ninety-nine in a hundred of his poems. The perplexity is in the departures from the standard of level merit which in general contented himself. Poets, the major even more commonly than the minor, are inured to failure. They descend as abruptly as Phaethon, apparently without concern or consciousness. The phenomenon is so ordinary as to be hardly worth notice. In Herrick's case the wonder is to see him, without ceasing to be himself, rise suddenly, as a lark from its nest, into the pure empyrean of inspiration. Fresh from diverting his readers with the discovery of 'hide or seek' carnations in Lucia's betraying cheek, from gambolling, innocently enough, with maidens who toss a cowslip ball, or from issuing orders to the entire human race to await the leave of 'my Julia' before venturing to 'dispose itself to live or die', he soars into three noble lyrics.

It is a mystery of mind, of inspiration, how the adorer of Perenna, Perilla, Silvia, Corinna, Electra, Lucia, Julia, and the rest, could have conceived the offer of knightly service to Anthea. How bravely it rings!

> Bid me to live, and I will live
> Thy Protestant to be,
> Or bid me love, and I will give
> A loving heart to thee.
>
> A heart as soft, a heart as kind,
> A heart as sound and free
> As in the whole world thou canst find,
> That heart I'll give to thee.
>
> Bid that heart stay, and it will stay
> To honour thy decree;
> Or bid it languish quite away,
> And 't shall do so for thee.
>
> Bid me to weep, and I will weep
> While I have eyes to see;
> And, having none, yet I will keep
> A heart to weep for thee.
>
> Bid me despair, and I'll despair
> Under that cypress-tree;
> Or bid me die, and I will dare
> E'en death to die for thee.
>
> Thou art my life, my love, my heart,
> The very eyes of me;
> And hast command of every part
> To live and die for thee.[33]

Then, wonder on wonder, we come upon Blossoms and Daffodils! The song to Anthea was of a refreshing vigour, downright and stirring. It gives a sense of open air, breezy sunshine, as we emerge from the half-lights and millinery of love ditties and Valentines. I do not pretend for it that we feel, as with great poetry, that it has descended upon us, we know not whence. The other two belong to another world than ours. They are of an ethereal beauty, sadness, and suggestiveness, difficult to match, and impossible to surpass. There is no indication of an intention in the author that they should be coupled ; yet a unity of spirit is traceable in them; and each, in its place in the Hesperides, stands a clear head and shoulders above its neighbours. Here are the lines on Blossoms :

> Fair pledges of a fruitful tree,
>   Why do ye fall so fast ?
>   Your date is not so past
> But you may stay yet here a while,
> To blush and gently smile ;
>   And go at last.
>
> What ! were ye born to be
>   An hour or half's delight,
>   And so to bid good-night ?
> 'Twas pity Nature brought ye forth
> Merely to show your worth,
>   And lose you quite.
>
> But you are lovely leaves, where we
>   May read how soon things have
>   Their end, though ne'er so brave ;
> And after they have shown their pride
> Like you a while, they glide
>   Into the grave.[34]

Are not sense and melody perfect ? Pass to Daffodils, and we wonder if perfection do not admit of degrees of comparison :

> Fair daffodils, we weep to see
>   You haste away so soon ;
> As yet the early-rising sun
>   Has not attain'd his noon.
>   Stay, stay,
>   Until the hasting day
>   Has run
>   But to the evensong ;
> And, having prayed together, we
>   Will go with you along.

> We have short time to stay, as you,
>   We have as short a spring;
> As quick a growth to meet decay,
>   As you, or anything.
>   We die,
> As your hours do, and dry
>   Away,
> Like to the summer's rain;
> Or as the pearls of morning's dew,
>   Ne'er to be found again.[35]

Together, the lovely pair, so various with the same conclusion—just thirty-eight short lines—set all the chimes in the heart playing at once! Labour to track the magic home. It is as impossible as for the anatomist to discover the footprints of a fled soul in a human corpse. The words, ninety per cent. of them, are of one syllable. They are on a text the oldest of all worn themes. Subtlest analysis has nothing else to show. The dry bones reunite; and a tongue of fire descends upon them, bringing all Heaven before our eyes.

Why are we not oftener blessed with this seraphic visitant in the harmonious legion, fourteen hundred strong, of the Hesperides and Noble Numbers? The only, and sufficient, answer is, I fear, Herrick's own:

> That things of greatest, so of meanest worth,
> Conceiv'd with grief are, and with tears brought forth.[36]

The delightful singer suffered from the malady of indolence, intellectual, moral, and spiritual, aggravated by nature's too great kindness. He knew he had but to let music flow from his pen, and it would flow. So he let it.

Robert Herrick: The Hesperides, and Noble Numbers, ed. Alfred Pollard, Preface by A. C. Swinburne. (The Muses' Library.) Two vols. Lawrence & Bullen, 1891.

[1] An Ode for Him (Ben Jonson) (Hesperides, 911, ii. 110, st. 1).

[2] (Hesperides, 1028.) His Tears to Thamesis, and (Hesperides, 715) His Return to London.
[3] Oberon's Feast (Hesperides, 293). [4] Ibid.
[5] Corinna's Going a Maying (Hesperides, 178), and The Wake (Hesperides, 763).
[6] Mrs. Eliz. Wheeler—the Lost Shepherdess (Hesperides, 263)
[7] The Cheat of Cupid (Hesperides, 81).
[8] Mrs. Eliz. Wheeler. See supra, 6.
[9] The Night-Piece—to Julia (Hesperides, 619).
[10] Delight in Disorder (Hesperides, 83).
[11] The Rock of Rubies, and the Quarry of Pearls (Hesperides, 75).
[12] How his Soul Came Ensnared (Hesperides, 878).
[13] The Captiv'd Bee (Hesperides, 182).
[14] Cherry-Ripe (Hesperides, 53).
[15] Upon Julia's Voice (Hesperides, 67 and 68).
[16] Upon Her Feet (Hesperides, 527).
[17] To the Virgins, to Make Much of Time (Hesperides, 208).
[18] To his Dying Brother, Master William Herrick (Hesperides, 186).
[19] The Kiss: A Dialogue (Hesperides, 329).
[20] The argument of his Book (Hesperides, 1), i. 3, and His Confession (Noble Numbers, 1-2).
[21] The Primrose (Hesperides, 580).
[22] Upon a Child (Hesperides, 640).
[23] The Bellman (Noble Numbers, 121).
[24] His Litany to the Holy Spirit (Noble Numbers, 41)
[25] His Winding-Sheet (Hesperides, 515).
[26] To His Sweet Saviour (Noble Numbers, 77).
[27] Ibid.
[28] Hesperides, 1129, ii. 165. His Creed (Noble Numbers, 78).
[29] To Primroses Filled with Morning Dew (Hesperides, 257).
[30] The Poet's Good Wishes for The Duke of York (Hesperides, 266).
[31] Another Grace for a Child (Noble Numbers, 95).
[32] The Widow's Tears; or, Dirge of Dorcas (Noble Numbers, 123), 216-19.
[33] To Anthea, who may Command him Anything (Hesperides, 267).
[34] To Blossoms (Hesperides, 467).
[35] To Daffodils (Hesperides, 316).
[36] To Primroses, &c. (Hesperides, 257).

SAMUEL BUTLER

1612—1680

A GREAT name in the history of mind, politics, and literature.

Dryden himself did not argue in rhyme with the elaborate dexterity of Hudibras. The mental eye is kept hard at work as it watches the swift thrusting and parrying. Now the Knight is answering his Squire's 'vitilitigation' on the respective merits of 'Synods or Bears';[1] and now debating with the Widow he was courting on Nature's ordinance of Marriage:

> Those heavenly attracts of yours, your eyes,
> And face, that all the world surprise,
> That dazzle all that look upon ye,
> And scorch all other ladies tawny,
> Those ravishing and charming graces,
> Are all made up of two half-faces,
> That in a mathematic line,
> Like those in other heavens, join,
> Of which, if either grew alone,
> 'Twould fright as much to look upon.
> The world is but two paths that meet
> And close at th' equinoctial fit;
> And so are all the works of nature;
> Stamped with her signature on matter;
> Which all her creatures, to a leaf,
> Or smallest blade of grass, receive.
> All which sufficiently declare
> How entirely marriage is her care.[2]

Then the text for discussion, as at a gathering of Christian Scientists, is the reality or nullity of

>   this thing call'd pain.
> It is—the learned Stoics maintain—
> Not bad simpliciter, nor good ;
> But merely as 'tis understood.
> Sense is deceitful, and may feign,
> As well in counterfeiting pain
> As other gross phaenomenas
> In which it oft mistakes the case.
> But since th' immortal intellect—
> That's free from error and defect,
> Whose objects still persist the same—
> Is free from outward bruise or maim,
> Which nought external can expose
> To gross material bangs or blows,
> It follows we can ne'er be sure
> Whether we pain or not endure ;
> And just so far are sore and grieved
> As by the fancy is believ'd.[3]

The logic-chopping jumps from one perplexing topic to another, as adroitly as if the whole were a show of circus riders. The aphorisms are at once wit, dazzling wit, and wisdom, practical wisdom, in disguise ; and both wisdom and wit, from two to three centuries old, are, for the most part, modern now. The wonder of it all is that, while no parallel to so heterogeneous a medley of folly and sagacity exists in the language, yet there is unity in the whole. It is made to appear entirely reasonable that sense and absurdity should walk hand in hand ; that depths of learning should be sounded to dredge up sewage ; and that the hero of the piece should possess the infallibility of Solomon, and act with the silliness of Simple Simon.

The book is an absolute treasure-house of phrases which have been incorporated into English. No author but Shakespeare has been more accommodating in this way, though Pope may compare. Isolated they are effective, and much more so in their proper places. Butler has uses for them all, and exact corners for which they seem severally to have been manufactured. Words, sentiments, rhythm, and rhymes assume for him a consummate Harlequin's apparent unconsciousness of the substantiality of joints and bones. Try to express the idea otherwise, and you find them hard and rigid as iron. I have been refreshing my recollections, dating from boyhood's explorations of a minute copy in my father's library; and I find the workmanship altogether wonderful. The brilliancy of the repartees! The discernment of every weak point in an opponent's armour, of the least opening for an instillation of red-hot oil! The delightfulness, even to dispassionate, protesting neutrals, of the insolence of the attack! Who could help being diverted by the Cavalier view of your true blue Presbyterians?

> that stubborn crew
> Of errant saints, whom all men grant
> To be the true church militant;
> Such as do build their faith upon
> The holy text of pike and gun;
> Decide all controversies by
> Infallible artillery;
> And prove their doctrine orthodox
> By apostolic blows and knocks;
> Call fire and sword, and desolation,
> A godly thorough reformation;
> More peevish, cross, and splenetic
> Than dog distract, or monkey sick,
> That with more care keep holiday
> The wrong, than others the right way;
> Compound for sins they are inclin'd to,
> By damning those they have no mind to,
> Still so perverse and opposite,
> As if they worshipp'd God for spite.

>The self-same thing they will abhor
>One way, and long another for.
>Free-will they one way disavow,
>Another nothing else allow;
>All piety consists therein
>In them, in other men all sin.
>Rather than fail, they will defy
>That which they love most tenderly;
>Quarrel with minc'd pies, and disparage
>Their best and dearest friend, plum-porridge;
>Fat pig and goose itself oppose,
>And blaspheme custard thro' the nose.[4]

Apart from the attractive rancour, the characters are portrayed with extraordinary vividness. The minuteness of detail is as striking. Readers are left with a satisfying sense of abundance of matter in the author, as well as in his theme. A feeling less satisfied of curiosity also is aroused; for a story, left alas! half-told, of knight-errantry is related, as well as a squib exploded. Fragmentary though it all be, it is of inestimable value as history; a monument of Cavalier revenge for the triumph of Puritanism; an explanation, unintended by Butler, of the second and final quenching of the Cavalier spirit. If it can be read with pleasure now, think of the enthusiasm in its own day, when every allusion was identified, every shot found its deadly billet!

With all that, with the deepest sense of the genius of the man, I have undergone grave searchings of heart, whether I could inscribe him among my poets. I am not pretending to dictate to others. I write for myself, to remind myself of the writers among whom I have to choose when I feel in the mood to read poetry. In the number of high literary qualities which distinguish Hudibras, I listen in vain for a half-note, a subtone, of tenderness, sympathy. The Knight and Ralph pass from misfortune to misfortune. They are subjected to all kinds of mockery and humiliation. Their chronicler parades his pleasure at their disasters. He extricates them only that he may plunge them deeper in the mire. The Knight displays singular philosophy in his afflictions. He is comparatively patient. He is always ready to improve the occasion. In most doleful dudgeon he finds a reserve in himself of energy enough to ply his obstinate Squire with a storm of syllogisms. A reader is inclined to admire and compassionate. Manifestly the author of Hudibras's existence is insensible to pity. He is incapable of admiration likewise; or, if ever he feel any, it is for the Billingsgate valour, in arm and tongue, of his heroine Trulla.

Nowhere, unless in irony, will be discovered a word of praise for men or women, for work of art or of nature. Passion, except in the shape of a cold fury of partisan indignation, is non-existent throughout. As there is no charity, neither is there sadness. Cervantes, in prose, while he steeps his masterpiece in mockery of the picturesque phases of mediaevalism, yet cannot resist the temptation to indulge in a climax of sweetest, affectionate melancholy. Our English comic epic tastes wholly of gall, from the beginning to the end of it. No pathos is in it, no sorrow, nor kindness, nor heroism, nor generosity; and how can beauty flower without them? And without beauty where is poetry?

Thus Hudibras is ruled out of Parnassus. Yet, there it stays, doggedly defiant; one of the world-poems. Many of its qualities are such as no poem ought to have. It wants many which no poem ought to be without. Nevertheless, though it will not conform to canons which must be obeyed if poetry is to be taken to the heart, it is impossible to deny its title to poetical rank. I suppose the reason is that real feeling is present, if not joy in virtue and beauty; that there is a whole-soul resentment of intolerance, hypocrisy, covetousness, ugliness, and meanness; with absorption in a theme, self-abandonment, the rapture of creation. Where these are, it is as difficult to say that verse can fail to be poetry, as it is to say that there can be poetry without beauty or virtue. Thus, poetry I am almost forced to recognize that Hudibras is; as also that Butler is a poet. A poet; and fashioned by nature—given the due circumstances—to have captivated the heart, as he storms the interest. The pity of it! And the more the pity, that any change in the structure which would have supplied the deficiencies without making Hudibras to be no longer Hudibras, is inconceivable!

Hudibras: in three Parts: Written in the Time of the late Wars, by Samuel Butler, Esq. Annotated by Zachary Grey, LL.D. Two vols. London, 1806.

[1] Part I, Canto iii, vv. 1261-8.
[2] Part III, Canto i, vv. 779-804.
[3] Part II, Canto i, vv. 183-200.
[4] Part I, Canto i, vv. 192-230.

EDMUND WALLER

1606—1687

WALLER is among the great names in the history of literature. He was a fine gentleman as well as wit, an enterprising, if not successful, amateur statesman, a brilliant courtier. Yet, unlike others of the previous, or of his own, generation, resembling him in social distinction, he was not ashamed to be a man of letters. Contemporary writers, even Ben Jonson, whose scholar he was proud to be,[1] acknowledged him as of the craft, a colleague as well as a patron. He is admitted to have preceded Dryden in the effort, for good or evil, to fix the language, to counteract the inconveniences, even the dangers, of continual change ; for

> who can hope his line should long
> Last in a daily changing tongue ?[2]

In effecting the transformation from Elizabethan into modern English his instrument was verse. As an author he has to be judged by that. Of his merit in it, at any rate during his younger days, he himself had no doubt :

> O, that I now could write as well as then ![3]

Critics and the reading public shared his candid belief in himself to the full. With scarce a dissenting voice they would have endorsed the description of him in Beaconsfield Churchyard as ' inter poetas sui temporis facilè princeps '.

It is a good working rule to accept contemporary opinion of literary worth as weighty evidence in a positive, if not in a comparative, sense. I will try to explain how far

I have satisfied myself of its applicability to Edmund Waller. His poems are not much in quantity. Society, with politics for a period, occupied a large part of his time. He was too careful of his reputation to be profuse or diffuse. Very many of his productions, it must be allowed, are grown cold-dead for us. It is impossible to moan with trees at Penshurst for my Lord of Leicester's absence in France ; or with its deer, that they fall to another crossbow than his,

> Whose arrows they would gladly stain ! [4]

The allusions constantly are to drawing-room gossip, to pinpricks of fashion, rather than to perennial, universal emotions of the heart. Obviously he is commonly thinking of individuals in the accidents of their individuality. So large an amount of his work is thus earmarked for an obsolete past, that, although in no body of verse can a large part expect immortality, one is visited by a special apprehension here of an excessive disproportion between the author's net achievement and his fame.

In the remainder, however, there is matter which still fights bravely for life. The three Cromwellian poems, the Panegyric, the victory at San Lucar,[5] with all its bombast, and the elegy on the Protector's death,[6] are historical monuments. The first in particular is admirable for the tact with which the least invidious features in a great career are singled out for especial praise—the pacification of civil strife, the grasp of the empire of the seas, and national exaltation. It never rises into hysterical passion, and seldom sinks into bathos :

> With a strong, and yet a gentle hand,
> You bridle faction, and our hearts command ;
> Protect us from ourselves, and from the foe,
> Make us unite, and make us conquer too.

Your drooping country, torn with civil hate,
Restor'd by you, is made a glorious state ;
The seat of empire, where the Irish come,
And the unwilling Scots, to fetch their doom.

The sea's our own ; and now, all nations greet,
With bending sails, each vessel of our fleet ;
Your power extends as far as winds can blow,
Or swelling sails upon the globe may go.

Hither th' oppressed shall henceforth resort,
Justice to crave, and succour, at your Court ;
And then your Highness, not for ours alone,
But for the world's Protector shall be known.

Fame, swifter than your winged navy, flies
Through every land that near the ocean lies ;
Sounding your name, and telling dreadful news
To all that piracy and rapine use.

Lords of the world's great waste, the ocean, we
Whole forests send to reign upon the sea ;
And every coast may trouble or relieve ;
But none can visit us without your leave.[7]

The new King, according to tradition, contrasted sarcastically the inferior benediction on the Restoration with the full flood of the grand encomium on the old Dictator. Posterity is more inclined to be indignant at the fervour of the compliments—paid by the burnt child of plottings against authority—to Charles's 'mighty' mind, and to 'matchless' James. There can indeed be but one apology both for the extravagance and for the poverty of sycophantic ideas and topics—the royal 'shape so lovely'—the monarch's strolls in St. James's sacred groves, where he 'resolves the fates' of neighbouring Princes— and his healing tears over his deserted Queen's sick-bed. They may testify at least that the courtier had, as poet, a soul too high to be inspired by an unworthy theme.

Elsewhere he could be eloquent ; and of his possession

of the gift of elegance there never was a question. The word Wit was used with a different significance in the seventeenth century from that it conveys now. I can understand its application to Waller when I read a poem like that to The Mutable Fair. His Muse was specially commissioned and equipped to play, for example, the comedy of a blasé victim's pretence of fury, but real relief, when the traitress

> Again deceives him, and again;
> And then he swears he'll not complain;
> For still to be deluded so,
> Is all the pleasure lovers know.[8]

His amatory fancy delighted to hover bird-like, without alighting at the risk of a cage; to be not more ready to drink than to be scared away; to flutter, in charmed suspense, between an

> Amoret, as sweet and good
> As the most delicious food,

and a

> Sacharissa's beauty's wine,
> Which to madness doth incline;[9]

blissfully to welcome martyrdom at the hands of Chloris tunefully slaying him with a song of his own!

> That eagle's fate and mine are one,
> Which, on the shaft that made him die,
> Espy'd a feather of his own
> Wherewith he wont to soar so high.[10]

Never did bard keep his inspiration more completely in hand. When Thyrsis bewails with Galatea the premature death of the beautiful Hamilton, as sweet as she was noble,

> So good, so lovely, and so young,[11]

an exquisite polish, an air of the best society, tempers common grief, as a soft, tepid rain subdues a troubled sea. Very generously he warns youthful Flavia's guardians to beware of the burning effect of a poet's breath upon a budding beauty, as upon an opening rose :

> Still as I did the leaves inspire,
> With such a purple light they shone,
> As if they had been made of fire,
> And spreading so, would flame anon :
> All that was meant by air or sun,
> To the young flower, my breath has done.[12]

So long as the incendiarism was confined to verse, they need not have taken alarm. Consider even the celebrated lines :

> That which her slender waist confin'd,
> Shall now my joyful temples bind ;
> No monarch but would give his crown,
> His arms might do what this has done.
>
> It was my heav'n's extremest sphere,
> The pale which held that lovely deer ;
> My joy, my grief, my hope, my love,
> Did all within this circle move !
>
> A narrow compass ! and yet there
> Dwelt all that's good, and all that's fair ;
> Give me but what this ribband bound,
> Take all the rest the sun goes round.[13]

For Waller, so perfect are the three stanzas, that, were all else of his lost, the whole essence of him would survive. But, like the rest, they are uninflammatory. Their luminousness actually by its defects stamps the piece as more ideally his. It less resembles cheerful sunlight than the dazzling reflection from Alpine snows.

His work lacks heat of its own ; it is no emanation from head and heart combined. On the other hand, precision, lucidity, completeness of harmony between a conceit and its expression, are invariable qualities. The ability to whip cream out of the thinnest milk is amazing. The slighter the subject—a slip on wet clay, a rouged cheek, the wedding of two dwarfs, an air on the lute—the fitter. A weighty thought required too much fining down. We almost see a real idea in the act of being ground down, pared, relieved of an excess of suggestiveness and boastful intellectuality. Poor thing! in as ill case as Mary of Modena, with nothing but a Royal wig to screen off all the King's Ministers from her bed! No allowance made for a delicate germ's modesty --the operator glorying in the exhibition of his remorseless skill!

An admirable artist—exulting in his dexterity—Edmund Waller had elected to be a poet; and is he? Well, take the Panegyric. That is a lofty, masculine declamation, abounding in rhetorical fire. It proves its author the master he unquestionably was of strong, pure, clear English. It indicates powers of expression which might have made him a commanding prose writer; perhaps an eminent orator. I am afraid I cannot perceive in it, and in other work of a similar order, the distinctive poetic vein. The love lyrics are refined in their moral tone; strangely so for the time at which their writer was born, and, yet more, for that into which he survived. They are irreproachable in rhythm, and as perfect in form and fashion as a Paris frock. To me all, with a single exception, want the nearly indescribable something which stamps essential poetry.

Still, the exception remains, and cannot—happily, cannot—be explained away. Compare the brilliant Girdle lyric with:

> Go, lovely Rose!
> Tell her, that wastes her time and me,
> That now she knows,
> When I resemble her to thee,
> How sweet, and fair, she seems to be.

> Tell her that 's young,
> And shuns to have her graces spy'd,
> That had'st thou sprung
> In deserts where no men abide,
> Thou must have uncommended dy'd.
>
> Small is the worth
> Of beauty from the light retir'd;
> Bid her come forth,
> Suffer herself to be desir'd,
> And not blush so to be admir'd.
>
> Then die! that she
> The common fate of all things rare
> May read in thee;
> How small a part of time they share
> That are so wondrous sweet and fair![14]

The fragrance in it—the atmosphere—the colour, issuing from inward warmth, and from inward life! Here we do not see—with what admiration we may—the consummate artist in language and metres carving, filing, veneering, inlaying, polishing, and gilding. The fabric, to its dying close, seems to grow before our eyes, touched by a light, a glow, as strange—we will hope, as delightful—to poet as to reader.

If the singer did not develop the poetic soul-germ as nature had designed, I am afraid it must have been that he would not. He was far from contemptuous of a poet's renown; he hoped and expected to be venerated as one in future ages; he chose to be crowned at once by his own generation, and in a lady's boudoir. A poet, to be ranked among the great, ought to let himself go, to suffer the spirit to carry him whither it will. Waller, I suspect, was always on guard to repress the least symptom of divine madness. He had a horror of becoming ridiculous. Here is, I believe, a clue to the frigidity which numbs the sympathy modern readers would gladly feel. I am not equally satisfied that it convicts his contemporaries of misplaced enthusiasm. As other creatures may possess faculties of which man has no conception, so it may be with other eras in literature. I confess to a suspicion sometimes, and a hope, that Waller's own period may have been endued with a poetic sensibility enabling it to find at the hearth of his sparkling wit a comfort beyond us. It is a curious question whether it appreciated the warmth as fully as the flame in the single instance in which we recognize in him the presence of both.

The Poems of Edmund Waller (Johnson's Poets, vol. xvi). 1790.
[1] Upon Ben Jonson.
[2] Of English Verse, v. 6.
[3] Of the Fear of God, v. 50.
[4] To my Lord of Leicester, v. 10.
[5] Of our late War with Spain.
[6] Upon the Death of the Lord Protector.
[7] A Panegyric to my Lord Protector, stanzas 1, 4, 5, 8, 9, 11.
[8] The Mutable Fair, vv. 63-6.
[9] To Amoret.
[10] To a Lady Singing a Song of his Composing, st. 2.
[11] Thyrsis, Galatea. [12] The Bud.
[13] On a Girdle. [14] Song.

SIR JOHN SUCKLING

1609—1642

SUCKLING'S was a short career, but eventful, passed in a blaze of notoriety. Son of a Secretary of State, he was born and bred in a Court, and early became a favourite of King Charles and Queen Henrietta. He inherited wealth, which he spent freely at the gaming table, and in the dissipations of fashionable life. His was a nature to carry him gaily into adventures, without sufficient sturdiness to see him safely through them. At the same time, it included enough elasticity for him to live down rebuffs. Thus a futile attempt to retrieve his embarrassed fortunes by a rich marriage brought him the disgrace of a cudgelling by a rival. The affront was not avenged by him; yet it neither clouded permanently his reputation as a gentleman, nor dashed his own self-confidence. He had served, with distinction, it is said, a campaign in Germany under Gustavus Adolphus. On the armed rising of the Scottish Covenanters under Lesley against the King's Church policy, he raised, at his own expense, a troop of horse. It ran away with the rest of the Royal Cavalry at Newburgh. Finally, having been a principal in a wild plot for the forcible rescue of Strafford from the Tower, he fled to France. In Paris, having used up his courage and hopefulness, as well as his estate, he ended his life, it is generally supposed, by suicide.

A scholar trained at Westminster and Trinity, and a wit, he played the author in the intervals of gallantry, gambling, soldiering, and political intrigues. A weighty epistle by him to Jermyn, afterwards Lord St. Albans, on the disputes between King and Parliament attracted much notice. His habits of life did not even hinder him from employing his pen in a defence of Religion by Reason. But it was as a poet—though, after the affectation of his day, he disclaimed the title—that he expected to be recollected; and it is as a poet that, if dimly, we must try to see him. A lyric poet; for of the plays he wrote—Aglaura, The Goblins, Brennoralt, and The Sad One—the two which are dimly remembered survive, each in virtue simply of a song: in Aglaura, of

>Why so pale and wan, fond Lover?

and, in the comedy of The Goblins, of

>A health to the Nut-brown Lasse,
>Let it passe—let it passe—

a rough draft for Sheridan's

>Let the toast pass!

I do not think that a survey of his active life assists us much to understand his career in letters. We should infer from his doings a character made up of warm impulses, without equivalent strength of will. Passion, both spiritual and sensual, is consistent with them. So is the refinement of fits of dissoluteness by an element of romance. The rioting might conceivably have been followed by stages of remorse. Spasms of religious exaltation might have ended, not as with Crashaw, in the Chapter of Loretto, but at la Trappe. The whole is compatible with a poet's genius, and work to correspond. Or, on the contrary, an adventurous nature, finding its field in action, might have suffered an extinction of any ethereal spark in the brain.

Neither one nor the other fate was Suckling's. He continued to the end man of the world, and of the pen. Contemporaries, many of them carping and jealous, recognized in him poetic powers of the highest. Posterity remains uncertain as to the degree ; it has never denied the reality of what there is ; and the reality has won its admiration, not its affection. There is seldom a glow, unless phosphoric, as of animal desire ; never a sigh of remorse, though many of satiety; only once a positive groan of Vanitas vanitatum ; nowhere a battle-cry, the joyousness of chivalry ; only one hint at a doubt that woman can be more than a beast of chase, if not, as oftener, among the hounds, or even a tigress and man-eater ; no glimpse of a God in Heaven, or a soul in nature. On the other hand, cut diamonds in profusion sparkle. Gaiety is present, not unmixed with malice, and sometimes malignity ; an air of good society ; a fine choice of pure diction ; if not a largeness of ideas, precision and sureness in their exposition ; more than enough of a poet's sensibility to surprise, disappoint, and trouble that there is none of the sympathy.

Wit, the sudden gleam from the flint, was what he valued in himself most ; and it abounds. It caught the Town in the Session of the Poets, not that there its occasional flashes any longer dazzle. Spite against his contemporaries is more durably apparent—against all but Lord Falkland, who in his passion for theology,

> had almost forgot his poetry.
> Though to say the truth—and Apollo did know it—
> He might have been both his Priest and his Poet.[1]

Better stuff of the kind may be found in the game of Love, Reason and Hate, at barley-break, with Folly, Fancy, and Pride for mates, where Love always ends by being coupled to Folly, and in Hell ;[2] in the sardonic advice to a lover to feast high :

> Spare diet is the cause love lasts ;[3]

in the glorying of a Constant Lover :

> Out upon it, I have loved
> Three whole days together ! [4]

and in the explanation of a lady's beauty-spots, as

> Mourning-weeds for hearts forlorn.[5]

Sheer delight in the ingenuity almost beguiles him into a semblance of amiability, in the invitation to a rival to share the joy of contemplating perfections manifestly too ecstatic for a single individual :

> Thou first shalt sigh, and say shee 's fair,
> And I'll still answer, past compare.
> Thou shalt set out each part o' the face.
> While I extol each little grace ;
> Thou shalt be ravish'd at her wit ;
> And I, that she so governs it ;
> Thou shalt like well that hand, that eye ;
> That lip, that look, that majesty ;
> And in good language them adore ;
> While I want words, and do it more.
> Yea, we will sit and sigh a while,
> And with soft thoughts some time beguile ;
> But straight again break out, and praise
> All we had done before, new ways.
> Thus will we do till paler death
> Come with a warrant for our breath,
> And then whose fate shall be to die
> First of us two, by legacy
> Shall all his store bequeath, and give
> His love to him that shall survive ;
> For no one stock can ever serve
> To love so much as shee'll deserve.[6]

Hardly less dexterous, with the skipping backwards and forwards, as if wooing were a course of gymnastics, is the comparison of love to a clock.[7] Certainly never Valentine bettered the denunciation of the criminal waste of a couple of breasts to lodge two hearts which could house much more warmly in one :

> I prythee send me back my heart,
>   Since I cannot have thine ;
> For if from yours you will not part,
>   Why then shouldst thou have mine ?
>
> Yet now I think on 't, let it lie,
>   To find it were in vain,
> For th' hast a thief in either eye
>   Would steal it back again.
>
> Why should two hearts in one breast lie,
>   And yet not lodge together ?
> O love, where is thy sympathy,
>   If thus our breasts thou sever ? [8]

Fancy can barb his habitual cynicism itself towards women so daintily, that—as in the song reminding of Jonson's Triumph of Charis—contempt has the effect of a caress :

> Hast thou seen the down i' the air,
>   When wanton blasts have toss'd it ?
> Or the ship on the sea,
>   When ruder waves have cross'd it ?
> Hast thou mark'd the crocodile's weeping,
>   Or the fox's sleeping ?
> Or hast view'd the peacock in his pride,
>   Or the dove by his bride ?
> O, so fickle, O, so vain, O, so false, so false is she ! [9]

The more pity that he should in general have been satisfied with mere play of wit like these pretty trifles, or even the still more biting and brilliant lyric in Aglaura—ice which scorches—

> Why so pale and wan, fond lover ?
>   Prythee, why so pale ?
> Will, when looking well can't move her,
>   Looking ill prevail ?
>   Prythee, why so pale ?

> Why so dull and mute, young sinner?
>   Prythee, why so mute?
> Will, when speaking well can't win her,
>   Saying nothing do't?
>   Prythee, why so mute?
>
> Quit, quit, for shame! This will not move,
>   This cannot take her;
> If of herself she will not love,
>   Nothing can make her;
>   The devil take her![10]

when he had it in him to create the four famous stanzas, and as many more as can well be quoted, in the Ballad on Lord Broghill's and little Lady Margaret Howard's marriage:

> Her feet beneath her petticoat,
> Like little mice stole in and out,
>   As if they feared the light:
> But O, she dances such a way,
> No Sun upon an Easter-Day
>   Is half so fine a sight.
>
> Her Cheeks so fair a white was on,
> No Daisy makes comparison,
>   (Who sees them is undone;)
> For streaks of red were mingled there,
> Such as are on a Catherine Pear,
>   (The side that's next the Sun.)
>
> Her lips were red, and one was thin,
> Compar'd to that was next her chin;
>   (Some Bee had stung it newly.)
> But, Dick, her eyes so guard her face,
> I durst no more upon them gaze,
>   Than on the Sun in July.
>
> Her mouth so small when she does speak,
> Thou'dst swear her teeth her words did break,
>   That they might passage get;
> But she so handled still the matter,
> They came as good as ours, or better,
>   And are not spent a whit.[11]

So bewitching indeed is grace as well as wit in Suckling at his best, that, after I have dwelt upon it for a time, the impression of its completeness almost overpowers judgement. The writer, I feel, has succeeded in doing just what he undertook to do. Convinced as I am that it is the duty of poetry to be something more and higher, I nevertheless am tempted to be satisfied with a series of consummate vers de société.

Perhaps he himself was visited by occasional self-questionings whether he had used his gift fully or aright. He is supposed to have regarded himself as belonging to the metaphysical school of poetry, with Donne, ' the great lord of it ',[12] for his master. It was, unless once, only externals he had caught—the Dean's trick of misogyny, and, to a certain extent, the diction, with its distinctions and refinements, of seventeenth-century hymnologists. Thus a song lamenting his incapacity, as being not in the least 'all soul', for spiritual union with one who was, might have figured in a sacred anthology but for its final pleading for an ad interim less immaterial alliance.[13] Similarly he can satirize vice; without convincing of his personal aversion. What a relief—a surprise—it is, when he appears to be honestly indignant, as at Calumny snarling at an affection which chanced to be pure :

> Thou vermin slander, bred in abject mind
> Of thoughts impure, by vile tongues animate,
> Canker of conversation ! could'st thou find
> Nought but our love whereon to show thy hate ?
> Thou never wert when we two were alone ;
> What canst thou witness then ? thy base, dull aid
> Was useless in our conversation,
> Where each meant more than could by both be said.
> Whence hadst thou thy intelligence ; from earth ?
> That part of us ne'er knew that we did love :
> Or from the air ? Our gentle sighs had birth
> From such sweet raptures as to joy did move :

Our thoughts, as pure as the chaste morning's breath,
When from the night's cold arms it creeps away,
Were cloth'd in words; and maiden's blush that hath
More purity, more innocence than they.
Nor from the water couldst thou have this tale;
No briny tear hath furrowed her smooth cheek,
And I was pleased; I pray what should he ail.
That had her love, for what else could he seek?
We shortened days to moments by love's art,
Whilst our two souls in amorous ecstasy
Perceived no passing time, as if a part
Our love had been of still eternity.
Much less could have it from the purer fire:
Our heat exhales no vapour from coarse sense,
Such as are hopes, or fears, or fond desire:
Our mutual love itself did recompense.
Thou hast no correspondence in heaven,
And th' elemental world thou seest is free;
Whence hadst thou then this talking monster? even
From hell, a harbour fit for it and thee.[14] .

Unhappily it is the single apparently genuine exception, in a life's songs devoted to amours, to a kaleidoscope of misrepresentations of woman:

There never yet was woman made,
  Nor shall, but to be curst;
And O, that I—fond I—should first
    Of any Lover
This truth at my own charge to other fools discover![15]

In the fireworks of an imagined siege, where he acknowledges that a woman may maintain her chastity for ' a year or more ', against

Great cannon oaths, and shot,

against starvation even,

By cutting off all kisses,
Praying and gazing on her face.
And all such little blisses,

he finds the defence has been nothing but a Point of Honour. Thereupon :

> March, march—quoth I—the word straight give,
>   Let 's lose no time, but leave her;
> That Giant upon air will live,
>   And hold it out for ever.
> To such a place our camp remove
>   As will no siege abide;
> I hate a fool that starves her love,
>   Only to feed her pride![16]

His parting attitude when, after taking a ghastly inventory of feminine departed attractions, comparable, without the piety, to Vaughan's Charnel-house, and for gloom, without the horizon of immortality, to Herbert's Mortification, he bids Farewell to Love,[17] is more degrading. It is that of a slave spurning under foot a dead master.

I dare say there was exaggeration in his invectives. I am inclined to doubt the sincerity of his declared hatred of women, as I doubt the sincerity of his pursuit of them. He was infatuated with society; and, woman being the gate to it, he had to storm her, or pretend it, in order to enter. She was a wit's natural text; and, resenting while admitting the necessity, he sang and reviled her. But whether he were the cynic he proclaims himself, or only playing a part, the sourness equally tainted his verse. As a result he has bequeathed to literature a battery of epigrams, and not a tear of tenderness.

Sir John Suckling—Poems, Plays, and Other Remains, edited by W. C. Hazlitt. Second Edition. Two vols. 1892.
[1] A Session of the Poets, stanza 25.
[2] Love, Reason, Hate.
[3] Against Absence.
[4] Out upon it, I have Loved.
[5] Upon the Black Spots worn by My Lady D. E.

[6] To My Dearest Rival.
[7] That none beguiled be.
[8] I prithee send me back my heart, Nos. 1-3.
[9] Fickle and False—Song to a Lute. Tragedy—The Sad One, Act IV, Sc. iii.
[10] Aglaura—Song, Act IV, Sc. i.
[11] A Ballade—Upon a Wedding, stanzas 8, 10, 11, and 12.
[12] To my Friend Will. Davenant on his other Poems.
[13] If you refuse me once.
[14] Detraction Execrated.
[15] Vol. i, p. 19.
[16] 'Tis now since I sat down before, stanzas 4, 5, 6, 7.
[17] Farewell to Love.

RICHARD LOVELACE
1618—1658

A BEAUTIFUL character. A modest second to Sidney among warrior poets. Though a Courtier, Cavalier, and Soldier, little tainted by the fashionable dissipations of his years, rank, and profession. Women's adorer and champion:

He who lov'd best, and them defended best.[1]

The 'best of brothers'.[2] Prodigal, not for his own pleasures, but for the sake of his family, his comrades, and a cause he esteemed holy. A valiant combatant for King and Church from the time he quitted, an early-ripe scholar, Gloucester Hall. In his slow death, from the effects of wearisome detention in London, and the privations of poverty, uncomplaining. Never murmuring even at misfortunes in love. In any and every phase of his brief but varied career, diligent and devoted, except, apparently, in the service by which alone his memory was to survive—that of the Muses.

Though I do not suppose, in the condescending spirit of an early editor, that he treated his productions as 'merely the amusements of an active soldier', I doubt if he ever regarded versifying seriously enough. The distaste for labouring over it was rather specially detrimental in the kind which he particularly favoured. The two Lucastas, the first printed in his lifetime, and the second published by his brother Dudley's pious care after his death, are a circle of songs on the single text of Love. On any one given theme fancy, which abhors compulsion, will spontaneously light up only a spot here and there. The dexterity of an artist, though one of nature's poets, like Shakespeare, or Sidney, Lovelace's own 'celestial' pattern, is needed to supply the necessary lapses. Lovelace had not the training or patience to perform the duty; and the consequence is that his verse sinks often to a low level. I confess myself to having been visited by an occasional doubt, when not under the spell of his best, whether he may have been only among the potentialities in poetry, not the actualities; whether there be but casual sparks, not the durable fire of a poetic soul. But the scepticism has been merely transient. I do not think it possible to consider his work as a whole without recognizing him as an inspired poet, not simply as the author of a few inspired poems.

Elsewhere, as well as in them, the waters, if not very deep, run over sands which will be found by those who search to contain gold. Amarantha's shining hair, braided no more, but let flutter with the freedom an audacious hand had restored to it, gleams in the sunshine,

> and scatters day,

three centuries after.[3] Gratiana, dancing and singing, still with each step, each note, raises and treads out a suitor's hopes, till—

> when she ceas'd, we sighing saw
> The floor lay pav'd with broken hearts.
> So did she move; so did she sing
> Like the harmonious spheres that bring
>   Unto their rounds their music's aid;
> Which she performèd such a way,
> As all th' enamour'd world will say
>   The Graces danced, and Apollo play'd.[4]

Lucasta weeps so enchantingly that the God of Day in sympathy, after having in vain

> With his handkerchief of light,
> Kiss'd the wet pearls away,

shrouds his rays in clouds of his own tears, until she smiles again, and he with her.⁵ There could not be a prettier picture in words than of two young children; the boy:

>Like Love in arms; he wrote but five,
>Yet spake eighteen, each grace did shine
>And twenty Cupids thronged forth,
>Who first should show his prettier worth.
>But oh, the nymph! did you e'er know
>Carnation mingled with snow?
>Or have you seen the lightning shroud,
>And straight break through th' opposing cloud?
>So ran her blood, such was its hue;
>So through her veil her bright hair flew,
>And yet its glory did appear
>But thin, because her eyes were near.⁶

When, from indolence, or carelessness, he has been extravagant or trite, we often are surprised by a sudden flash; such as, in Love Made in the First Age, by the retrospect of primaeval innocence:

>No palace to the clouds did swell,
>Each humble princess then did dwell
> In the piazza of her hair;⁷

or by the lovely anticipation, in Lucasta's Rose, of Tennyson's Maud:

>See! rosy is her bower,
>Her floor is all this flower:
> Her bed a rosy nest
> By a bed of roses press'd.⁸

Strange that even a beauty's cold heart, which had thus been wooed, should, on the idle rumour of such a lover's death, have hurried to the altar with a rival!

And he has other notes than of love, though rarer. Not many nobler, more sympathetic, epitaphs have been inscribed than that to Mrs. Elizabeth Filmer, possessed of a form fit index to a soul as fair :

> Chaste as th' air whither she 's fled,
> She making her celestial bed
> In her warm alabaster lay
> As cold as in this house of clay ;
> Nor were the rooms unfit to feast
> Or circumscribe this angel-guest ;
> The radiant gem was brightly set
> In as divine a carcanet ;
> For which the clearer was not known,
> Her mind, or her complexion ;
> Such an everlasting grace,
> Such a beatific face
> Incloisters here this narrow floor
> That possess'd all hearts before.
>
> Thus, although this marble must,
> As all things, crumble into dust,
> And though you find this fair-built tomb
> Ashes, as what lies in its womb ;
> Yet her saint-like name shall shine
> A living glory to this shrine,
> And her eternal fame be read,
> When all but very virtue 's dead.[9]

To The King's Painter he gives the exact praise an artist would value, whatever the present age may think of its justice in the particular instance :

> See ! what a clouded majesty ! and eyes
> Whose glory through their mist doth brighter rise !
> See ! what an humble bravery doth shine,
> And grief triumphant breaking through each line
> How it commands the face ! so sweet a scorn
> Never did happy misery adorn !
> Thou sorrow canst design without a tear,
> And with the man his very hope or fear ;
> So that th' amazèd world shall henceforth find
> None but my Lily ever drew a mind.[10]

Even himself he can measure, worthily, not vainly :

> Yet can I music too ; but such
> As is beyond all voice or touch ;
> My mind can in fair order chime,
> Whilst my true heart still beats the time.
> Take all notes with your skilful eyes,
> Hark, if mine do not sympathize !
>
> Sound all my thoughts, and see express'd
> The tablature of my large breast ;
> Then you'll admit that I too can
> Music above dead sounds of man ;
> Such as alone doth bless the spheres,
> Not to be reach'd with human ears.[11]

A large heart indeed his, which was not ashamed of acknowledging gratitude to a benefactress, ' a living saint ', and hymned old age as warmly, and as sweetly, as if it were youth and beauty :

> Slow time with woollen feet make thy soft pace,
> And leave no tracks i' th' snow of her pure face ! [12]

Although I will not lay stress on the barrack-room panegyric of Bacchus :

> What of Elysium's missing ?
> Still drinking, and still kissing ;
> Adoring plump October ;
> Lord ! what is man, and sober ? [13]

I cannot refrain from noting the humour of the addresses to the ant, a ' great good husband ',[14] and the ' sage, compendious snail ',

> Large Euclid's strict epitome ; [15]

with the grave serenity of the Ode to the Grasshopper,[16] from which I should like to quote, were not its ten stanzas of an excellence delightfully even.

Crown finally the whole with the two glorious songs,

VOL. I M

178 FIVE CENTURIES OF ENGLISH VERSE

Going to the Wars, and To Althea from Prison, which shine like stars in the firmament even of English Poesy. Apparently unconnected, they are one in essence; for they sum up a spirit, and a man. With what gay hopefulness he bids his mistress farewell as he rides forth to war!

> Tell me not, sweet, I am unkind,
>   That from the nunnery
> Of thy chaste breast, and quiet mind,
>   To war and arms I fly.
>
> True; a new mistress now I chase,
>   The first foe in the field;
> And with a stronger faith embrace
>   A sword, a horse, a shield.
>
> Yet this inconstancy is such
>   As you too shall adore;
> I could not love thee, dear, so much,
>   Lov'd I not honour more.[17]

How, again, the courage leaps, and the inspiration flames, as the Cavalier, persecuted and in prison, rejoices to have suffered for his King!

> When love with unconfinèd wings
>   Hovers within my gates;
> And my divine Althea brings
>   To whisper at the grates;
> When I lie tangled in her hair
>   And fetter'd to her eye:
> The birds that wanton in the air
>   Know no such liberty.
>
> When flowing cups run swiftly round
>   With no allaying Thames,
> Our careless heads with roses bound,
>   Our hearts with loyal flames,
> When thirsty grief in wine we steep,
>   When healths and draughts go free,
> Fishes that tipple in the deep
>   Know no such liberty.

When—like committed linnets—I
  With shriller throat shall sing
The sweetness, mercy, majesty,
  And glories of my King;
When I shall voice aloud, how good
  He is, how great should be;
Enlargèd winds that curl the flood
  Know no such liberty.

Stone walls do not a prison make,
  Nor iron bars a cage;
Minds innocent and quiet take
  That for an hermitage;
If I have freedom in my love,
  And in my soul am free;
Angels alone that soar above
  Enjoy such liberty.[18]

What a sense of buoyancy the verses give, of infinite space in the realm of poetry for fancy to disport itself without fear of collision with other winged things! The soldier had a flight of emotions to send abroad; he tossed them forth; and they fly and sing still. A thousand songs may contain the same ideas; yet Lovelace's will never be superseded or superannuated. As I recall the two, I am disposed to be indignant with myself for having ever questioned the title of the bright, generous, gracious, luckless soul to occupy an honoured place on the English Parnassus.

Blessings on the memory of Mr. Edmund Wyld, who, according to Aubrey's kindly, ungrammatical gossip, had, when the poet was dying in a cellar—in Gunpowder Alley, near Fetter Lane—a little before the Restoration, ' made collections for him, and given him money. He was of —— in Kent, £500 or more. He was an extraordinary handsome man, but prowd. Geo. Petty, haberdasher, in Fleet Street, carryed twenty shillings to him every Munday morning from Sir ——— Many and Charles Cotton, Esq., for months.'[19] And not the less blessed be he or they, that the doles escaped the bathos of being ever 'repayd'!

Lucasta: Epodes, Odes, Sonnets, Songs: to which is added Alamantha, a Pastoral, by Richard Lovelace, Esq. New Edition. Chiswick: C. Whittingham, 1817; and Lucasta: Posthumous Poems of Richard Lovelace, Esq. With Poems to his Memory. New Edition. Chiswick: C. Whittingham, 1818.
 [1] Marvell's Poems (The Muses' Library).
 [2] Col. Francis Lovelace, Lucasta, xiv.
 [3] To Amarantha (Lucasta), stanza 4.
 [4] Gratiana Dancing and Singing (Lucasta), stanzas 3-4.
 [5] Lucasta Weeping (Lucasta).
 [6] Amputor's Grove. His Chloris, Arigo, and Gratiana (Lucasta).
 [7] Love Made in the First Age: To Chloris (Lucasta: Posthum. Poems).
 [8] To Lucasta—The Rose (Lucasta).
 [9] On the Death of Mrs. Elizabeth Filmer (Lucasta)
 [10] To Mr. Peter Lilly, on the Picture of His Majesty and the Duke of York, Drawn by him at Hampton Court (Lucasta).
 [11] To a Lady who desired me I would bear my part with her in a Song (Lucasta).
 [12] The Lady A. L. My Asylum in a Great Extremity (Lucasta).
 [13] A Loose Saraband (Lucasta: Posthum. Poems).
 [14] The Ant (Lucasta: Posthum. Poems).
 [15] The Snail (ibid.).
 [16] The Grasshopper (Lucasta).
 [17] To Lucasta—Going to the Wars (Lucasta).
 [18] To Althea—from Prison (Lucasta).
 [19] John Aubrey: and Anthony à Wood: Athenae Oxonienses, ed. P. Bliss.

ABRAHAM COWLEY

1618—1667

Is it the fault of our age, or of Cowley's, of himself, or nobody's, that the ordinary reader has no longer eyes for the merits of a writer accounted in his own time ' incomparable ', ' most incomparable ', ' Prince of Poets ' ? When first I really studied him in early middle life, I came to the conclusion that he had greatness in him. On an independent review now of my past judgement, I find little or nothing to recall, though something perhaps to add.

Sweetness stands high among the qualities of genuine poetry ; and Cowley can be sweet. Sweetness in him is not of springtide, as Chaucer's, ' of whom '. Dryden reports, ' he had no taste '. It is autumnal, measured, and lingering ; a fragrance, as from stately, ancient gardens. That is my feeling as I read the lovely fifth and sixth stanzas of the elegy on William Hervey :

> Say, for you saw us, ye immortal lights,
> How oft unweary'd have we spent the nights,
> Till the Ledaean stars, so fam'd for Jove,
>   Wonder'd at us from above !
> We spent them not in toys, in lusts, or wine ;
>   But search of deep Philosophy,
>   Wit, Eloquence, and Poetry,
> Arts which I lov'd, for they, my friend, were thine.
>
> Ye fields of Cambridge, our dear Cambridge, say
> Have ye not seen us walking every day ?
> Was there a tree about which did not know
>   The love betwixt us two ?

> Henceforth, ye gentle trees, for ever fade;
> Or you sad branches thicker join,
> And into darksome shades combine,
> Dark as the grave wherein my friend is laid![1]

The lines can compare in tenderness with Lycidas, or with The Scholar Gipsy. But thoughtfulness, rising, deepening, to sublimity, was his forte; as in his rebuke of the scoffers at the infant Royal Society;

> The things which these proud men despise, and call
>   Impertinent, and vain, and small,
> Those smallest things of nature let me know,
> Rather than all their greatest actions do!
> Whoever would deposèd Truth advance
>   Into the throne usurp'd from it,
> Must feel at first the blows of Ignorance,
>   And the sharp points of envious Wit.
> So, when, by various turns of the celestial dance,
>   In many thousand years
>   A star, so long unknown, appears,
> Though heaven itself more beauteous by it grow,
> It troubles and alarms the world below;
> Does to the wise a star, to fools a meteor, show.[2]

The same qualities mark his congratulations to Hobbes on his Leviathan:

> I little thought before
> That all the wardrobe of rich Eloquence
>   Could have afforded half enough
>   Of bright, of new, and lasting stuff
> To cloathe the mighty limbs of thy gigantic sense;[3]

his elegy on Crashaw, Poet and Saint, whom he had saved from something like starvation to be wafted by Angels to Loretto, like its black Virgin:

> 'Tis surer much they brought thee there; and they
> And thou, their charge, went singing all the way;[4]

and the eulogium, in the Ode to the Royal Society, of Bacon, chosen by his King, and by Nature,

Lord Chancellor of both their laws;
who, in Science,
 Like Moses, led us forth at last;
 The barren wilderness he past;
 Did on the very border stand
 Of the blest, promis'd land;
 And from the mountain's top of his exalted wit,
 Saw it himself, and shew'd us it.[5]

Grand conceptions these, yet hardly so overflowing, teeming, as that of the noble Hymn to Light:

 Thou, Scythian-like, dost round thy lands above
  The sun's gilt tents for ever move,
  And still, as thou in pomp dost go,
 The shining pageants of the world attend thy show;
 Nor amidst all these triumphs dost thou scorn
  The humble glow-worms to adorn,
  And with those living spangles gild—
 O greatness without pride!—the bushes of the field:
 When, Goddess! thou lift'st up thy waken'd head,
  Out of the morning's purple bed,
  Thy quire of birds about thee play,
 And all the joyful world salutes the rising day.
 All the world's bravery that delights our eyes,
  Is but thy several liveries.
  Thou the rich dye on them bestow'st,
 Thy nimble pencil paints this landscape as thou go'st.
 A crimson garment in the rose thou wear'st;
  A crown of studded gold thou bear'st;
  The virgin lilies in their white
 Are clad but with the lawn of almost naked light.
 The violet, Spring's little infant, stands
  Girt in thy purple swaddling bands;
  On the fair tulip thou dost doat;
 Thou cloath'st it in a gay and party-colour'd coat.[6]

Again, to measure the force, the compass of his fancy, savour his scorn of the abuse of the term Life:

> Life's a name
> That nothing here can truly claim;
> This wretched inn, where we scarce stay to bait,
> We call our dwelling-place!
> And mighty voyages we take,
> And mighty journeys seem to make,
> O'er sea and land, the little point that has no space.
> Because we fight and battles gain,
> Some captives call, and say, 'the rest are slain';
> Because we heap up yellow earth, and so
> Rich, valiant, wise, and virtuous seem to grow;
> Because we draw a long nobility
> From hieroglyphic proofs of heraldry,
> And impudently talk of a posterity—
> We grow at last by Custom to believe,
> That really we Live;
> Whilst all these Shadows, that for Things we take,
> Are but the empty Dreams which in Death's sleep we make.[7]

Yet again—how we feel the breeze tossing his proud fancy round the globe, as he sits and drinks in the Chair constructed of timber from Drake's ship!

> Cheer up, my mates, the wind does fairly blow;
> Clap on more sail, and never spare;
> Farewell all lands, for now we are
> In the wide sea of drink, and merrily we go.
> Bless me, 'tis hot! another bowl of wine,
> And we shall cut the burning Line:
> Hey, boys! she scuds away, and by my head I know
> We round the world are sailing now.
> What dull men are those that tarry at home,
> When abroad they might wantonly roam,
> And gain such experience, and spy too
> Such countries and wonders, as I do!
> But pr'ythee, good pilot, take heed what you do,
> And fail not to touch at Peru!
> With gold there the vessel we'll store,
> And never, and never be poor,
> No, never be poor any more.

He wakes from his dream, to find the last timber of the gallant ship a dry motionless log, but consoles himself and it nobly :

> Great relick ! thou too, in this port of ease,
> Hast still one way of making voyages ;
> The breath of Fame, like an auspicious gale,
>   The great trade-wind which ne'er does fail,
> Shall drive thee round the world, and thou shalt run.
>   As long around it as the sun.
> The streights of Time too narrow are for thee ;
> Launch forth into an undiscover'd sea,
> And steer the endless course of vast Eternity !
> Take for thy sail this verse, and for thy pilot, me ! [8]

His subtlety was only too eager, as Cowper laments :

> splendid wit
> Entangled in the cobwebs of the schools.

But, much as he was addicted to high, bewildering speculation, curiosity as to his own powers impelled him to play with them all. He tried them upon every sort of subject. His fancy he held as if in a leash. He could let it slip upon any theme, with a fair certainty that it would run it down. Being a Cavalier, and a Courtier, as well as by profession a Poet, he esteemed it a duty to sing of Love. He discoursed of it under many aspects, and with an extraordinary ingenuity. Few prettier sketches have been drawn of natural womanly fascinations than in the opening stanza of The Change :

> Love in her sunny eyes does basking play ;
> Love walks the pleasant mazes of her hair ;
> Love doth on both her lips for ever stray,
> And sows and reaps a thousand kisses there. [9]

Seldom has a compliment been more delicately insinuated than when he deprecates embellishment by a Waiting-Maid's appliances :

Th' adorning thee with so much art
  Is but a barbarous skill;
'Tis like the poisoning of a dart
  Too apt before to kill.[10]

Often, I regret to say, he condescended to the fashionable licence of seventeenth-century speech and sentiment. In the extravagant, but more innocent, boisterousness of The Chronicle he pretends to a primacy for himself in its practical indulgence:

Margarita first possest,
  If I remember well, my breast,
    Margarita first of all;
But when awhile the wanton maid
With my restless heart had play'd,
  Martha took the flying ball.

Martha soon did it resign
  To the beauteous Catharine.
    Beauteous Catharine gave place—
Though loth and angry she to part
With the possession of my heart—
  To Eliza's conquering face.

Eliza to this hour might reign,
  Had she not evil counsels ta'en.
    Fundamental laws she broke,
And still new favourites she chose,
Till up in arms my passions rose,
  And cast away her yoke.

Mary then, and gentle Anne,
  Both to reign at once began;
    Alternately they sway'd;
And sometimes Mary was the fair,
And sometimes Anne the crown did wear,
  And sometimes both I obey'd.

Another Mary then arose,
   And did rigorous laws impose;
   A mighty tyrant she!
Long, alas! should I have been
Under that iron-scepter'd queen,
   Had not Rebecca set me free.

When fair Rebecca set me free,
   'Twas then a golden time with me;
   But soon those pleasures fled:
For the gracious princess dy'd,
In her youth and beauty's pride,
   And Judith reigned in her stead.

One month, three days, and half an hour,
   Judith held the sovereign power:
   Wondrous beautiful her face!
But so weak and small her wit,
That she to govern was unfit,
   And so Susanna took her place.

But when Isabella came,
   Arm'd with a resistless flame,
   And th' artillery of her eye;
Whilst she proudly march'd about,
Greater conquests to find out,
   She beat out Susan by the bye.

But in her place I then obey'd
   Black-ey'd Bess, her viceroy-maid;
   To whom ensued a vacancy:
Thousand worse passions then possest
The interregnum of my breast:
   Bless me from such an anarchy!

Gentle Henrietta then,
   And a third Mary next began;
   Then Joan, and Jane, and Audria:
And then a pretty Thomasine,
And then another Catharine,
   And then a long et cetera.

> But I will briefer with them be,
>   Since few of them were long with me.
>   An higher and a nobler strain
>   My present Emperess does claim,
>   Heleonora, first o' th' name ;
>   Whom God grant long to reign ![11]

The insolence, no less than the gaiety, of the confession is irresistible. But it need not overmuch shock serious readers who would like to respect the man as well as admire the poet. Both here and elsewhere in Cowley's amatory effusions, I find abundance of wit ; I fail to discern passion. Disappointing as to some may be the theory, I am fully persuaded of the decorum of his life, loose as may be some of his verse. The freedom of his talk about women probably was little more than a flourish of intellectual audacity. By choice he pursued his amours in the free and safe communion of his own imagination, where he could

> careless and unthoughtful, lying,
>   Hear the soft winds, above me flying,
>   With all their wanton boughs dispute,
>   And the more tuneful birds to both replying,
>   Nor be myself, too, mute.

For society he needed only that

> A silver stream shall roll his waters near,
>   Gilt with the sunbeams here and there ;
>   On whose enamel'd bank I'll walk,
>   And see how prettily they smile, and hear
>   How prettily they talk.[12]

If he permitted any material passion to divert his thoughts from ' life's incurable disease ', it was gardening :

> God the first garden made, and the first city Cain.[13]

When he meditates on womanly companionship ; on

> A mistress moderately fair,
> And good as guardian-angels are,
> Only belov'd, and loving me!

the wish, carefully toned down as it is, comes distinctly second to his primary longing:

> Ah, yet, ere I descend to th' grave,
> May I a small house and large garden have![14]

In praising a wife, he can devise no higher compliment than to discover

> The fairest garden in her looks,
> And in her mind the wisest books.[15]

I can read more satisfaction with the floral charms which are left to him, than despair at the departure of a beloved female guest, in the polite endeavour, in The Spring, to account for his garden's stolid complacency at its and his bereavement:

> Though you be absent here, I needs must say
> The trees as beauteous are, and flowers as gay
>   As ever they were wont to be;
>   Nay, the birds' rural musick too
>   Is as melodious and free,
>   As if they sung to pleasure you;
> I saw a rose-bud ope this morn—I'll swear
> The blushing morning open'd not more fair.[16]

Gardening itself he loved chiefly because it excused his retirement from affairs to hold converse with books and his own thoughts. His translations from the Classics demonstrate him an accomplished scholar, if not with Dryden's imperious strength of adaptation, richer in occasional felicities of diction; if without Milton's profound learning, more on a level than he with contemporary and applied science. For catching the spirit of Anacreon in particular, he has never had a superior; for instance:

The thirsty earth soaks up the rain,
And drinks, and gapes for drink again.
The plants suck in the earth, and are
With constant drinking fresh and fair;
The sea itself—which one would think
Should have but little need of drink—
Drinks twice ten thousand rivers up,
So fill'd that they o'erflow the cup.
The busy sun—and one would guess
By 's drunken fiery face no less—
Drinks up the sea, and when he 's done,
The moon and stars drink up the sun:
They drink and dance by their own light;
They drink and revel all the night.
Nothing in nature's sober found,
But an eternal health goes round.
Fill up the bowl then, fill it high,
Fill up the glasses there; for why
Should every creature drink but I;
Why, man of morals, tell me why? [17]

He was a master of prose, as of verse, and its reformer; at once metaphysician and orator. His essays, jewelled with rhyme, especially on gardens, charm still. History contains no written character more grandly outlined, and more deeply graven, than his of Protector Oliver. Ponderous he can be, both in Pindarics, and in Heroics; witness, his failures—On the late Civil war, as recognized by himself; the Resurrection; the noisy Plagues of Egypt; the Ecstasy; and the ambitious, and tiresomely respectable, Davideis. Often even in his finest efforts inspiration appears to be lagging. But we always may hope for a break. The Muse, after dozing in a dull grey twilight, suddenly awakes. The mist parts. Ears, eyes, and soul open in response to a burst of sunshine, and grave, rich harmony, as in the monody on Richard Crashaw. At any rate, his own period, while not insensible of his shortcomings, pardoned them in consideration of his general greatness. It held that he had wholly succeeded in fulfilling his own aspiration :

> What shall I do to be for ever known,
> And make the age to come my own ?[18]

It believed his Muse immortal. If an educated public now suffers moss to grow over his monumental grave, it must be that he wanted some quality which his own period could do without, and ours cannot.

Poetic inspiration has two forms, inspiration of the head, and of the heart. The brilliancy of Cowley's genius is indisputable. His fertility of ideas is inexhaustible, as is his power of developing and combining them. The children of his brain pace forth, frequently dance, in shining raiment. His own times were content to be dazzled, feeling themselves enlightened as well. Upon a new age, which Chaucer, his senior by three centuries, still warms, he strikes cold ; scarcely does he even illuminate it ; for it knows already the learning he could teach, and more. Intellect, high intellect, must be added to sympathy to win recognition for a poet anywhere. By a conjunction of the manifold resources which intellect commands, he may, without more, satisfy his contemporaries. Cowley satisfied his. To survive their tastes a writer needs a heart to thrill humanity. By that alone can he appeal to common emotions earmarked by no date. It has, I am afraid, to be conceded that Cowley's pulse beat too temperately for a poet thus of all time, even when some chord in himself is most stirred. His enthusiasm, when entirely genuine, when his wit most pierces, remains intellectual only. It is a pity that in consequence place may no longer be made for him by the hearth where some hardly his peers in mental loftiness sit secure. Yet his name could not be omitted from the first rank in the Golden Roll of English poets without the sense of a wrong to literature no less than to him.

The Poems of Abraham Cowley (Johnson's Poets, vols. vii, viii, ix, 1790).
 [1] On the Death of Mr. William Hervey, stanzas 5-6.
 [2] To the Royal Society.　　　[3] To Mr. Hobbes
 [4] On the Death of Mr. Crashaw.　　[5] To the Royal Society.
 [6] Hymn to Light, stanzas 8, 9, 16, 18, 19, 20.　　[7] Life.
 [8] Ode—Sitting and Drinking in the Chair made out of Relicks of Sir Francis Drake's Ship.
 [9] The Change, st. 1.　　[10] The Waiting-Maid, st. 4.
 [11] The Chronicle, A Ballad.　　[12] Of Solitude.
 [13] The Garden—to J. Evelyn, Esq.　　[14] The Wish, st. 2.
 [15] The Garden.　　[16] The Spring. st. 1.
 [17] Drinking (II. Anacreontiques—translated paraphrastically out of Anacreon).
 [18] The Motto.

SIR JOHN DENHAM

1615—1668

In what respected upper shelf can I safely sequester the poetical remains of the Honourable Sir John Denham, K.B., secure from curious eyes, which certainly, if tempted to disturb the Knight's repose, would abuse me the innocent cause of their disgust?

I can imagine that his satires, now tediously innocent, may once, especially the ironical argument attributed to Roundheads Against Peace at the Close Committee, have had a poisonous vitality :

> Princes we are if we prevail,
> And gallant villains if we fail;
> When to our fame 'tis told,
> It will not be our least of praise,
> Since a new state we could not raise,
> To have destroyed the old.[1]

Some spirit diversifies the adulation, disgraceful as it is, though hardly more so than Waller's, of the description in Cooper's Hill of a royal hunt. I can feel force in the lamentation for the doom of 'Great Strafford', at whose trial

> Each seem'd to act that part he came to see,
> And none was more a looker-on than he![2]

Though the heavy sermonizings by the worn man of the world on Prudence, Justice, the Progress of Learning, and the duties and pleasures of Old Age, must have palled even upon contemporaries, it is possible still to dwell respectfully —not even here enthusiastically—on the dirge for a comrade —Cowley—in perilous political intrigues, whom a 'fatal hour' had

> plucked, the fairest, sweetest flower
> That in the Muses' garden grew.

The elegy not only shows due appreciation of eminent genius; incidentally, it testifies to fair critical discernment by the mourner of the special gifts of his dead friend's fore-runners in the shrine, where

> poets near our princes sleep,
> And in one grave their mansion keep.

As the funeral cavalcade passes, he lays grateful wreaths on the tombs, of ' old Chaucer ', who

> like the morning star,
> To us discovers day from far;

of Spenser,

> Whose purple blush the day foreshews;

and of Ben Jonson, Shakespeare, and Fletcher, exemplars in art, mother-wit, and nature.[3]

Unfortunately, this tribute to bygone bards is the high-water mark of Denham's poetic sensibility. With one minute exception, hereafter to be noted, it is the utmost of distinctive literary accomplishment, and then not super-eminent, which I can put to his credit.

Taking his all in all, good, bad, and indifferent, and considering the load which even the Great, in their many uninspired intervals, impose upon Pegasus of verse delighting nobody, I approve most sincerely the friendly counsel of King Charles the First. Charles happened to see verses of his to Sir Richard Fanshawe, and, " though he liked them well ', advised him to write no more. Young men, he said, ' with little else to do might vent the overflowings of their fancy that way ', but should cease ' when they were thought fit for more serious employments '.[4] Often, recently, as I laboured through Sir John's rhymes, I felt tempted to take it for granted that he had complied with his old master's 'commands'.

In truth, I could easily, and without fear of protest, have acted as if he had, but for a singular impediment. I might have passed over the youthful Pope's laudation of him as 'lofty', and 'majestic'.[5] Even I might have been deaf to Dryden's weightier reference to his authority, as 'a famous wit', 'loved living, and reverenced dead',[6] 'the standard of good writing', who, in conjunction with Waller, reformed, superfluously, in my opinion, the language of literature. But it is impossible to forget that in his sketch of the course of the Thames, incidental in fact to the account, already mentioned, of a Stag-hunt, he happened to stumble upon four deathless lines :

> O could I flow like thee, and make thy stream
> My great example, as it is my theme !
> Though deep, yet clear; though gentle, yet not dull;
> Strong without rage, without o'erflowing full.[7]

How consign their author to a limbo of poets 'unbaptized for the dead' !

Yet—four lines, and hospitality for aye on Parnassus ! Such the inscrutable lottery of Fame !

Poems and Translations, by the Honourable Sir John Denham, Knight of the Bath (Johnson's Poets), vol. ix, 1790.

[1] A Speech against Peace at the Close Committee, st. 17.

[2] On the Earl of Strafford's Trial and Death, vv. 13-14.

[3] On Mr. Abraham Cowley's Death, and Burial amongst the Ancient Poets.

[4] Dedication to the King.   [5] Pope, Windsor Forest.

[6] Preface concerning Ovid's Epistles (Aldine British Poets, Dryden, vol. v, pp. 8 and 10).

[7] Cooper's Hill

ANDREW MARVELL

1621—1678

A DOZEN years younger than Suckling, three than Lovelace; in death preceded only four years by Herrick; and half a century of thought and feeling between all three and Marvell. They were Elizabethans. Herrick, though he survived the Restoration by fourteen years, belonged in spirit to his birth time. Marvell was at the meeting of the waters, partaking somewhat of the one tendency, more of the other. A period had opened which was to continue without any positive break till the reign of the third George. Poets had been gay and reckless; at once romantic and artificial. They sang of love with deliberate extravagance. In their verse it is represented as the one worthy object in life, unless they were devotees. Then Religion took its place, and its emotions. In either case they had the art of seeming to absorb their whole souls into the pursuit. They were not afraid of being considered, and knowing that they were, abnormal, eccentric, even absurd. As one of nature's poets himself, Marvell had a vein in him which now and again startles the reader with a tone, an idea, recalling the rush and sparkle of the youth of English verse. The outbursts are only occasional. They subside, leaving a thinker who had reasons for his strains; one intellectually of the second half of the seventeenth century; morally too, though on its sober, Puritan side.

Tradition, and practice almost contemporary, perhaps also some insurgent impulses, were powerful enough with him to force him as a poet to be a lover. His amatory fancies necessarily were expressed decorously; for he was a member of a pious and well-conducted household. He dwelt with the great citizen-soldier, Fairfax, an earlier Washington, at Billborow amid the quiet Yorkshire pastures. There he taught the classics and 'holy mathematics' to the daughter, reckless Buckingham's future bride. She,

> yet more pure, sweet, straight, and fair,
> Than gardens, woods, meads, rivers are,

was so 'judicious', at shy fifteen, that the flaunting sun himself,
> lest she should see him go to bed,
> In blushing clouds conceals his head.[1]

Nevertheless, even in such company he had to do his duty as a bard. Though, as I cannot but believe, against the grain, he affected raptures; and what raptures! Clorinda coquets solemnly with demure Damon. Love defines itself by the help of a planisphere. Thyrsis invites his Dorinda to feast her ear with astronomical melodies, till they shall find leisure from shepherding to make poppy wine, and

> drink on't even till we weep,
> So shall we smoothly pass away in sleep.[2]

So intoxicating are the charms of the absent Juliana that her swain mows into his own ankle.[3] When Daphnis and Chloe are on the verge of being ever so little incorrect, after five and twenty stanzas, their minstrel knows how to check his Pegasus's wild career. One wonders if the warm panegyrist of soaring Richard Lovelace[4] were conscious of the abyss which separated their respective lyrics.

Marvell, however, is a genuine poet, when not tempted by custom to trespass on ground otherwise appropriated. He paints to the life pleasant, homelike scenes. We see the Billborow hill:
> how courteous it ascends,
> And all the way it rises bends.[5]

A nymph's sorrow over her fawn, murdered by troopers, is so delicate that one could no more be offended with its excess than with the overflow of a fountain after a June shower:

> With sweetest milk and sugar first
> I it at my own fingers nursed;
> And as it grew, so every day
> It waxed more white and sweet than they.
> It had so sweet a breath! And oft
> I blushed to see its foot more soft
> And white shall I say than my hand?
> Nay, any lady's of the land.
> I have a garden of my own,
> But so with roses overgrown,
> And lilies, that you would it guess
> To be a little wilderness;
> And all the spring-time of the year
> It only lovèd to be there.
> Upon the roses it would feed,
> And then to me 'twould boldly trip,
> And print those roses on my lip.
> Had it lived long it would have been
> Lilies without, roses within.
>   O help! O help! I see it faint
> And die as calmly as a saint!
> See how it weeps! the tears do come
> Sad, slowly, dropping like a gum.
>   I in a golden vial will
> Keep these two crystal tears, and fill
> It till it do o'erflow with mine,
> Then place it in Diana's shrine.[6]

The epitaph upon a young girl too modest to be commemorated by name, is a model of pensive beauty.

> To say, she lived a virgin chaste
> In this age loose and all unlaced;
> Nor was, when vice is so allowed,
> Of virtue or ashamed or proud;
> That her soul was on Heaven so bent,
> No minute but it came and went;

> That, ready her last debt to pay
> She summed her life up every day;
> Modest as morn, as mid-day bright,
> Gentle as evening, cool as night:
> 'Tis true; but all too weakly said;
> 'Twas more significant, she 's dead.[7]

With dainty simplicity he gathers in four lines a nosegay of rustic charms:

> A tender shepherdess, whose hair
> Hangs loosely playing in the air,
> Transplanting flowers from the green hill
> To crown her head and bosom fill.[8]

He can float a gossamer conceit as dexterously as any courtier-poet of his age. Listen, for instance, to him complimenting a Fair Singer,

> Whose subtle art invisibly can wreathe
> My fetters of the very air I breathe;[9]

or he will draw an analogy—a whole theological philosophy in miniature—between a Drop of Dew, which, Heaven-born,

> Gazing back upon the skies,
> Shines with a mournful light,
> Like its own tear,
> Because so long divided from the sphere,

and

> the soul, that drop, that ray
> Of the clear fountain of eternal day,

which,

> Remembering still its former height,
> Shuns the sweet leaves and blossoms green,
> And recollecting its own light,
> Does, in its pure and circling thoughts, express
> The greater heaven in an heaven less.[10]

Like all true poets he has magic at his command. Who can explain why the Bermuda boat-song goes on carolling in the belfry of every brain it has once charmed?

Where the remote Bermudas ride,
In the ocean's bosom unespied,
From a small boat, that row'd along,
The listening winds received this song :
  ' What should we do but sing His praise,
  That led us through the watery maze,
Unto an isle so long unknown,
And yet far kinder than our own ?
He lands us on a grassy stage,
Safe from the storms, and prelate's rage.
He gave us this eternal spring,
Which here enamels everything ;
He hangs in shades the orange bright.
Like golden lamps in a green night,
And does in the pomegranates close
Jewels more rich than Ormus shows ;
He makes the figs our mouths to meet,
And throws the melons at our feet ;
But apples plants of such a price,
No tree could ever bear them twice ;
With cedars chosen by His hand,
From Lebanon, he stores the land,
And makes the hollow seas that roar.
Proclaim the ambergris on shore :
He cast—of which we rather boast—
The Gospel's pearl upon our coast,
And in these rocks for us did frame
A temple where to sound His name.
Oh ! let our voice His praise exalt,
Till it arrive at Heaven's vault,
Which, thence, perhaps, rebounding, may
Echo beyond the Mexique Bay.'
  Thus sung they in the English boat
An holy and a cheerful note ;
And all the way, to guide their chime,
With falling oars they kept the time.[11]

Cowley could not have conjured up a ' delicious solitude ',
' garlands of repose ', to beat Marvell's version from his

own Latin original of the Garden, a Buddha's paradise of endless contemplation :

> What wondrous life is this I lead !
> Ripe apples drop about my head ;
> The luscious clusters of the vine
> Upon my mouth do crush their wine ;
> The nectarine, and curious peach,
> Into my hands themselves do reach ;
> Stumbling on melons, as I pass,
> Insnared with flowers, I fall on grass.
>   Meanwhile the mind, from pleasure less,
> Withdraws into its happiness ;
> The mind, that ocean where each kind
> Does straight its own resemblance find ;
> Yet it creates, transcending these,
> Far other worlds, and other seas,
> Annihilating all that 's made
> To a green thought in a green shade.
>   Here at the fountain's sliding foot,
> Or at some fruit-tree's mossy root,
> Casting the body's vest aside,
> My soul into the boughs does glide ;
> There, like a bird, it sits and sings,
> Then whets and combs its silver wings,
> And, till prepared for longer flight,
> Waves in its plumes the various light.
>   Such was that happy garden-state,
> While man there walked without a mate ;
> After a place so pure and sweet,
> What other help could yet be meet !
> But 'twas beyond a mortal's share
> To wander solitary there :
> Two paradises 'twere in one,
> To live in paradise alone ! [12]

Such ethereal melodies were his diversions, as I can scarcely believe the heavy flirtations of his Damon and Thyrsis with Dorinda and Clorinda ever to have been.

But he put his Muse to combative work also ; and then he is a master. He ranks among the earliest of political poets ; and Dryden does not surpass him at his best. Savage, often incredibly brutal, and even unjust, he could be, when his indignant broodings on the chances restored kingship had been given, and had squandered, exploded in the red-hot lava of Nostradamus's Prophecy, an Historical Poem, Clarendon's House-warming, Britannia and Ralegh, the Dialogue Between Two Horses, The Last Instructions to a Painter About the Dutch Wars ! How exalted when, still a politician, he found it in his conscience to praise !

The welcome to Cromwell returning from Ireland is magnificent throughout ; a loud song of exultation in the three-forked lightning of adventurous war, as well as in the victor's equal, and less lofty, capacity, alas, for the cunning of statesmanship :

> When, twining subtle fears with hope,
> He wove a net of such a scope,
>   That Charles himself might chase
>   To Caresbrooke's narrow case.

And then a hush !—We forget the Republican Conqueror and his craft.—A greater for the instant mounts ' the tragic scaffold ' ; a prouder throne than its victim in his splendour had ever pressed ! Every faithful Royalist, persecuted, down-trodden, must have felt his blood stir, and himself to be a glorified martyr, as he read the incomparable tribute from a Roundhead to the majesty of his King by right divine :

> He nothing common did, or mean,
> Upon that memorable scene,
>   But with his keener eye
>   The axe's edge did try :

> Nor called the gods with vulgar spite
> To vindicate his helpless right;
> But bowed his comely head
> Down, as upon a bed.[13]

Poetry here beats history on its own ground.

The passage is the one sublime, by no means the only eminent, example of Marvell's faculty for realistic imagining. Frequently—as in his Blake's Teneriffe victory and The Loyal Scot—crude, clumsy, and bombastic, at times ridiculous, he yet always utters something worth saying. In The Loyal Scot, for example, what a grand anachronism of scorn for topographical heartburnings:

> One king, one faith, one language, and one isle.
> English and Scotch, 'tis all but cross and pile!

Take, again, the death-scene of Captain Douglas—bravely resigned to fate on board the burning ship he had striven to the last to save:

> Down on the deck he laid himself, and died,
> With his dear sword reposing by his side,
> And on the flaming plank so rests his head
> As one that warmed himself, and went to bed.[14]

The First Anniversary may be ponderous, and more rhetorical than poetical. At the same time, it is at once a brilliant controversial defence of the title of Cromwell to reign, and a courtly recognition of him as Royal, though with no other crown than one of silver hairs:

> For to be Cromwell was a greater thing
> Than aught below, or yet above, a king.[15]

The Lament for his death, if not showing more prescience in the poet than among statesmen as to the durability of that strange palace of ice, the Protectorate, indicates a remarkable faculty for reading human nature. A portrait as true as it is beautiful is there drawn of the invincible soldier, the sagacious, astute, and stern ruler, dying, not of age, or disease, but of sorrow for a child ; a sacrifice to

> the wondrous softness of his heart.
> . . . . .
> Like polished mirrors, so his steely breast
> Had every figure of her woes expressed ;
> Fate could not either reach with single stroke,
> But, the dear image fled, the mirror broke ; [16]

a man and a father in tenderness ; yet in death a sovereign still, and of iron will :

> I saw him dead : a leaden slumber lies,
> And mortal sleep over those wakeful eyes ;
> O, human glory vain ! O, Death ! O, wings !
> O, worthless world ! O, transitory things !
> Yet dwelt that greatness in his shape decayed,
> That still though dead, greater than Death he laid ;
> And in his altered face you something feign
> That threatens Death he yet will live again.[17]

Too disdainful of wealth to care to be a man of affairs ; too truthful for a professional diplomatist ; too thoughtful —silent for twenty years, not dumb, on the benches of the Commons—for an orator ; too good a Christian to be a fanatic ; too loyal a patriot to be a partisan—Andrew Marvell neither asked nor would accept honours or possessions. Too sensible—'easy philosopher', as in youth he described himself [18]—to burn with sensibility ; too sincere a moralist—just 'an old, honest countryman ' [19]—to masquerade as a mad lover ; too apt even as a singer to damp down with his reason the furnace of his real inspiration— with a little more, or a little less, he might have ranked high in the inner circle of poets—or he might not have been among them anywhere. But about him, such as he is, though he heralds the descent of the grey light of common day upon English poetry for close upon a century and a half, the sunshine flickers still. His verse, if without the halo of romance, which beams from the brows of those he championed, 'noble Lovelace', and 'mighty' Milton, blind, yet bold,[20] has struck out from sympathy with genius like theirs sparks of fancy peculiarly his own. Literature would have been sadly the poorer without the Garden, the Bermudas, and the Death-song of King Charles.

The Poems of Andrew Marvell, edited by G. A. Aitken, 1898. Satires of Andrew Marvell, edited by G. A. Aitken, 1892. London: Lawrence & Bullen (The Muses' Library).

[1] Upon Appleton House (Poems), vv. 603-4 and 695-6.
[2] Dialogue between Thyrsis and Dorinda (Poems), vv. 47-8.
[3] Damon, the Mower (Poems), vv 73-80.
[4] To his Noble Friend, Mr. Richard Lovelace (Poems).
[5] The Hill and Grove at Billborow (Poems), vv. 21 2.
[6] The Nymph Complaining for the Death of her Fawn (Poem).
[7] An Epitaph upon —— (Poems), vv. 9-20.
[8] The Gallery (Poems), vv. 53-6
[9] The Fair Singer (Poems), vv. 11-12.
[10] On a Drop of Dew (Poems), vv. 11-14, 19-20, 22-6.
[11] Bermudas (Poems).
[12] The Garden (Poems), vv. 33-64.
[13] An Horatian Ode—Upon Cromwell's Return from Ireland (Poems), vv. 49-52 and 57-64.
[14] The Loyal Scot. Upon the Death of Captain Douglas, burned on his ship at Chatham (Poems), vv. 142-3 and 53-6.
[15] The First Anniversary of the Government under His Highness the Lord Protector (Poems), vv. 225-6
[16] Upon the Death of his late Highness the Lord Protector (Poems), vv. 20 and 73-6.
[17] Ibid. (Poems), vv. 247-60.
[18] Upon Appleton House (Poems), v. 561.
[19] Translated from Seneca. Thyestes (Poems), Chorus ii, v. 11
[20] On Paradise Lost (Poems), v. i.

JOHN DRYDEN

1631—1700

Who now habitually reads Dryden, unless it be for Alexander's Feast, and some hundred lines in Absalom and Achitophel? Who did not read him until well into last century?

His contemporaries envied, abused, persecuted, starved, but admired and studied, him. They tolerated his threadbare love-songs, though Waller and Herrick were still among them. They echoed his judgement that

> Our ladies and our men now speak more wit
> In conversation than those poets writ,

the poets being Ben Jonson 'in his height', and his famous fellows. They agreed with him in thinking Chaucer no longer 'harmonious', and that Chapman—Keats's Chapman!—had 'thrown Homer down as low as harsh numbers, improper English, and a monstrous length of verse could carry him'.[1] The Annus Mirabilis has fine features. It is spacious, audacious, and breezy, if often ridiculous. The absurdities were not apparent to the eyes of 1666, any more than the ugliness of the conceit, in a juvenile poem, of the small-pox weeping scarring tears for its murder of young Lord Hastings. Dryden from boyhood to grey hairs knew his age, and was intensely of his age; and his age was absolutely 'modern'. It believed devoutly in the perfection of its own taste and manners, in the eternal importance of its controversies. Dryden accepted and accentuated its characteristics. He enrolled his genius in its service. For a period like ours, 'modern' also, though, it is to be hoped against hope, less bigoted in its modernity, it is difficult to appreciate the fury of partisan feeling with or against violent pamphlets in verse, such as The Medal, Religio Laici, or the Hind and the Panther, if not Absalom and Achitophel. But we must try to understand the writer's point of view, or a whole chapter in literature will be closed to us.

The wonder now is that the Georgian era esteemed him scarcely less highly than his own. Pope venerated him as Elisha Elijah. For fastidious Gray, who passes Pope by, his car

> Wide o'er the fields of glory bear
> Two coursers of ethereal race;
> With necks in thunder clothed, and long-resounding pace.

Scott, half a century later, did him homage as to a reigning monarch. In part-explanation we must remember that the contests in which he had vigorously combated, continued to rage, though the current had set adversely to his side. He had the benefit also of a long stagnation of poetical genius. Lovers of poetry, weary, if not of Pope, of his caricaturists, were almost compelled to travel a generation further back. Then finally, for the later age, as for his own, there was the natural title to admiration of a great writer, of great writing.

There after all is to be found the clue to the riddle of the Dryden-cult of a century and a half. From one motive or another he mixed himself up with matters alien to poetry. He sold himself to play-writing for bread. In that capacity itself he tampered knowingly with 'Shakespeare's magic'. With, and leading, his pauper profession, which

> must live by Courts, or starve,

he helped to

> Taint the Stage for some small snip of grain

Whether in pursuit of patrons, from contempt of the chiefs of the opposite camp, many of them turncoats and hypocrites, or from an element of honest, if mistaken, conviction, he threw himself into the discords of Whig and Tory, the State Church, Dissent, and Rome. He was a disputant of weight and renown. Wellington assured the British Cabinet that Napoleon's individual presence in the Peninsula would be equivalent to a French reinforcement of forty thousand men. Dryden's aid to either side meant as mighty an armament. Never writer, except Butler, argued like him in rhyme, whether in Absalom and Achitophel, The Medal, Religio Laici, or The Hind and the Panther. If, for instance, a preacher would borrow a sermon against Deism, he must search far before he discovered one loftier, or more apt, than the lines in Religio Laici, addressed to any one who fancies that :

    Man by his own strength to Heaven would soar,
    And would not be obliged to God for more.
    Vain, wretched creature, how art thou misled
    To think thy wit these godlike notions bred !
    These truths are not the product of thy mind,
    But dropp'd from Heaven, and of a nobler kind.
    Reveal'd Religion first inform'd thy sight,
    And Reason saw not, till Faith sprung the light.
    Hence all thy natural worship takes the source ;
    'Tis revelation what thou think'st discourse.
    Else how com'st thou to see these truths so clear,
    Which so obscure to Heathens did appear ?
    Not Plato these, nor Aristotle found ;
    Nor he whose wisdom oracles renowned ?
    Hast thou a wit so deep, or so sublime,
    Or canst thou lower dive, or higher climb ?
    Canst thou by reason more of Godhead know
    Than Plutarch, Seneca, or Cicero ? [2]

But Dryden nowhere is a mere debater. He is a poet throughout, and fights in a poet's panoply, with a poet's generous impulses. Doubtless it was a joy to him to launch, though, as we may well believe, in a wrong cause, the grand protest against theological intolerance :

> Of all the tyrannies on human kind,
> The worst is that which persecutes the mind.
> Let us but weigh at what offence we strike :
> 'Tis but because we cannot think alike.
> In punishing of this we overthrow
> The laws of nations and of nature too.[3]

While the politician denounces Monmouth, the rebel, the poet appeals for a father's compassion to, and pride in, the son :

> Whate'er he did was done with so much ease,
> In him alone 'twas natural to please :
> His motions all accompanied with grace ;
> And Paradise was open'd in his face.[4]

It is again to the poet's sense of equity, resisting the politician's vindictiveness, that, as I will, in spite of jealous gossip, believe, we owe the magnanimous testimony to the incorrupt judge in the withering blast at the statesman turned demagogue.[5]

It is highly to the credit of eighteenth-century intelligence that it condoned the partisanship, and recognized golden grains of inspiration like those. The nineteenth's and twentieth's literary curiosity is less strong. Unless in the form of elegant extracts it rejects the Court manifestoes ; and so far the neglect is not surprising. It is less excusable when it extends to the witty brimstone of Emperor Mac Flecknoe's devise of the Crown of Nonsense to a forgotten poetaster ; for the reason that

> Shadwell alone, of all my sons, is he
> Who stands confirm'd in full stupidity.
> The rest to some faint meaning make pretence,
> But Shadwell never deviates into sense.[6]

The Amboyna Sea-fight, again, ought not to be forgotten.

In its boisterous, rugged variety, it is an excellent, if rather too deliberate, example of onomatopoeia.

> Who ever saw a noble sight,
> That never view'd a brave sea-fight!
> Hang up your bloody colours in the air,
> Up with your fights, and your nettings prepare;
> Your merry mates cheer, with a lusty bold spright,
> Now each man his brindice, and then to the fight.
> St. George, St. George, we cry,
> The shouting Turks reply.
> Oh now it begins, and the gun-room grows hot,
> Ply it with culverin and with small shot;
> Hark, does it not thunder? no, 'tis the guns roar.
> The neighbouring billows are turn'd into gore;
> Now each man must resolve to die,
> For here the coward cannot fly.
> Drums and trumpets toll the knell,
> And culverins the passing bell,
> Now, now they grapple, and now board amain;
> Blow up the hatches, they're off all again;
> Give them a broadside, the dice run at all,
> Down comes the mast and yard, and tacklings fall;
> She grows giddy now, like blind Fortune's wheel,
> She sinks there, she sinks, she turns up her keel.
> Who ever beheld so noble a sight,
> As this so brave, so bloody sea-fight![7]

We are meant to feel, and, more or less, we do feel, from the British side, the surging backwards and forwards of the fortunes of the battle. It is a drama in two dozen lines.

The Epistle to Kneller—

> Thy pictures look a voice—

illustrates Dryden's wonderful capacity for simultaneous versifying and thinking.[8] The fine lament for John Oldham's premature death possesses every quality of an epitaph, except pathos. That, always a rare emotion in him, sweetens the personal appeal, in the Epistle to Congreve, by the veteran,

worn with cares and age,
And just abandoning the ungrateful stage,
To you, whom every muse and grace adorn,
Whom I foresee to better fortune born.
Be kind to my remains: and O defend,
Against your judgment, your departed friend!
Let not the insulting foe my fame pursue,
But shade those laurels which descend to you.[9]

Such pieces go far towards explaining a general admiration which outlived their writer by more than a century. Unlike much brilliant work of his, which is strictly earmarked for a period, they have a certain inherent vitality. Unfortunately, common readers are able nevertheless to live without them; and we exercise the right.

There are others, though few, which admit of no option. We have grown up beside them. Verse, like the character of Shaftesbury, is inscribed on the memory in fire:

Of these the false Achitophel was first;
A name to all succeeding ages curst;
For close designs, and crooked councils fit;
Sagacious, bold, and turbulent of wit;
Reckless, unfix'd in principles and place;
In power unpleas'd, impatient of disgrace;
A fiery soul, which, working out its way,
Fretted the pigmy-body to decay,
And o'er-informed the tenement of clay.
A daring pilot in extremity;
Pleas'd with the danger, when the waves went high
He sought the storms; but for a calm unfit,
Would steer too nigh the sands to boast his wit
Great wits are sure to madness near allied,
And thin partitions do their bounds divide;
Else why should he with wealth and honour blest,
Refuse his age the needful hours of rest?
Punish a body which he could not please;
Bankrupt of life, yet prodigal of ease?

And all to leave what with his toil he won,
To that unfeather'd two-legg'd thing, a son ;
Got while his soul did huddled notions try ;
And born a shapeless lump, like anarchy.
In friendship false, implacable in hate ;
Resolv'd to ruin or to rule the state.
To compass this the triple bond he broke ;
The pillars of the public safety shook ;
And fitted Israel for a foreign yoke :
Then seiz'd with fear, yet still affecting fame,
Usurp'd a patriot's all-atoning name.
So easy still it proves in factious times
With public zeal to cancel private crimes.
How safe is treason, and how sacred ill,
Where none can sin against the people's will ?
Where crowds can wink, and no offence be known,
Since in another's guilt they find their own.
Yet fame deserv'd no enemy can grudge ;
The statesman we abhor, but praise the judge.
In Israel's courts ne'er sat an Abethdin
With more discerning eyes, or hands more clean,
Unbrib'd, unsought, the wretched to redress,
Swift of dispatch, and easy of access.
Oh ! had he been content to serve the crown,
With virtues only proper to the gown ;
Or had the rankness of the soil been freed
From cockle, that oppress'd the noble seed ;
David for him his tuneful harp had strung,
And heaven had wanted one immortal song.[10]

Rhetoric ? Yes ; just enough to clothe the ideas, as a body the soul ; more than a suspicion of inspiration 'to order'—something, may be, of patchwork—but the maker of the song is right ;—it is 'immortal' ! Never was there so terrible a process of vivisection—a slicing of living cell from cell—with the visible working on the operator of a fascination at the sense of power, of a sort of greatness in the then helpless subject ! Why was there no German Dryden for Bismarck !

And from the same pen and fancy proceeded the majestic pageant of the passions, embodied in Alexander's Feast. Here was no Royal or Ministerial requisition to veneer, encrust, pull down. Lord of himself, his imagination, his conscience, his art, his soul, the cashiered, emancipated courtier bade them work in freedom. See the wonder they have reared! The harmony, the proportions, are perfect. The least change would be desecration. The poet had flattered the painter:

> Thy pictures think, and we divine their thought.

With more truth it might be claimed for the Ode on St. Cecilia's Day that every stanza paints a scene; that the result is a series of moving, pictorial pageants, such as the Doge's Palace or Versailles could not parallel. The Ode is one of the world's masterpieces, with not a flaw, unless that it may not be said of it, 'We cannot tell whence it emanated.' We can discern it issuing straight from Dryden's brain:

> And what Timotheus was is Dryden now.[11]

He transfigures the Conqueror into a God—and the God of Wine, with his army of Beauties and Revellers. It is his lyre which evokes the shade of Darius:

> great and good
>   By too severe a fate,
> Fallen, fallen, fallen, fallen,
> Fallen from his high estate,
>   And welt'ring in his blood;
> Deserted, at his utmost need,
> By those his former bounty fed;
> On the bare earth exposed he lies;
> With not a friend to close his eyes.

He is the musician, the magician, who summons the demon of revenge to lay the

> Grecian ghosts, that in battle were slain,
>   And unburied remain,

by kindling for their funeral pyre the glories of Persepolis,

And glittering temples of the hostile gods.[12]

So, there are at all events two products of Dryden's Muse, in the enjoyment of a bright immortality, not like that of Tithonus. As much cannot, I am afraid, be claimed for his Translations, which nevertheless merit life also, and life with youth. Among our poet-translators he stands pre-eminent. Much the larger half of his poems, apart from his plays, consists of versions from Greek, Latin, Italian, and early English. To translating he resorted after he had ceased to hire out his Muse to political and religious wranglings, or, worse, to what he knew to be an unworthy and dissolute Stage. His curiosity as to the working of other rich and earlier fancies was extreme. He indulged it in tracing their expatiations line by line, often by intentional deviations. For nature had moulded him critic as well as poet. If he is first of translators, it is that he is first of critics.

As critical exercises his prefaces to the several translations are admirable for English as correct as Addison's, and racier, the earliest actually modern English in our literature ; for insight into the spirit of his authors, and discrimination among them ; for sympathetic and decisive judgements. Yet more critically instructive are the versions themselves. Few more useful courses in literary art could be pursued than a verbal comparison of the originals and his renderings, and an inquiry into his motives for modifications. Frequently it would probably have to be recognized that Homer, Virgil, Ovid, Chaucer were themselves, and Dryden just himself ; that being himself, and a master-poet like them, he is not so successful as he seems to have hoped, in ' maintaining the character of an author, which distinguishes him from all others'. Ovid and Virgil, with the rest, I confess, as Englished by him, appear to me, independently of the subject-matter, much nearer to being identical in his manner than they were in their own. Still, it cannot but be borne in upon readers that everywhere he in spirit felt the differences, the individuality of each separate poet; and he makes us feel that he felt them.

After all, our business is with Dryden; our primary object is to study the collection as Dryden's work; and as such its merits are transcendent. With Horace alone in the few Odes he has attempted, he seems to me to have failed; that is, he shares the universal failure. In his Theocritus, competent as it is, one is conscious of the want of a dialect, both in temper and tongue. A Burns is needed. The plentiful specimens of the Metamorphoses, if not in smoothness, are, in sparkling and charm, completely Ovidian. We must search long among translations to parallel for ease, power, melody, variety, the Ceyx and Alcyone, and despairing Polyphemus's prayer to Galatea. For Dryden's sake, if not for shameless Ovid's, I pass by the worse than wasted skill in the version of the Art of Love. The treatment of the first book of the Iliad shines out in comparison with Pope's. It is less polished. Sometimes it is slovenly; Pope could not have printed

> For yesterday the Court of Heaven with Jove
> Remov'd; 'tis dead vacation now above;

or

> Brave Hector went to see
> His virtuous wife, the fair Andromache.
> He found her not at home.

In exchange, it is far and away more resounding, various, vigorous, and vivid.

Over and over again in the Juvenal there is mighty verse. None of the regiment of Dryden's followers has surpassed, for example, the majesty of his rendering of the grand epitaph on Hannibal. The pity is that something awry in his nature, as in Swift's, wrenched his pen towards physical uncleanness. Coarse as is the Roman, he coarsens him. He revels in grossness. The propensity spots his noble Lucretian anthology, to his blame, not that of his author who wrote as a physiologist, no longer a poet. It must have been a gigantic capacity for transmuting philosophy into poetry, which yet in the Lucretius extorts indulgence even for that blur. Finally the gift, in another of its phases, triumphed over the intellectual crabbedness of Persius. At all times there it fairly smooths out the creases. Often it adds a grace, to which the Latin fancy would never have risen, or, perhaps stooped, as, of a mistress's power, that it

> Can draw you to her with a single hair.[13]

Sometimes it points a sermon from a heathen text to Christian formalists:

> O souls, in whom no heavenly fire is found,
> Fat minds, and ever grovelling on the ground!
> We bring our manners to the blest abodes,
> And think what pleases us must please the Gods.[14]

The success with Lucretius, and, as a feat of art more completely still with Persius, is remarkable. For pure delightfulness the Tales from Boccaccio and Chaucer may be rated higher. A time was when it would have been disgraceful not to be versed in the redemption by invincible love from loutishness of Cymon, who

> Whistled as he went, for want of thought;[15]

in the unforgiving, haughty father's vengeance upon his daughter Sigismonda, and her lowly bridegroom; and in Guido Cavalcanti's fiendish hunt. The present neglect is waste of a heritage of national literature. If the translations or paraphrases of several of Chaucer's Tales are equally overlooked, an excuse may be that they are known now in the original. Far be it from me to suggest that Chaucer's adorable naïveté, the infinite surprises of his flexible rhythm, could ever have been fully replaced by later substitutes. It remains no less true that Dryden's more measured, but never monotonous, harmony is a creation which it is a sin to lose. Nor is it words alone that he interpreted, but spirit, and with a view to modern intelligence. Thus, for one who might and ought to have enjoyed the Knight's Tale, ninety-nine, at all events in the seventeenth century, to appreciate it, needed to have it passed through a more recent understanding, and stamped with its accent. If the proportion happily is changed in our times, there is still a majority of readers to whom Dryden's version is more congenial.

Let me quote a few lines for comparison. Chaucer is describing Emelye in the garden, as she appeared to the two prisoners :

> In the gardin, at the sonne up-riste,
> She walketh up and doun, and as hir liste
> She gadereth floures, party whyte and rede,
> To make a sotil gerland for hir hede,
> And as an aungel hevenly she song.[16]

The passage happens to be unusually free from archaisms ; yet see how Dryden transforms it, while he doubles the length :

> At every turn she made a little stand,
> And thrust among the thorns her lily hand
> To draw the rose, and every rose she drew
> She shook the stalk, and brush'd away the dew .
> Then party-colour'd flowers of white and red
> She wove, to make a garland for her head :

> This done, she sung and caroll'd out so clear,
> That men and angels might rejoice to hear:
> E'en wond'ring Philomel forgot to sing:
> And learn'd from her to welcome in the spring.[17]

For myself I prefer Chaucer always; but I could not resign Dryden.

Dryden is like the image in Nebuchadnezzar's dream, with 'the feet part of iron, and part of clay'. Much of his work is worse than clay, mere mud. Adulations, hardly to be excused by official duty, occupy a large space; a dismal Threnodia Augustalis, in which one eye weeps for a dead monarch, while the other beams on the successor; an Astraea Redux; a Britannia Rediviva. There are hireling condolences, dear at any price, with an Earl the poet did not know, on the decease of a Countess he had never seen. There are weary Prologues and Epilogues, which, if paid for by weight, would have been lucrative. For background and foreground, Tragedies, tearing passion to rags, alternate with Comedies, as much cause as effect of the social degeneracy. A poet proud of the name—as he boasts to a cousin:

> Nor think the kindred muses thy disgrace;
> A poet is not born in every race—[18]

allowed himself to be crowned King of Grub Street; to sell what did duty for inspiration that he might revel at a tavern.

So much is a lamentable, not an unprecedented, stain upon a lofty career and fame. Other writers of eminence have discredited their greatness by misusing it for base purposes. The phenomenon with Dryden is that after any fall he could redeem, not so much his dignity, as his powers themselves, to whatever work he had anew pledged them. The toughness, the fierceness of his robust and masculine spirit, would doubtless have made the ungentle topics of politics and casuistry equally his theme had he rivalled Andrew Marvell in incorruptness and simplicity. Nature moulded him for a flail to thresh away chaff, a tornado to tear through a forest. He is the Rubens of poetry, admirable for the certainty of his touch, the overpowering tenacity of his grasp of an idea. A misfortune of his genius was to belong so wholly to his period, which he dominated, with its passions, and fashions, to be so wrapped up in it and them, as often to be liable to burial with it and them in its grave. Its happy peculiarity was to be able to emerge again and again.

He employed poetry as a weapon of affairs. None are poets who cannot absorb themselves into their theme for the time being. He was a born fighter, as he was a born poet. His imagination set the atmosphere of controversy on fire. It is impossible wholly to regret that he descended from Parnassus into the arena of political and theological controversy. If that has rusted with age much of his work, a whole period of history, the prey else of dullness and darkness, has been illuminated by the radiance of his imagination. In another direction literature has gained by this habit in him of regarding poetry as a craftsman his tools. He had to earn his living. The public would pay for Tales; and he wrote Tales for it. It was a happy necessity which drove him to such an exercise of his journeyman's industry. They reveal stores in him of sweetness, sublimity, the true poet's infinity of sympathy. Unfortunately the public was ready to pay, and yet more eagerly, for Plays after its taste; and he has written Plays to suit it.

Thus far he acted equally after his manner with the specific instrument nature had bestowed upon him. But it is impossible to measure by strict rule either the potentialities, or the humours, of supreme imaginativeness. None can predict when and how Heaven in the Prophet will begin to speak. At the age of sixty-six, exiled from Court, stripped

220   FIVE CENTURIES OF ENGLISH VERSE

of his appointments—and in Shadwell's favour!—out of touch with popular feeling, impoverished, and sick, he blazed, as we have seen, upon a forgetful world with his Alexander's Feast. No English Ode can match it but Milton's Hymn on the Morning of Christ's Nativity. The smell of the lamp hangs about Gray's Progress of Poesy and the Bard, even about Collins's Ode to the Passions. They have not the same fire, the spontaneity. Well that the captive and blind Samson, after grinding and making sport for a dissolute Court and public all the best years of his life, should have been moved before he died to sing a Song like this!

And yet—as we read it, how more and more we feel with his brother poet—as it were, his successor—'Unhappy Dryden!'

The Poetical Works of John Dryden (Aldine Edition of the British Poets). William Pickering, 1832. Five vols.

[1] Translations from Ovid's Metamorphoses.
[2] Religio Laici; or, A Layman's Faith, vv. 62-79.
[3] The Hind and the Panther, vv. 239-44.
[4] Absalom and Achitophel, Part I, vv. 27-30.
[5] Ibid., vv. 188-97.
[6] MacFlecknoe, vv. 17-20.
[7] Song of the Sea-fight, in Amboyna.
[8] To Sir Godfrey Kneller, Epistle 14.
[9] To my Dear Friend, Mr. Congreve, on his Comedy, The Double Dealer, Epistle 10, vv. 66-75.
[10] Absalom and Achitophel, Part I, vv. 150-97.
[11] Pope, Essay on Criticism, Part I.
[12] Alexander's Feast; or, The Power of Music: Ode in Honour of St. Cecilia's Day.
[13] Persius, Sat. v, v. 247.
[14] Ibid., Sat. ii, vv. 110-13.
[15] Cymon and Iphigenia, v. 95.
[16] The Knightes Tale (Canterbury Tales), ed. Skeat, vv. 1051-5.
[17] Palamon and Arcite (Tales from Chaucer), vv. 191-200.
[18] To my Honoured Kinsman, John Dryden, of Chesterton, Epistle 13, vv. 201-2.

MATTHEW PRIOR

1664—1721

It is a truism that a man may have had a successful career, yet be, from his own point of view, a failure. I am not sure that Prior did not so regard his literary laurels. Very possibly he would even have deemed the ripple of personal kindliness which still gurgles about his score of gay lyrics, poor compensation for the foundering of his more serious poems in the stream of fame. He himself, under the guise of a would-be intimate, affects to be diverted by the refusal of the public to recognize sublimity in the gravity of dull Solomon :

> Indeed, poor Solomon in rhyme
> Was much too grave to be sublime.[1]

It is more likely that he was sincerely disappointed. Of the epic a single couplet is popularly remembered :

> Abra was ready ere I called her name ;
> And, though I call'd another, Abra came.[2]

Scarcely so much survives of Henry and Emma.

But he has proved elsewhere that he had a right to feel able to measure swords with masters, as in his youth. To the satiric mockery, excellent of its kind, of the Story, principally his, of the Country-Mouse and the City-Mouse, he added later real fire of fancy in the brilliant ballad on King William's recapture of Namur in 1695. It is a retort to Boileau's paean on its capture by the French in 1692. Every stanza rustles and roars with the whizzing of the triumphant cannonade. For an instance, not an exceptional one, take the fourth :

> Full fifteen thousand lusty fellows
>   With fire and sword the fort maintain ;
> Each was a Hercules you tell us ;
>   Yet out they march'd, like common men.
> Cannons above, and mines below,
>   Did death and tombs for foes contrive ;
> Yet matters have been order'd so,
>   That most of us are still alive.[3]

Alma in another sort exhibits power to break and ride with a light hand a philosophical theme as bravely. Lines of Prior's are of the substance of our language. Who, for instance, is not familiar, if not with the whole ballad of the thief on his way to be hanged, at any rate with the disagreement between him and his spiritual adviser on the merits of dispatch ; how he

>   whose good grace was to open the scene,
> Seem'd not in great haste that the show should begin ;
> Now fitted the halter, now travers'd the cart ;
> And often took leave, but was loth to depart.[4]

His epigrams gleam even now with not unamiable malice. On the whole, I am willing to believe, and doubtless with his own full concurrence, that, but for the counter attractions of ambition, always social rather than political, he might have attained, as a partisan poet, a position in literary history resembling, with less weight of metal, that occupied by Dryden's self.

As it was, he thought he had earned a monument in Westminster Abbey, and made handsome provision for one by will. Whatever the coolness of contemporary opinion, he looked, I dare say, to posterity to grow enthusiastic over 'poor Solomon' and its like. Hard as it may be to fix limits to hopefulness in respect of posthumous fame, there is no reason to suppose that he anticipated immortality for his minor poems. They are the earliest unmistakable vers de société enshrined in classical English literature. Ben Jonson, Donne, Herrick, Suckling, Lovelace, Waller, even Cowley, and saintly Crashaw, had sung the praises of love and wine. Their songs had passion, or ideas. They were impersonal, and were born with an intention of living. It might have been thought that Prior's, which had no lofty pretensions, had answered their purpose if they praised a friend or patron, and brought to their author a momentary vogue. The coloured bubbles he blew would not have been futile had they burst with the shock of a coffee-house's or a boudoir's applause. Somehow, on they went glittering, fluttering, like butterflies, as with a life of their own; and they flutter and glitter still.

Modern taste braves Johnson's scorn of what he accounted mawkish delicacy,[5] and has shelved several poems, once on every one's lips, as too full-flavoured; but two centuries have not superannuated 'Kitty, beautiful and young', who, overruling Mamma's judgement in keeping her yet awhile within her nursery,

> at heart's desire,
> Obtain'd the chariot for a day,
> And set the world on fire—[6]

inclusive of the Duke of Queensberry. They have not worn the edge off Cloe's all-sufficient explanation to an Angry Lover of her breach of an appointment;[7] Euphelia's very natural displeasure that,

> My lyre I tune, my voice I raise,
>   But with my numbers mix my sighs;
> And, whilst I sing Euphelia's praise,
>   I fix my soul on Cloe's eyes;[8]

Cupid's unfortunately matricidal mistake of Venus for her likeness, the same Cloe; [9] or the superhuman wisdom of a bachelor's advice to a jealous husband:

> Wait on her to the park and play,
> Put on good-humour; make her gay;
> Be to her virtues very kind;
> Be to her faults a little blind;
> Let all her ways be unconfin'd;
> And clap your padlock—on her mind.[10]

He renders a 'blubbered face' still adorable, and his own scandalous grammar in apologizing, in turn, to Cloe, for his miscellaneous amorousness in verse:

> Then let us like Horace and Lydia agree:
> For thou art a girl as much brighter than her,
> As he was a poet sublimer than me!

more delightful than good English, as probably it was better in keeping with her own.[11]

His fancy is an inexhaustible spring. At a touch the fountain plays at love of a five-year-old Lady Mary, who

> makes her silk-worms beds
> With all the tender things I swear;
> Whilst all the house my passion reads
> In papers round her baby's hair.[12]

An instant, and another Child of Quality draws from the mature, yet never hardened, wit, a gush of honest, thoughtful affectionateness:

> My noble, lovely, little Peggy,
> Let this my first epistle beg you,
> At dawn of morn, and close of even,
> To lift your heart and hands to Heaven,
> In double beauty say your prayer—
> Our Father, first; then, Notre Pere—
> And, dearest child, along the day,
> In every thing you do and say,

> Obey and please my lord and lady,
> So God shall love, and angels aid ye,
>   If to these precepts you attend,
>   No second letter need I send,
>   And so I rest your constant friend.[13]

Gaiety, innocence, elegance, neatness, sweetness—even, when required, a passing flush of tenderness—are native to Prior's pen. Note, for a combination of these qualities, the pretty and graceful, but far from profound, Garland—the simple, yet well-dressed ease, 'simplex munditiis,' of the transition from smiles to melancholy :

> Ah me ! the blooming pride of May,
>   And that of Beauty are but one ;
> At morn both flourish bright and gay ;
>   Both fade at evening, pale and gone.
>
> At dawn poor Stella danc'd and sung ;
>   The amorous youth around her bow'd ;
> At night her fatal knell was rung ;
>   I saw, and kiss'd her in her shroud.[14]

The artifice is well known in poetry, a mortal experiment with an infinity of failures. As the reader feels an approach to the attempt, he has an emotion akin to that of an Alpine climber on a slender snow-ledge. There is the perilous, intoxicating joy of being an inch off a violent death—the imminence of a bathos lying in wait for an excess of pathos.

That is the distinction, the wonder, of 'Mat Prior's easy jingle'. At one moment he obliges us to be surprised at the commonplace. At another he appears to be riding for a fall, and does not tumble. One can no more be angry with him for an invitation to a walk on slippery ground than with a child who puts his elders to the blush. The attractiveness, almost the fascination, is certain ; and yet, after all, the things, as I have said, are mere vers de société. True; but such as no Englishman in his own time, or for a hundred years after, if ever, has matched; such as our literature could not dispense with now; in one way or another irresistible!

Well, and a poet then? Forty years ago I put the question to myself, and seemingly had no doubt of the fit answer: 'Without thought or passion no writer can long keep his rank among poets; and Prior had neither.' The latter part of that verdict I am not inclined to dispute. His poems contain little more thought than is needed to save them from vacuity, and no passionateness, except such as may attend irony. But they possess a quality which vindicates their title to be poetry nevertheless; and that is, atmosphere. In it they live and breathe; it travels down the current of time with them; and it ensures them an independent being. It is a quality which at once veils and reveals. It affords space for the singer's idea to move about, define, amplify; and for the reader's fancy as well. Associations house themselves within. It is like a Spaniard's cloak, a comrade, a confidant, something of a home, an universal provider. Rather thin in texture it may be; but it is elastic, agreeable, and companionable. On the whole, while within its influence, I am ready to believe that the inmate of the tomb in the Abbey deserved the honour, though, as a rule, it is better for a poet to have been put than to put himself there.

The Poems of Matthew Prior (Johnson's Poets, vols. xxxii, xxxiii, and xxxiv. London, 1790).

[1] The Conversation. A Tale.
[2] Solomon, Book II, vv. 362–3.
[3] An English Ballad—on the Taking of Namur by the King of Great Britain, 1698, st. 4.

[4] The Thief and the Cordelier. A Ballad, st. 5.
[5] Boswell's Johnson, vol. vii, pp. 10-11. Murray, 1835.
[6] The Female Phaeton, st. 8.
[7] A Lover's Anger.
[8] An Ode, st. 3.
[9] Cupid Mistaken.
[10] An English Padlock. vv. 76-81.
[11] A Better Answer to Cloe Jealous, st. 7.
[12] To a Child of Quality, Five Years Old, st. 4.
[13] To the Honourable Lady Margaret Cavendish Harley, when a Child.
[14] The Garland, stanzas 8-9.

DR. JONATHAN SWIFT

1667—1745

How either include, or exclude Swift? He wished, thought, knew, declared himself to be a poet. He owned, and displayed many of a poet's qualities. Versifying was as natural to him as breathing. His imagination was extraordinarily, extravagantly, ready and lively. Whatever the topic, it searched every dusty hole and corner. For the purposes of criticism, almost invariably cruel, it exhausted the utmost capabilities of caricature. With the propensity, or in spite of it, the man himself seemed to have been designed for a poet in feeling, as in intellect. His heart was at bottom warm and loving, misunderstood as it has been by writers who might have been expected to know better. Never was a wiser and more constant friend. When he raged it was with a poet's intensity; and his caprices, his piques, his attachments, were a poet's too.

From the happy afternoon on which, a child, I was led by my father to read Gulliver, my affections have always gone out to Swift. In my later investigations of history, by predilection I chose tracks on which I could meet his familiar figure. Everywhere, unless when, for an unwilling instant, I chanced upon his verse, I was sensible of the poet in him. Never did it occur to me to consider him as a writer of poetry. I should have been glad still to waive discussion altogether of the question whether work of his attain to that rank, or not. But he himself autocratically insists upon an answer. I have now been scrutinizing afresh the volumes of his metrical compositions, that I may have a right to reply. The result is that I will not deny, and cannot definitely affirm, but—almost resentfully—hope.

Manifestly he can chronicle with dramatic power; as, for example, a Modern Lady's day or night, until unlucky Madam, in tears,

> With empty purse, and aching head,
> Steals to her sleeping spouse to bed.[1]

In fits of more or less righteous wrath his rhymes lash, till the blood flows, antagonists, secular or ecclesiastical, bishops, lawyers, soldiers, even fellow men of letters in the opposite camp.[2] Nay, he has a store of charming cajoleries for friends and allies; for Peterborough, who

> Shines in all climates like a star,
> In senates bold, and fierce in war;[3]

for Pope,

> A genius for all stations fit,
> Whose meanest talent is his wit;[4]

for the late Lord Treasurer, in the Tower, who

> Nor stoops to take the staff, nor lays it down,
> Just as the rabble please to smile or frown.[5]

As a maid-of-all-work for the sweeping-out of the lumber-room of a mind occupied in general with affairs really serious, no Muse was ever more useful than the great Dean's. Rarely indeed does it seem to have occurred to himself that poetry is among the gravest, the noblest, of all affairs; that its ministers, set apart and consecrated, are under an obligation to offer up heart and brain on its altar.

Had Swift been incapable of flights beyond the Furniture of a Woman's Mind,[6] or a ballad narrating how the renowned highwayman,

> Clever Tom Clinch, while the rabble was bawling,
> Rode stately through Holborn to die in his calling,[7]

literature might have accepted such bitter-gay whimsicalities from him as it greeted playful trifles from Prior, with the smiling thankfulness they merit. It might respectfully have recognized hints of a loftier spirit in the sarcastic outbursts against a Marlborough, a Walpole. But

facit indignatio versus,

not poetry. Lovers of that would have marked, and passed on. They have a real right to feel aggrieved when, in the heap of leaflets, squibs, and sportive nothings, they come upon pieces like the autobiographical elegy—I had almost written, autopsy—On the Death of Dr. Swift.[8] We are forced to suspect that its author had more than

a kind of knack at rhyme ; [9]

that it was a poet's heart, and not a wit's gall, which accounted it the hardest penalty of his exile to have to

> spend his life's declining part ;
> Where folly, pride, and faction sway,
> Remote from St. John, Pope, and Gay ; [10]

and his chief solace to cling, under a show of not caring, to a hope that, when his friends should hear of his death :

> Poor Pope will grieve a month, and Gay
> A week, and Arbuthnot a day.
> St. John himself will scarce forbear
> To bite his pen, and drop a tear.[11]

Such glimpses within reveal to us much more than an egotist labouring to condense into five hundred lines his own epitaph.

In verse still more intimate, the epistle to Stella Visiting me in my Sickness, we are permitted something of insight into his true relations to the one woman he cared for, and—nobody knows why—sacrificed. It shows us a poet's understanding of female worth—the courage, the wit and sense :

> The world shall in its atoms end,
> Ere Stella can deceive a friend.
> By honour seated in her breast
> She still determines what is best;
> What indignation in her mind
> Against enslavers of mankind!
> Base kings, and ministers of state,
> Eternal subjects of her hate!
> Say, Stella, was Prometheus blind,
> And, forming you, mistook your kind?
> No: 'twas for you alone he stole
> The fire that forms a manly soul;
> Then, to complete it every way,
> He moulded it with female clay;
> To that you owe the nobler flame,
> To this the beauty of your frame.

He had experienced her devotion:

> When on my sickly couch I lay,
> Impatient both of night and day,
> Lamenting in unmanly strains,
> Call'd every power to ease my pains;
> Then Stella ran to my relief
> With cheerful face and inward grief;
> And though, by Heaven's severe decree,
> She suffers hourly more than me,
> No cruel master could require,
> From slaves employ'd for daily hire.
> What Stella, by her friendship warm'd,
> With vigour and delight perform'd.[12]

'Her Friendship'! The only thing about her he seems not to have learnt till it was too late was that her friendship was a woman's love; and that she thirsted for his love in return. Somehow that was an emotion nature would appear to have denied, or to have failed to ripen in, him. With it his big soul might have borne twenty-fold, a hundred-fold, the meagre poetic harvest it has chosen to yield.

A few pages of genuine, if undressed, poetry, out of some seven hundred devoted, otherwise, partly, to scorching up, or freezing, but, mainly, to miscellaneous mocking at things sacred and profane, equally at natural necessities and at social corruptions of human life! Still, a score or two. If only he had been as enthusiastic for virtue as he was scornful of imposture, had opened his eyes to see visions, had gazed at the stars instead of raking in mud!

The Poems of Dr. Jonathan Swift (Johnson's Poets, vols. xlii, xliii, xliv. London, 1790).
[1] The Journal of a Modern Lady.
[2] Irish Bishops; a late famous General; The Upright Judge; The Yahoo's Overthrow; John Dennis's Invitation to Richard Steele.
[3] To the Earl of Peterborough, st. 11.
[4] A Libel on Dr. Delany and Lord Carteret.
[5] To the Earl of Oxford, in the Tower.
[6] The Furniture of a Woman's Mind.
[7] Clever Tom Clinch.
[8] On the Death of Dr. Swift.
[9] Ibid., v. 264.
[10] Ibid., vv. 495-8.
[11] Ibid., vv. 207-10.
[12] To Stella--Visiting Me in My Sickness

ALEXANDER POPE
1688—1744

WHAT a fiery spirit in those fetters of rhyming heroics! How bravely still the carcass, only half dead, clanks its chains by the busy highway, with a sneer, a jeer, a curse at the law and order to which its creaking bones testify! Defiance is writ large over Pope's whole life and genius. He trampled on the pretensions of the least flexible of all the instruments of poetry to regulate his intellect or temper. He scorned the physical checks of abiding pain racking his incubus of a body. He paraded a persecuted faith, when no longer really his, in the face of an intolerant age. Who can look up at London's glaring, staring column without a thought of admiration for the puny, professing Papist, who ventured to affront the tall bully lifting its brazen head with a lie![1] In death as in life he lorded it over an age, and compels literature still to trace its lineage through him. His sovereignty may have ceased to be acknowledged; the memory of it has ingrained itself in the language. We perpetually are using coinage stamped with his image.

He had his vices. They were no mere accidents of physical ailments, transient moods, circumstance. They were essentially his own, bred and born in the bone. He had fondled and nursed them. Unless in a narrow circle of intimates—and then sometimes—he was venomous as a wasp, fascinatingly spiteful as a humming-bird. Seldom did he forgive an injury, and never a slight. Lady Mary made an enemy of him for life by her virtue, Queen Caroline by coquetting with other wits, and Ambrose Philips by daring to emulate his Pastorals. Much of the scornfulness, wholly justifiable as criticism, in the tremendous Dunciad has the sourness of a personal grievance. Literature, which has gained by a matchless hurricane of explosive bullets, has never discovered a rational explanation of the outburst against Addison ;

        Were there one whose fires
True genius kindles, and fair fame inspires,
Bless'd with each talent and each art to please,
And born to write, converse, and live with ease ;
Should such a man, too fond to rule alone,
Bear, like the Turk, no brother near the throne ;
View him with scornful, yet with jealous, eyes,
And hate for arts that caus'd himself to rise ;
Damn with faint praise, assent with civil leer,
And without sneering teach the rest to sneer ;
Willing to wound, and yet afraid to strike,
Just hint a fault, and hesitate dislike ;
Alike reserv'd to blame or to commend,
A timorous foe, and a suspicious friend ;
Dreading e'en fools ; by flatterers besieg'd,
And so obliging that he ne'er oblig'd ;
Like Cato, give his little senate laws,
And sit attentive to his own applause ;
While wits and templars every sentence raise,
And wonder with a foolish face of praise —
Who but must laugh if such a man there be ?
Who would not weep if Atticus were he ?[2]

I have often wondered at the apparent serenity with which acquaintances stood the ordeal. They must have continually felt themselves in front of a masked battery of spitfire suspicion, ready at any moment, on any or no pretext, to open, and shatter them to pieces.

His poetical deficiencies were as deeply rooted. For wild, natural beauty he had no genuine feeling. Windsor Forest itself—a wonderful work for a boy—indicates little or none, though he was too diffident of his footing with nature to stumble into blunders. With freedom for the most part from incongruous absurdities, the barrenness of his favourite Pastorals is dreadful. He could have written for the purpose to as much effect when, at the age of twelve, he hymned Solitude. For so dexterous a craftsman, for so great a genius, it is extraordinary how helpless he was outside his habitual forms, and how insensible he seems to be to the incapacity. Occasionally he tried other metres than the heroic with deplorable results. The Universal Prayer is sustained and justified by fine thoughts, rather philosophical than strictly poetical. The Ode for Music on St. Cecilia's Day, lauded once as only second to, if not the equal of, Alexander's Feast, has reached its proper dead level in opinion now. The last four lines alone rise above mediocrity. We have learnt better than to waste applause on such as

> Music can soften pain to ease,
> And make despair and madness please;
> Our joys below it can improve,
> And antedate the bliss above![3]

Playing his own special instrument he turns out very different work from that of St. Cecilia's poetaster. In his hands the decasyllabic couplet became a full orchestra. He had trained it to barb an epigram in every second line. For him it could expound a theology:

> All are but parts of one stupendous whole,
> Whose body Nature is, and God the soul;
> That chang'd through all, and yet in all the same,
> Great in the earth as in th' ethereal frame,
> Warms in the sun, refreshes in the breeze,
> Glows in the stars, and blossoms in the trees;

236 FIVE CENTURIES OF ENGLISH VERSE

> Lives through all life, extends through all extent,
> Spreads undivided, operates unspent;
> Breathes in our soul, informs our mortal part.
> As full, as perfect, in a hair as heart;
> As full, as perfect, in vile man that mourns
> As the rapt seraph that adores and burns:
> To him no high, no low, no great, no small;
> He fills, he bounds, connects, and equals all!
> Submit —In this or any other sphere,
> Secure to be as bless'd as thou canst bear;
> Safe in the hand of one disposing Power,
> Or in the natal or the mortal hour.
> All nature is but art unknown to thee:
> All chance direction, which thou canst not see;
> All discord, harmony not understood;
> All partial evil, universal good.[4]

It could sum up a life, a character, a tragedy. Equally it immortalized fame and infamy, affection and glory.

Whatever the subject, he could warrant it to supply appropriate music. Courage was needed to charge the heavy jingle with The Rape of the Lock; and the trust was justified. Nothing could be lighter and daintier. The setting is preposterously and delightfully monumental. An archaeologist might draw up from the poem a treatise on the toilette service of a lady of fashion in the golden days, when, near the scene of the epic,

> Great Anna, whom three realms obey,
> Did sometimes counsel take—and sometimes tea.[5]

If no record survived of the game of ombre, it could be reconstructed from the encounter here between the heroine and the Baron. The description of the race of Sylphs, the tutelary guardians of sovereign beauty, is as ample. There would seem even to be danger of suffocation of the plot by its sumptuous properties. Yet the nicest proportion is maintained between accessaries and principals. Belinda, the object of universal care by the powers of air and of drawing-rooms, down to obsequious

> Sir Plume, of amber snuff-box justly vain,
> And the nice conduct of a clouded cane,
> With earnest eyes, and round unthinking face,[6]

reigns in the tale supreme. For conquest of hearts she hardly needs the spell of the two unequalled locks, whence the temptation to a shameless outrage, and to mortal strife, only to be healed by the snatching-up of the radiant trail of hair into the starry heavens. Her general charms would have sufficed:

> On her white breast a sparkling cross she wore,
> Which Jews might kiss, and infidels adore,
> Bright as the sun her eyes the gazers strike,
> And like the sun they shine on all alike.
> Yet graceful ease, and sweetness void of pride,
> Might hide her faults, if belles had faults to hide;
> If to her share some female errors fall,
> Look on her face, and you'll forget them all.[7]

The prettiest of fantastic trifles; and it wears its panoply of iron heroics as if of gossamer!

But a still bolder application of the measure was to the translation of the Iliad. For an indifferent scholar to have undertaken the work at all was in itself audacious; his choice of the heroic metre was almost an insult. Nothing, however, succeeds like success; and indisputably the adventure succeeded. During a century and a half Pope's version held the field; who can say that it has been superseded yet? Even the learned have been in the habit of dealing gently with its sciolism. The facile consistency of the rhythm, though regular to monotony, was accepted in exchange for the long sinuous sweep of the old Ionic. A consciousness that deep down lay the germ of a poet's genuine fellowship with the great original has acted on criticism as an opiate.

There the clue will be found to the wonders he wrought in the realm of poetry at large ; to the evils to which his triumphant example conduced. Partly the fashion set by Dryden, partly the decay of Elizabethan spontaneity, and the divorce of verse from music, put the heroic couplet into his hands for his instrument. He accepted it, with less choice perhaps even than his mighty predecessor. At all events, he soon learnt it would serve him well. But it was no chance, no necessary property of the metre, that, under his touch, it reflected almost every human mood. Multitudes of other writers have declared how jaundiced they were with their fellows and with existence ; and have never been heeded. The world was compelled to mark every jeer and groan of his :

> Behold the child, by Nature's kindly law,
> Pleas'd with a rattle, tickled with a straw ;
> Some livelier plaything gives his youth delight,
> A little louder, but as empty quite.
> Scarfs, garters, gold, amuse his riper stage ;
> And beads and prayer-books are the toys of age ;
> Pleas'd with this bauble still, as that before,
> Till tir'd he sleeps, and life's poor play is o'er.[8]

Disposition and circumstances inclined him to unmask and mock at weaknesses. But there was genius also in whatever phase his cross-grainedness assumed. It might be virulence, as at Duchess Sarah :

> From loveless youth to unrespected age,
> No passion gratified, except her rage.[9]

Sometimes it was less contempt than malicious amusement at the manifold forms—all crazy—which social folly may take :

ALEXANDER POPE

    A salmon's belly, Helluo, was thy fate;
The doctor call'd, declares all help too late.
'Mercy,' cried Helluo, 'mercy on my soul!
Is there no hope? Alas! then bring the jowl.'
The frugal crone whom praying priests attend,
Still strives to save the hallow'd taper's end,
Collects her breath, as ebbing life retires,
For one puff more, and in that puff expires.
'Odious in woollen! 'twould a saint provoke'—
Were the last words that poor Narcissa spoke—
'No, let a charming chintz and Brussels lace
Wrap my cold limbs, and shade my lifeless face;
One would not, sure, be frightful when one's dead—
And—Betty—give this cheek a little red.'
The courtier smooth, who forty years had shin'd
An humble servant to all humankind,
Just brought out this, when scarce his tongue could stir;
'If—where I'm going—I could serve you, Sir?'
'I give and I devise,'—old Euclio said,
And sighed—'my lands and tenements to Ned.'
'Your money, Sir?'—'My money, Sir! What, all?
Why, if I must,'—then wept—'I give it Paul.'
'The manor, Sir?' 'The manor! hold,' he cried;
'Not that—I cannot part with that'—and died.[10]

Rarely, something may be infused warmer than sarcasm:

    In the worst inn's worst room with mat half hung,
The walls of plaster, and the floors of dung,
On once a flock-bed, but repair'd with straw,
With tape-tied curtains never meant to draw,
The George and Garter dangling from that bed
Where tawdry yellow strove with dirty red,
Great Villiers lies—alas! how changed from him,
That life of pleasure, and that soul of whim!
Gallant and gay, in Cliveden's proud alcove,
The bower of wanton Shrewsbury and love;
Or just as gay at council, in a ring
Of mimic statesmen and their merry King.

> No wit to flatter left of all his store.
> No fool to laugh at, which he valued more.
> There, victor of his health, of fortune, friends,
> And fame, this lord of useless thousands ends ! [11]

Is there not a spice of pity here for the wasted life—perhaps for the teller of the tale too, to whom every gift thrown away upon the profligate had been denied, and, in fancy, it seemed, would have been a joy?

A first impression of Pope is of a satirist visiting the blame for his many infirmities and privations on the whole of society, and finding in his habitual metre an instrument dedicated to his vindictiveness. It is indisputable that he commonly used criticism as a hangman's noose. But in a fine, if chequered, nature like his a spring of tenderness will rise hard by one of bitterness. The thundercloud of wrath which darkens the Elegy on an Unfortunate Lady breaks to let tears shower down :

> What can atone, oh, ever injured shade !
> Thy fate unpitied, and thy rites unpaid ?
> No friend's complaint, no kind domestic tear
> Pleas'd thy pale ghost, or grac'd thy mournful bier.
> By foreign hands thy dying eyes were clos'd,
> By foreign hands thy decent limbs compos'd,
> By foreign hands thy humble grave adorn'd,
> By strangers honour'd, and by strangers mourn'd !
> What though no friends in sable weeds appear,
> Grieve for an hour, perhaps, then mourn a year,
> And bear about the mockery of woe
> To midnight dances, and the public show ?
> What though no weeping loves thy ashes grace,
> Nor polish'd marble emulate thy face ?
> What though no sacred earth allow thee room,
> Nor hallow'd dirge be mutter'd o'er thy tomb ?
> Yet shall thy grave with rising flowers be dress'd,
> And the green turf lie lightly on thy breast ;

> There shall the morn her earliest tears bestow,
> There the first roses of the year shall blow;
> While angels with their silver wings o'ershade
> The ground, now sacred by thy relics made.[12]

He wrote as he saw. When he saw good, he sang of it; and inspiration, descending, illuminated fond regret as magically as condemnation. Few epitaphs surpass in pathetic ingenuity the Harcourt one:

> To this sad shrine, whoe'er thou art, draw near;
> Here lies the friend most lov'd, the son most dear;
> Who ne'er knew joy but friendship might divide,
> Or gave his father grief but when he died.
> How vain is reason, eloquence how weak!
> If Pope must tell what Harcourt cannot speak.
> Oh, let thy once-lov'd friend inscribe thy stone,
> And with a father's sorrows mix his own![13]

The accustomed snarl could be exchanged for a soul-stirring tribute to desert, even in a peer:

> And you, brave Cobham! to the latest breath
> Shall feel your ruling passion strong in death:
> Such in those moments as in all the past,
> 'O save my country, Heaven!' shall be your last.[14]

Or some thirty decasyllabics would raise an eternal monument to a humble citizen of a country town:

> But all our praises why should lords engross?
> Rise, honest Muse, and sing the Man of Ross!
> Who hung with woods yon mountain's sultry brow?
> From the dry rock who bade the waters flow?
> Whose causeway parts the vale with shady rows?
> Whose seats the weary traveller repose?
> Who taught that heaven-directed spire to rise?
> 'The Man of Ross,' each lisping babe replies.
> Behold the market-place with poor o'erspread;
> The Man of Ross divides the weekly bread;
> He feeds yon almshouse, neat, but void of state,
> Where age and want sit smiling at the gate;

> Him portion'd maids, apprentic'd orphans blest,
> The young who labour, and the old who rest.
> Is any sick ? The Man of Ross relieves,
> Prescribes, attends, the medicine makes and gives.
> Is there a variance ? Enter but his door,
> Balk'd are the Courts, and contest is no more.
> ' And what ? no monument, inscription, stone,
> His race, his form, his name almost unknown ? '
> Who builds a church to God and not to fame,
> Will never mark the marble with his name ;
> Go search it there, where to be born and die,
> Of rich and poor makes all the history.[15]

How generously, delicately, can this misanthrope, manipulating a stiff and starched measure, mingle admiration with commiseration for the victim of a Court, the great singer, who

> taught to join
> The varying verse, the full resounding line,
> The long majestic march, and energy divine ; [16]

and warm tears with both for yet another poet-plaything of fashion, whom it had fondled and would have starved :

> Bless'd be the great ! for those they take away.
> And those they left me—for they left me Gay ;
> Left me to see neglected genius bloom,
> Neglected die, and tell it on his tomb.[17]

How he devoted his heart and his Muse to any who had shown him kindness—the prouder of their friendship if they were in disgrace, and persecuted !—to Harley alike, and his successful rival, all-accomplished St. John, in their common fate ; to the attainted Bishop :

> How shin'd the soul, unconquer'd, in the Tower ! [18]

to him,

> Whose lightning pierc'd th' Iberian lines,[19]

to Swift, flicked with a caress :

> who charms us with his spleen,[20]

to the mother, who had watched over his troubled childhood ; and to the physician :

> Friend to my life, which did not you prolong,
> The world had wanted many an idle song ;[21]

without whose affectionate art and care even his faithful Muse would have been too hard tasked,

> To help me through this long disease my life![22]

No wonder that he ruled ; an absolute monarch. More than half a recluse, waging incessant war with society, he all the while possessed the genius of it in the most vivid, elastic form. He had an instinct for penetrating its breast, and for lighting up its most secret recesses. No one who aspires to reach the heart and brain of the eighteenth century can neglect the study of him ; of the man in and through his works. He is its foremost representative. Of a large field in its development he was, in fact, owner and creator. We are continually speaking him ; using his wit and wisdom. His conquests, in connexion especially with his favourite weapon in making them, had indeed an ill side. His own generation, and that which succeeded, like savage artists enraptured by the exactness of Birmingham machine goods, were overcome by the regularity, seldom broken, of his smooth rhythm. The small fry of minor poets easily caught the trick of the measure. They mimicked cheaply his cynicism in attacking fashion, while infusing servility. He had used his apparatus ; and it used them. For apprentices, without his 'musical finesse '—without the fang and poison-bag behind—above all, without the soul—poetry was degraded into

> a mere mechanic art;
> And every warbler had his tune by heart.[23]

Finally, a long-suffering age rebelled, and flung the tyrant-engine into outer darkness, where it was picked up by University prizemen and the like. The author of its excessive acceptance, it cannot be denied, suffered in fame from being confounded with his uninspired followers. It was but a partial obscuration. Goldsmith, Rogers, Campbell, Byron, from time to time reminded the world that the measure Pope was accused of having stereotyped wants only a meaning and a mind at its back to be a living voice again. It is, and always has been, the same with himself. In direct contradiction of the law that nothing in literature is mortal like fashion, Pope's Muse seemed to be nothing, at her prime, if not in the fashion, yet never dies. She may close her eyes, as if having drawn her last breath. In favouring circumstances, even at the spurn of an insolent hoof, she returns in an instant to lusty life. I open a volume of Pope, with a sigh at its stilted, artificial, superannuated, icy rhetoric; within five minutes the mildew dries off, the dust has flown, the frost melts; the page sparkles again, with its own poetic standard re-established; I could almost believe that the epigrammatic vitriol was a gush of spontaneous melody, that the writer might have been Byron, or Tennyson, if only he had been born a century or so later, and had willed the metempsychosis.

And for the man himself—listen to every sneer and curse; to every half-stifled groan; to every appeal for a licence to be perverse; to every muttered whisper how grateful he would have been, had nature but fashioned him kindly;— and resist, if you can, the impulse to assent, admire, forgive —yes, and even love!

The Poetical Works of Alexander Pope (Aldine British Poets). Three vols. William Pickering, 1835.
[1] To Lord Bathurst, Epistle III.
[2] To Dr. Arbuthnot, Satires, Prologue.
[3] Ode for Music on St. Cecilia's Day.
[4] An Essay on Man, Epistle I.   [5] The Rape of the Lock, Canto iii.

[6] Ibid., Canto iv.
[7] Ibid., Canto ii.
[8] An Essay on Man, Epistle II.
[9] Moral Essays, Epistle II.
[10] Ibid., Epistle I, Part iii.
[11] Ibid., Epistle III.
[12] Elegy to the Memory of an Unfortunate Lady.
[13] On the Hon. Simon Harcourt.
[14] Moral Essays, Epistle I, Part iii.
[15] Ibid., Epistle III.
[16] The First Epistle of the Second Book of Horace.
[17] Epistle to Dr. Arbuthnot, Prologue to the Satires.
[18] Epilogue to the Satires, Dialogue ii.
[19] The First Satire of the Second Book of Horace.
[20] Moral Essays, Epistle 1
[21] Epistle to Dr. Arbuthnot, Prologue, &c.
[22] Ibid.
[23] Cowper, Table Talk.

JOHN GAY

1685—1732

Gay has been one of my perplexities. Can I put him anywhere among our poets—and if anywhere, where, and how?

When I search for proofs of his title to a place, I can discover but two or three songs to give the merest colour to a claim. Without his name to them, I think it doubtful how I should have classed even them. At highest they would have had to be content with a corner among the Waifs and Strays.

Yet, omit Gay from the noble assembly of Poets! I should blush before the Shade of Pope. Certainly Swift would quit the party, and prefer Limbo with, to Elysium without, him!

The man manifestly was a poet. Poets in any age would have loved him, and have insisted on keeping him in their fellowship. So, there he must abide; to be made the best of. The comfort, since he has to be there, is that any twentieth-century reader will find, as found Pope, Bolingbroke, Swift, Peterborough, Addison, Atterbury, and Prior, besides Queen Caroline, in the eighteenth, that whatever his rank poetically, he is himself very good company indeed.

Go with him fishing, with the fly, not Izaak Walton's bait:

> Around the steel no tortur'd worm shall twine,
> No blood of living insect stain my line;

JOHN GAY

I warrant he will provide pleasant sport with him, though in vain you

> cast the feather'd hook
> With pliant rod athwart the pebbled brook.[1]

Are you curious in feminine adornments, of early eighteenth-century fashion? Accompany him without more heed than he personally takes of his warning not to

> dare
> The toilette's sacred mysteries declare.

He will show you no little of

> the nursery of charms,
> Completely furnish'd with bright Beauty's arms;
> The patch, the powder-box, pulville, perfumes,
> Pins, paint, a flattering glass, and black-lead combs.[2]

With him, in instructive Trivia, explore the Town he knew so well. You must not mind, however, being, though in St. James's Street itself, jostled at night off flinty, lantern-less pavements with open sewers, by brawny chairmen, who

> the wall command—

or by the bully, coward at heart, who

> with assuming pace,
> Cocks his broad hat, edg'd round with tarnish'd lace.[3]

Even from the safe pages of a book, long before your promenade is over, you will sigh thankfully for having been born centuries later, in the days of stalwart police, and gas lamps.

Never was there a more complaisant fancy. It produced, at will, didactic discourses, epistles, eclogues, and the Beggar's Opera. From it fables, too, flowed by the score, in easy cheerful verse, with irreproachable morals for the diversion and, we will hope, edification, of numberless generations of childhood, down, at all events, to mine. He was the philosopher and showman of the nursery, with his Elephant and the Bookseller, the Monkey who had seen the World, the Courtier and Proteus, the Jugglers, the Hare and Many Friends, and a whole menagerie besides! At the same time, his sly innuendoes in the famous Opera alarmed a Ministry, and took the public by storm. Snatches of verse in it have been incorporated into the language; for instance, the parental lament over a wrongheaded daughter:

I wonder any man alive will ever rear a daughter!
For she must have both hoods and gowns, and hoops to swell her
    pride,
With scarfs and stays, and gloves and lace, and she'll have men
    beside;
And when she's drest with care and cost, all-tempting, fine and gay,
As men should serve a cucumber, she flings herself away;[4]

and the petulant embarrassment of a too attractive gallant:

> How happy could I be with either,
> Were t'other dear charmer away!
> But while you thus tease me together,
> To neither a word will I say.[5]

Whatever the topic, it reeled itself off into rhyme. It might be a useful Receipt for Stewing

> a knuckle of veal—
> You may buy it, or steal;[6]

or a panegyric on the charms of a Wokingham innkeeper's daughter:

> The heart when half wounded is changing,
> It here and there leaps like a frog;
> But my heart can never be ranging,
> 'Tis so fix'd upon sweet Molly Mog.[7]

Occasionally this born trifler was pleased to coquet with the Muse of Poetry a little more in accordance with direct

JOHN GAY

conventions. He wrote words to Handel's airs in the Serenata of Acis and Galatea. Everybody is familiar with them, if not with the authorship. There is Acis's song :

> Love in her eyes sits playing,
>   And sheds delicious death :
> Love on her lips is straying,
>   And warbling in her breath ;
> Love on her breast sits panting,
>   And swells with soft desire ;
> Nor grace nor charm is wanting
>   To set the heart on fire ;[8]

and it is well matched by Polypheme's :

> O ruddier than the cherry !
> O sweeter than the berry !
>   O Nymph more bright
>   Than moonshine night,
> Like kidlings blithe and merry !
> Ripe as the melting cluster !
> No lily has such lustre ;
>   Yet hard to tame
>   As raging flame,
> And fierce as storms that bluster.[9]

What grace in each without the least attempt at sense !

In the latter respect we might have found relief in emerging upon the ballad on Nelly :

> Oh ! the turn'd neck, and smooth white skin,
>   Of lovely dearest Nelly !
> For many a swain it well had been
>   Had she ne'er been at Calai.
>
> For when as Nelly came to France—
>   Invited by her cousins—
> Across the Tuilleries each glance
>   Kill'd Frenchmen by whole dozens.[10]

But unfortunately, though Dr. Johnson assigns it to Gay,

probably it is by Arbuthnot, on Miss Nelly Bennett. At all events, Gay touches his high-water mark, for sheer poetic power, inclusive of a sufficiency of coherence, in the ballad of Sweet William's Farewell to Black-eyed Susan, certainly his own :

> All in the Downs the fleet was moor'd,
>   The streamers waving in the wind,
> When black-ey'd Susan came aboard.
>   Oh ! where shall I my true love find ?
> Tell me, ye jovial sailors, tell me true,
> If my sweet William sails among the crew.
>
> William, who high upon the yard
>   Rock'd with the billow to and fro,
> Soon as her well-known voice he heard,
>   He sigh'd, and cast his eyes below :
> The cord slides swiftly through his glowing hands,
> And—quick as lightning—on the deck he stands.
>
> So the sweet lark, high pois'd in air,
>   Shuts close his pinions to his breast—
> If chance his mate's shrill call he hear—
>   And drops at once into her nest.
> The noblest Captain in the British fleet
> Might envy William's lip those kisses sweet.
>
> O Susan, Susan, lovely dear,
>   My vows shall ever true remain ;
> Let me kiss off that falling tear ;
>   We only part to meet again.
> Change, as ye list, ye winds ; my heart shall be
> The faithful compass that still points to thee.
>
> Believe not what the landmen say,
>   Who tempt with doubts thy constant mind.
> They'll tell thee, sailors, when away,
>   In every port a mistress find :
> Yes, yes, believe them when they tell thee so,
> For thou art present wheresoe'er I go.

JOHN GAY

If to far India's coast we sail,
    Thy eyes are seen in di'monds bright,
Thy breath is Africk's spicy gale,
    Thy skin is ivory so white.
Thus ev'ry beauteous object that I view,
Wakes in my soul some charm of lovely Sue.

Though battle call me from thy arms,
    Let not my pretty Susan mourn;
Though cannons roar, yet safe from harms,
    William shall to his dear return.
Love turns aside the balls that round me fly,
Lest precious tears should drop from Susan's eye.

The boatswain gave the dreadful word,
    The sails their swelling bosom spread;
No longer must she stay aboard:
    They kiss'd, she sigh'd, he hung his head.
Her lessening boat unwilling rows to land:
Adieu! she cries; and wav'd her lily hand.[11]

Excellent! yet by the merit itself testifying how near Gay came to inspiration without being inspired. Songs like this, and the airs of the Opera, even Trivia and the rest of its kind, are so good as to be continually crying out upon him for the contrast between capability and performance. Delightful, intellectually indolent 'lapdog', as he has been fondly called, he always shunned the particular species of exertion which might have turned the versifier into a poet. He was willing to do much of a high sort of what I must reluctantly call hack work—The Fan, Rural Sports, Fables, and the like. He would not, or he could not, set his fancy on fire. Nor was he, with his nature, likely to try, when without exposing his gifts to so crucial an ordeal, he was assured of admiration and affection. He was content, as was his own age also; and as it happens, posterity has been ready to continue something of the same kindness to his memory. A little less self-satisfaction, or a little more self-dissatisfaction; and literature might have boasted in John Gay a second Herrick.

The Poems of Gay (Johnson's Poets, vols. xxxvi and xxxvii), 1790.
[1] Rural Sports, Canto i, vv. 265-8.
[2] The Fan, Book I, vv. 127-30 and 235-6.
[3] Trivia, Book I, v. 62, and Book II, vv. 59-60.
[4] The Beggar's Opera, Act i, Sc. 1, Mrs. Peachem.
[5] Ibid., Act ii, Sc. 2, Macheath.
[6] A Receipt for Stewing Veal.
[7] Molly Mog; or, The Fair Maid of the Inn.
[8] Acis and Galatea. A Serenata. Air.
[9] Ibid., Air.
[10] Ballad.
[11] Sweet William's Farewell to Black-eyed Susan.

EDWARD YOUNG

1683—1765

NOBODY, I suppose, in these days would by choice read Young. His seven Satires have lost the attraction they once exercised through their transparent allusions. As poems they remind too much of Pope, their model, without, though very far from being good-humoured, the zest of the sharp snappings of his vengeful fancy. The Last Day is remarkable chiefly for noise, and the Force of Religion for tedious sentimentality. Of his other considerable productions, the Paraphrase of Part of the Book of Job might impress persons not conversant with the sublime prose of the Authorized Version. In Reflections on the Public Situation of the Kingdom there is as much of the poetical as the title indicates. The Ode on the Death of Queen Anne is as dead as she. As for the deplorable Ocean and Resignation, one in seventy stanzas, the other in four hundred and five, both testify only to the author's utter want of comprehension of the 'spirit' of their form, which he believes himself to have 'hit'.

The work on which his reputation depends, Night Thoughts, remains. Several reasons are on the surface for the neglect which has overtaken that formerly illustrious publication. He himself speaks of his exhortations as

> Truths which at Church, you might have heard in prose.[1]

A natural comment is, why not then have been satisfied by preaching them there? The remonstrances with gay Lorenzo on undisclosed misdeeds of his pour down like a rain of buffets by a muscular evangelist, who is acutely sensible that

> A God all mercy is a God unjust.[2]

Never was the gospel of Christ delivered with less of persuasive sweetness. Somehow also, it must be added, a suspicion will beset the student of a deficiency in sincerity. Not even has the metre, monotonously heavy, if correct, any variety or vivacity to compensate for dearth of the same in the sense.

Yet how condemn as false pretenders to the name of poetry, productions acclaimed by their own and several later generations? As I have remarked elsewhere, the educated judgement of the age in which a poem appeared is entitled to high respect. A writer's contemporaries read between the lines. They can most easily appreciate his intentions, and the degree in which he has carried them into effect. They have measured by their own standard of taste, which, for all that we know, may be better than our own. That another period cares less, does not tell equally as evidence of inferiority.

Thus the liking in Young's day for rhetoric in verse may fairly be set off against the modern distaste for it. The charge of being rhetorical is not indeed ever necessarily damning, as it is a common fashion to assume. Reprobation on that ground would warn off the British Parnassus some eminent poets. Rhetoric so called, in poetry as in prose, may be seasonable as well as unseasonable, worthy as well as unworthy. Not a few of Young's outbursts may be rhetorical, but have a robust beauty besides, and beyond a doubt are spirited and impressive. Take, for instances, his lament for the beloved step-daughter he styles Narcissa:

> Sweet harmonist ! and beautiful as sweet !
> And young as beautiful ! and soft as young !
> And gay as soft ! and innocent as gay !
> And happy—if aught happy here—as good !
> For fortune fond had built her nest on high.
> Like birds quite exquisite of note and plume,
> Transfixt by fate—who loves a lofty mark—
> How from the summit of the grove she fell,
> And left it unharmonious ! [3]

And, again, the impassioned rebuke of Roman Catholic bigotry for its refusal of a grave to her in consecrated earth at Lyons:

> Denied the charity of dust, to spread
> O'er dust—a charity their dogs enjoy !
> What could I do ? What succour ? What resource ?
> With pious sacrilege, a grave I stole ;
> More like her murderer than friend, I crept
> With soft suspended step, and muffled deep
> In midnight darkness, whisper'd my last sigh.
> I whisper'd what should echo thro' their realms ;
> Nor writ her name, whose tomb should pierce the skies.
>   Glows my resentment into guilt ? What guilt
> Can equal violations of the dead ?
> The dead how sacred ! Sacred is the dust
> Of this heaven-labour'd form, erect, divine !
> This heaven-assum'd majestic robe of earth,
> He deigned to wear, who hung the vast expanse
> With azure bright, and cloth'd the sun in gold.
> When ev'ry passion sleeps that can offend ;
> When strikes us ev'ry motive that can melt ;
> When man can wreak his rancour uncontroll'd,
> That strongest curb on insult and ill-will ;
> Then, spleen to dust ? the dust of innocence ?
> An angel's dust ? [4]

Contemporaries applauded, and rightly. Pathos, and still reasonably, they found in his fond complaint of his dying wife's pretence of cheerful hope:

> How oft I saw her dead, while yet in smiles!
> In smiles she sunk her grief to lessen mine.
> She spoke me comfort, and increas'd my pain.[5]

Eighteenth-century readers dwelt on, and fondled, a multitude of Young's epigrammatic phrases, till they have become crystallized into household words. Few now recognize him as the author of honoured axioms with which most of us have been familiar from childhood. None can deny that they are admirable. Speech continues to be full of them—if often not his in the thought, assuredly currency of his coinage. My difficulty has been in rejecting. Here are some casual specimens:

> Procrastination is the Thief of Time.[6]
> All men think all men mortal but themselves.[7]
> Man wants but little, nor that little long.[8]
> By night an atheist half believes a God.[9]
> Pygmies are pygmies still, tho' percht on alps.[10]
> An undevout astronomer is mad.[11]
> Nature is the glass reflecting God.[12]
> A fool at forty is a fool indeed.[13]
> You read with all the malice of a friend.[14]

Why has a writer possessed of wit, thought, fire, and imagination, forfeited the place in literature which he won, and long kept? It is not as if his language, or even his moral and religious views, though they may have come to be considered in details somewhat strait-laced, were grown antiquated. I would rather explain the collapse by revolutions, in the mode of regarding poetry and poets, and in the impulse to their production. From the birth, or rebirth, of poetry in the sixteenth century until well into the seventeenth, the poet, as distinguished from the dramatist, sang because his fancy made him. Poetry was not the business of the age, or of the singer. If he had no regular vocation, probably he wrote for the stage. Dryden, followed by Pope, each of them, as it happened, inspired, discovered the use of poetry as a business of life. It became a profession, and, for the most part, a militant profession. The aspirant to the title of poet trained himself to the practice of arms. The cause to be defended or attacked differed with men and circumstances. For Dryden the subject was party politics; for Pope it was society, or social morals; it was religion for Young. Herbert, Crashaw, and Vaughan had equally exercised their poetic powers on religious themes; but how dissimilarly!

Nothing illustrates more forcibly the abyss between the earlier and later ideas of the poetical vocation, than the spirit in which Young and the earlier three religious poets respectively approached the subject. The three handle it as a lover in a transport over a dream of his mistress's eyes or girdle. To Young the composition of Night Thoughts was a Clerical function; the inspiration was the hope of capturing ecclesiastical preferment by sonorous orthodoxy, engineered with courtship of possible patrons, even such as Bubb Dodington. Versifying being his accepted calling, neither he nor his public would think his application of it to advancement in the Church in the least inappropriate. Neither, again, would expect the pen to wait for a spark to descend and kindle emotion.

Our day, as Young's, looks upon versifying as a vocation to be pursued at least as seriously as law or medicine. So far it has accepted, and has developed, the new departure of two centuries and a half since. It attempts to impose no heavy yoke upon the professors of the art, in respect of themes, lawful and unlawful, for the Muse to treat. With delight it follows the technicalities of a criminal trial. It explores strange countries, and stranger faiths and philosophies. It is willing to be plunged into the mysteries of Heaven and Hell. The one condition it exacts is that poetry shall be making use of the subject-matter, and not the subject-matter be making use of it.

The requisition does not seem very rigorous; in fact, it cuts at the root of a large proportion of Georgian verse. For real compliance with it, in order that the thing written shall be poetry, it must be the work of one who versifies because he cannot help himself. A man may write much which is not poetry, and be a poet nevertheless. A composition may contain much which is poetical, yet not be a poet's. The true poet writes because he has a message to deliver to the world, and feels that poetry is the essential, the only fitting, vehicle for it. In the eighteenth century it was not understood that a writer, before acting as a poet, should have felt, and be able to show, he had received a special commission for the purpose. In its darkest days genuine poets doubtless arose and wrote. Neither they nor their age understood the elementary difference between them and a host of others who conceived themselves to be, and were accepted as, poets, chiefly because they had found it convenient to clothe their thoughts in metre.

I do not think that Young had any clear perception of a versifier's need for a commission, or knew whether he possessed one or not. Simply he wrote in verse because he hoped to be more generally audible so—and to a fit congregation for his purpose—than in the pulpit. As I read him I am continually aware of a strong despotic intellect striving, often in vain, to flog the heart into a white heat of passion. But, as with some other writers of verse, his failures perplex me less than episodes of occasional inspiration. Suddenly a gust of pure poetic sensibility will snatch him from self

EDWARD YOUNG

and from contemplation of the Christian virtues of a Dodington, a Chesterfield, a Walpole. It wings his theology, as the ostrich's pinions, though not permitting it to soar, accelerate its course upon earth. I recollect

This King of Terrors is the Prince of Peace.[15]
Hast thou ever weigh'd a sigh,
Or studied the philosophy of tears?[16]
Life's a debtor to the grave,
Death's lattice, letting in eternal day.[17]
Too low they build who build beneath the stars.[18]
O be a man, and thou shalt be a God.[19]
What is Hell?
'Tis nothing but full knowledge of the truth.[20]

Then I wonder whether somewhere, deep within the Court Chaplain's breast, a song-bird may not have been caged.

The Poetical Works of Edward Young (Aldine Edition of the British Poets). Two vols. William Pickering, 1852.
[1] The Complaint; or, Night Thoughts: Night VIII.
[2] Ibid., Night IV. [3] Night III. [4] Ibid.
[5] Night VI. [6] Night I. [7] Ibid.
[8] Night IV. [9] Night V. [10] Night VI.
[11] Night IX. [12] Ibid. [13] Love of Fame, Sat. ii.
[14] Sat. iii. [15] Night III. [16] Night V.
[17] Night III. [18] Night VIII. [19] Night IX.
[20] Ibid.

JAMES THOMSON
1700—1748

I ONCE was attacking to Mark Pattison the poetry of the period I will call Hanoverian. After his manner he assented until I began upon the Seasons, when he demurred. He considered that its author wrote with personal knowledge. Thomson I still think stilted and artificial. He prefers pedantic Latinisms—such as amusive, delusive, diffusive, effusive, elusive, prelusive—to racy Saxon. He confounds verbal solecisms with new ideas. His upstrokes are as broad as his downstrokes. Not rarely he is delicate to the verge of comedy, as in Damon's belated respect for the modesty of fair Musidora. Finally, he adopts an air of having studied Nature in books rather than in situ. Nevertheless, his love for her was real. He had, I now fully agree, observed her at first hand, although he hides his familiarity underneath a coating of literary tradition and fashion.

He had followed the mowers, as

> they rake the green-appearing ground,
> And drive the dusky wave along the mead.[1]

His own eyes had noted the reluctant approach of the summer night, with faint erroneous ray:

> While wavering woods, and villages, and streams,
> And rocks, and mountain-tops, that long retain'd
> The ascending gleam, are all one swimming scene,
> Uncertain if beheld.[2]

He had seen how in autumn :

> The huge dusk, gradual, swallows up the plain;
> Vanish the woods; the dim-seen river seems
> Sullen, and slow, to roll the misty wave.
> E'en in the height of noon oppress'd, the sun
> Sheds weak, and blunt, his wide-refracted ray;
> Whence glaring oft, with many a broaden'd orb,
> He frights the nations. Indistinct on earth,
> Seen through the turbid air, beyond the life
> Objects appear; and, wilder'd, o'er the waste
> The shepherd stalks gigantic. Till at last
> Wreath'd dun around, in deeper circles still
> Successive closing, sits the general fog
> Unbounded o'er the world; and mingling thick,
> A formless grey confusion covers all.[3]

Though not himself a witness, he must have learnt from men, not books, how,

> where the Northern ocean, in vast whirls,
> Boils round the naked melancholy isles
> Of farthest Thule, and the Atlantic surge
> Pours in among the stormy Hebrides,

the migratory birds swarm in preparation for their southern flight; at the given moment departing,

> Infinite wings! till all the plume-dark air,
> And rude resounding shore are one wild cry.[4]

In the home of his boyhood, among the borderland moors and pastures, animated nature had been his school. The birds had warned him of the coming of a blast:

> A blackening train
> Of clamorous rooks thick urge their weary flight.
> Assiduous in his bower the wailing owl
> Plies his sad song. The cormorant on high
> Wheels from the deep, and screams along the land.
> Loud shrieks the soaring hern; and with wild wing
> The circling seafowl cleave the flaky clouds.[5]

Their lessons he repaid with tenderness and pity. Charmingly he touches a theme

> Unknown to fame—the passion of the groves.[6]

The imprisonment in cages of the songsters of 'boundless air' revolted him. Translating Virgil, he denounces the robbery of nests—above all, the nightingale's, who returning to her desolated home—for the singer remained for the eighteenth-century Philomela—tells

> Her sorrows through the night; and on the bough,
> Sole-sitting, still at every dying fall
> Takes up again her lamentable strain
> Of winding woe; till, wide around, the woods
> Sigh to her song, and with her wail resound.[7]

All English childhood once was familiar with his welcome to the robin, who,

> sacred to the household gods,
> Wisely regardful of the embroiling sky,
> In joyless fields and thorny thickets, leaves
> His shivering mates, and pays to trusted man
> His annual visit. Half afraid, he first
> Against the window beats; then, brisk, alights
> On the warm hearth; then, hopping o'er the floor,
> Eyes all the smiling family askance,
> And pecks, and starts, and wonders where he is.[8]

He overflowed with kindliness to everything sensible to pleasure and pain. If a century had to pass before a system more profitable as well as more humane of hive-keeping was introduced, it was no fault of the poet of the Seasons. As eloquently as wisely he had pleaded against the wasteful yearly massacre of myriads of honey-bees, stifled,

> while, not dreaming ill,
> The happy people, in their waxen cells,
> Sat tending public cares.[9]

With contemptuous anger he protests against sport with guns and dogs:

> the triumph o'er the timid hare;
> The falsely cheerful, barbarous game of death.[10]

His instinct of equity, in days before the horse had replaced the bullock at the plough, was, again like Virgil's, troubled at the slaughter of the plain, harmless, honest ox,

> To swell the riot of the autumnal feast,
> Won by his labour.[11]

Exaggerated sentiment there may be; but it will be forgiven in return for the quick succession of pictures, suffused with kindness, and generally as true as they are gracious. They are oases in the poetic Sahara of the parched central eighteenth century, which the supercilious present age thinks itself sufficiently better supplied to afford to neglect.

Neglected, even the noble concluding Hymn, by a generation which continually uses phrases from the Seasons as naturally as if they were its daily literary food; yet, the whole, buried in oblivion far less entire than has overwhelmed other work of the same pen. Dr. Johnson declared it a hard task to read through the poem of Liberty. Contemporary, no less than later, public opinion acted on his judgement. Probably the subject was too democratic for its own time, and too declamatory for the present. At any rate, the author, whose favourite it was, might have offered fair reasons for his liking, if not for his preference.

He has studded it with grand passages, a flotilla of splendid images descending the current of universal history. He acknowledges a world's debt to Phoenicia for letters

> That paint the voice, and silent speak to sight.[12]

The friend of the whole 'living chain' is grateful to the philosopher of Magna Graecia, who

> into his tender system took
> Whatever shares the brotherhood of life;[13]

the man of taste and letters renders obeisance to Hellas, mother of the arts,

> Which to bright science blooming fancy bore;[14]

and in the birth of Rome's supremacy the enthusiast for Liberty chooses to discover the stimulus to fervent energy which a sense of freedom furnishes. He fondly believes that, inspired by it, the citizen-soldiers:

>   one band of friends unconquerable,
> Thus up the hill of empire slowly toil'd;
> Till, the bold summit gain'd, the thousand states
> Of proud Italia blended into one;
> Then o'er the nations they resistless rush'd
> And touch'd the limits of the failing world.[15]

But he does not fail to recognize with sad reprobation that, emancipated themselves, they enslaved a universe. It does not surprise him that the penalty has been paid by their country. What survives of the glory, the dominion, they grasped, but a little wreckage from a flood of art, with—environing the proud seat of their empire—the Campagna,

>   All one desert, desolate and grey,

and within,

>   the still ruins of dejected Rome![16]

Thomson's muse had a general tendency to be didactic, and, it may be called, rhetorical. Such characteristics were no crimes in the author's period. They are in ours. It is unfortunate for him since his merits of insight into nature, and occasional sublimity in description, being involved in those qualities, have lost their credit along with them. Lyrical genius, had he possessed it, might have redeemed his fame. He attempted the class of composition often, and always lamentably failed. Amanda and Myra never succeeded in firing his or any other imagination. Britannia herself, when he, if it were not Mallet, played her into her Rule, ascended her throne like a clodhopper.[17] But how is it that the modern public has practically forgotten he once upon a time borrowed Spenser's harp of romance, and touched it as a master?

The Castle of Indolence, his latest work, is by far the most remarkable. It is a phenomenon. To take the first Canto, which is less moral than the next, and infinitely more poetical, he is Hanoverian no longer. On the instant he has turned an Elizabethan. His model could not have imagined for the gardens of Acrasia a more balmily soporific domain:

> A pleasing land of drowsy head it was,
> Of dreams that wave before the half-shut eye;
> And of gay castles in the clouds that pass,
> For ever flushing round a summer-sky; [18]

its severest toil—in preparation for the feast at will,

> Even undemanded by a sign or sound, [19]

to delude

> Along the brooks the crimson-spotted fry,— [20]

specially excepted for philosophic and hygienic purposes from the Canon of the Seasons against butchery for sport— with a gentle saunter now and then amid

> Sleep-soothing groves, and quiet lawns between;
> And flowery beds that slumbrous influence kest,
> From poppies breathed; and beds of pleasant green,
> Where never yet was creeping creature seen.
> Meantime, unnumber'd glittering streamlets play'd,
> And hurled every where their waters sheen;
> That, as they bicker'd through the sunny glade,
> Though restless still themselves, a lulling murmur made.
>
> Join'd to the prattle of the purling rills
> Were heard the lowing herds along the vale,
> And flocks loud bleating from the distant hills,
> And vacant shepherds piping in the dale:
> And, now and then, sweet Philomel would wail,

Or stock-doves plain amid the forest deep,
That drowsy rustled to the sighing gale;
And still a coil the grasshopper did keep;
Yet all these sounds y-blent inclined all to sleep.
Full in the passage of the vale, above,
A sable, silent, solemn forest stood;
Where nought but shadowy forms was seen to move,
As Idless fancied in her dreaming mood:
And up the hills, on either side, a wood
Of blackening pines, aye waving to and fro,
Sent forth a sleepy horror through the blood;
And where this valley winded out, below,
The murmuring main was heard, and scarcely heard, to flow.[21]

And for lodgings—a palace, which, as Chatsworth in the last century,
knew no shrill alarming bell;
where
endless pillows rose to prop the head;
So that each spacious room was one full-swelling bed;
with walls hung with costly tapestry:
Where was inwoven many a gentle tale;
Such as of old the rural poets sung,
Or of Arcadian or Sicilian vale:
Reclining lovers, in the lonely dale,
Pour'd forth at large the sweetly tortured heart;
Or, sighing tender passion, swell'd the gale,
And taught charm'd echo to resound their smart;
While flocks, woods, streams around, repose and peace impart;[22]
and
Near the pavilions where we slept, still ran
Soft tinkling streams, and dashing waters fell,
And sobbing breezes sigh'd, and oft began—
So work'd the wizard—wintry storms to swell,
As heaven and earth they would together mell;
At doors and windows, threatening, seem'd to call
The demons of the tempest, growling fell,
Yet the least entrance found they none at all;
Whence sweeter grew our sleep, secure in massy hall.[23]

A beautiful abode well befitting the bard its tenant, as—with the exception of his own first line—delineated by a friend :

>   more fat than bard beseems ;
> Who void of envy, guile, and lust of gain,
> On virtue still, and nature's pleasing themes,
> Pour'd forth his unpremeditated strain ;
> The world forsaking with a calm disdain,
> Here laughed he careless in his easy seat ;
> Here quaff'd, encircled with the joyous train,
> Oft moralizing sage ; his ditty sweet
> He loathèd much to write, ne carèd to repeat.[24]

Alas ! that he should have overcome his own repugnance to penmanship, and followed up sufficing Canto I with Canto II ; that it should have occurred to him to evoke his superfluous and pestilent Knight of Arts and Industry to lay waste the delightful Fairyland he had conjured into being, where he might, as in the flesh, have gone on sauntering for ever, hands in pocket, along garden-walls, eating from off the trees the sunny sides of peaches !

He was born, in truth, under an unlucky star. His lot should have been cast altogether in a period when Fancy danced as the May fly in the sun's beams on the face of the waters. He was ill suited for being harnessed by his age to theologies and moralities, for plodding instead of flying. Too indolent to struggle against the literary fashion of his period, he was tempted to lecture, preach, and propound truisms, instead of singing. But—gladly I recognize—a root of positive poetic feeling was in him. Blow away the frequent froth, like the

> gentle Spring, ethereal Mildness,[25]

scorned of Wordsworth ; and you find honest nature-love underneath ; frequently an aspiring thought ; even a vein of romance, with a breath of Keatsian grace and melody, within the Palace of Dreams, in which, between sleep and waking, his real genius blissfully reposes.

The Poetical Works of James Thomson (Aldine Edition of the British Poets). Two vols. William Pickering, 1830.

[1] Summer, vv. 365-6.
[2] Ibid., vv. 1689-92.
[3] Autumn, vv. 716-29.
[4] Ibid., vv. 860-3 and 867-8.
[5] Winter, vv. 140-7.
[6] Spring, v. 578.
[7] Ibid., vv. 721-5.
[8] Winter, vv. 246-54.
[9] Autumn, vv. 1173-5.
[10] Ibid., vv. 401 and 384.
[11] Spring, vv. 368-9.
[12] Liberty, Part ii.
[13] Ibid., Part iii.
[14] Ibid., Part ii.
[15] Ibid., Part iii.
[16] Ibid., Part i and Part v.
[17] Rule, Britannia. Masque of Alfred, by Thomson and Mallet. Song.
[18] The Castle of Indolence, Canto i, st. 6.
[19] Ibid., st. 34.
[20] Ibid., st. 18.
[21] Ibid., stanzas 3, 4, 5.
[22] Ibid., stanzas 33 and 36.
[23] Ibid., st. 43.
[24] Ibid., st. 68.
[25] Spring.

THOMAS GRAY

1716—1771

Gray, if he rose from the grave, would have no reason to complain of neglect. It is as difficult to forget his verse as for eyes not to be attracted by a diamond necklace, whatever the throat it clasps. Brilliancy, as of jewels—this is the first impression of his poetry. Light of all colours, as from diverse stones splendidly set in precious metal, flashes from Hymn and Ode. Necessarily the primary sensation is of creations—with one supreme exception—as wholly artificial as they are extraordinarily fascinating.

In one way the feeling is well founded. The finished work is a product of art, art so high that the artist does not affect to conceal it. Gray had abundance of leisure for polishing and perfecting the minute amount of literary work which he prepared for publication—some seven hundred lines, in all, exclusive of forgotten elegancies in Latin. He used it with scrupulous and most successful diligence. Take each poem line by line to pieces; and nothing seems simpler, even more commonplace, than the component phrases and thoughts. They are the merest pebbles, scarcely ordinary crystals. An imitator may flatter himself that he has detected the secret. Reset by him they are despised as 'Brighton diamonds'. As they drop back into the sockets Gray fashioned for them, it is forgotten that they had ever been despised elsewhere. They have recovered all their lustre.

Art with Gray was a necessity of his period and circumstances. In an earlier age, and with other environings, he might have been of the school of Spenser or Milton, of

Cowley or Dryden. He could not but have been a poet. As he sings, at once humbly and proudly:

> Oh! lyre divine, what daring spirit
>   Wakes thee now? Tho' he inherit
> Nor the pride, nor ample pinion,
>   That the Theban eagle bear,
> Sailing with supreme dominion
>   Through the azure deep of air;
> Yet oft before his infant eyes would run
>   Such forms as glitter in the Muse's ray
> With orient hues, unborrow'd of the sun;
> Yet shall he mount, and keep his distant way
> Beyond the limits of a vulgar fate,
> Beneath the Good how far!—but far above the Great.[1]

The eighteenth century, and Cambridge, however, made him the specific type of poet he was; as period and training in general make every poet what he is in manner. As the spirit moved him to write, so two counter influences acted on fashion and form. On one side an immense conversance with books was perpetually suggesting diction, and conceptions as well. On another he was always conscious of gossip, in the Covent Garden and Fleet Street taverns and coffee-houses, and the Cambridge and Oxford Common-rooms, preparing to scan and question every line. His natural genius, his inspiration, were resolved to have their own way. His shyness and his sensitiveness to opinion, on the other hand, abetted by his weight of learning, while resenting the tyranny of imposed canons of taste, were equally determined that contemporary criticism should have no fair pretext to convict him of offence.

It was indeed his own instinct to be on the watch for such inquisition; to be pleased to justify the coruscations of his fancy by their correspondence with the inspiration of earlier writers; to provide clues for the help of critics and commentators in tracing epithets, thoughts, images, to possible sources, ancient and modern. The lines of his are few which do not trail around them clouds of gold and purple dust, the essence of a hundred libraries. It might be the service of rosy-crowned Loves and Graces to their Mistress :

> Now in circling troops they meet ;
> To brisk notes in cadence beating,
> Glance their many-twinkling feet.
> Slow-melting strains their Queen's approach declare ;
> Where'er she turns, the Graces homage pay.
> With arms sublime that float upon the air,
> In gliding state she wins her easy way ;
> O'er her warm cheek, and rising bosom, move
> The bloom of young Desire and purple light of Love.[2]

Virgil and Ovid, even Apuleius, even one Barton Booth, are supposed to have been laid under contribution for the divine mode in which Venus and her Loves dance, for the tint of the impassioned air. When the Muse's track,

> where'er the goddess roves,
> Glory pursue, and gen'rous Shame,
> Th' unconquerable Mind, and freedom's holy flame,[3]

Pindar has to be vouched in defence of the liberty poetry has taken with the number of a verb. So are half a dozen other authorities on behalf of phrases in the magnificent anthem saluting the descent of Shakespeare's laurel crown successively to Milton and Dryden :

> Nor second He, that rode sublime
> Upon the seraph-wings of Extasy,
> The secrets of th' abyss to spy.
> He pass'd the flaming bounds of place and time ;
> The living throne, the sapphire blaze,
> Where angels tremble while they gaze,
> He saw ; but, blasted with excess of light,
> Clos'd his eyes in endless night.

> Behold, where Dryden's less presumptuous car,
> Wide o'er the fields of glory bear
> Two coursers of ethereal race,
> With necks in thunder cloth'd, and long-resounding pace.
> Hark, his hands the lyre explore!
> Bright-eyed Fancy, hov'ring o'er,
> Scatters from her pictur'd urn
> Thoughts that breathe, and words that burn.
> But ah! 'tis heard no more—[4]

The lurid splendours of The Bard are equally provided with defences and parallels, new and old; for the aspect of the seer, as:

> Robed in the sable garb of woe,
> With haggard eyes the poet stood,
> —Loose his beard, and hoary hair
> Stream'd like a meteor, to the troubled air—
> And with a master's hand, and prophet's fire,
> Struck the deep sorrows of his lyre;[5]

for the dirge over his murdered fellows in song; and for his exultation at the vengeance preparing for the victor and his line:

> 'Weave the warp, and weave the woof,
> The winding-sheet of Edward's race.
>   Give ample room, and verge enough
> The characters of hell to trace.
> Mark the year, and mark the night,
> When Severn shall re-echo with affright
> The shrieks of death, thro' Berkley's roof that ring,
> Shrieks of an agonizing King!
>   She-wolf of France, with unrelenting fangs,
> That tear'st the bowels of thy mangled mate,
>   From thee be born, who o'er thy country hangs
> The scourge of heav'n. What terrors round him wait!
> Amazement in his van, with flight combin'd,
> And sorrow's faded form, and solitude behind.'[6]

Verse like that was strong enough to need no borrowed light from older classics, or excuse for having 'conveyed' words or suggestions from them. It shines apart and independently, like a Play by Shakespeare, whencesoever he may have taken the plot. To apologize, however, was not Gray's intention. He did not regard a debt to Pindar or Callimachus, Lucretius, or Virgil, as derogatory, or as plagiarism. At all times he preferred fame for learning to fame for verse. I am not sure but that he agreed with Elizabethans in being a little ashamed of the name of poet, while he loved a poet's inspiration. In any case, as soon as nature, a poet's genius, had supplied the motive and basis of a piece, he would set to work as scholar-artist to polish and complete. We become impatient at the exquisite elaboration. Under it grand thoughts run a danger of being buried. There are degrees. Moments of quiet occur; in the footnotes, for example, to the Ode to Adversity:

> When first thy sire to send on earth
>   Virtue, his darling child, design'd,
> To thee he gave the heav'nly birth,
>   And bade to form her infant mind.
> Stern rugged nurse! thy rigid lore
> With patience many a year she bore;
> What sorrow was thou bad'st her know,
> And from her own she learn'd to melt at others' woe.[7]

In The Progress of Poesy, we sigh in vain for the linked golden chain of pageantry to be let without comment coil gloriously along. It is mere vexation to have a halt called at every other line that we may admire some exquisite inlay from kindred inspiration in the past.

It is a pardonable regret. A poet, however, has to be accepted as he is; and we recognize that Gray is an amalgam of art and nature. More apparent in The Bard,

The Progress of Poesy, the Ode for Music, the art is felt shaping, if less obtrusively, also the lamentations for departed boyhood, fleeting Spring, and pensive Selima's unfortunate absence of aversion to fish. Its handiwork is visible in the unfinished tragedy of Agrippina, in didactics on Education and Government which stirred the enthusiasm of Gibbon, in translations from Eddas or Aneurin, and in sarcasms hurled at a Sandwich or a Holland. We almost see a fragment like the Ode on the Pleasure Arising from Vicissitude waiting in tremulous, smiling suspense to be informed whence its original beauties had their being, and for the lingering, loving pen to star it all over with other lines as luminous as the description of a convalescent's surprised delight in everyday life :

>The meanest floweret of the vale,
>The simplest note that swells the gale,
>The common sun, the air, the skies,
>To him are opening Paradise.[8]

An infinite capacity for taking pains has been alleged to be identical with genius. I doubt the universality of the rule. The combination is true at all events of Gray, whose genius is indisputable. So is his refinement, almost superstition, in the improvement and embellishment of his verse. It is open and manifest everywhere—except in the Elegy.

The rest of his poems in any case must have lived, and been applauded. Hardly would they have been loved. As a theme, the Elegy was an accident of inspiration. Accident, if that can be so called which selects merit for its object and rewards it, tells in literature, as well as in the start of millionaires and lawyers. Never was there a happier chance than that which directed Gray's steps to the Buckinghamshire churchyard when the poetic fit was upon him. Without the six-score lines of the Elegy it

THOMAS GRAY

would have been impossible to discover the reserve in him of native tenderness. His wealth of imagination and learning, his fire, his wit and humour, could not have been hidden or slighted. But posterity would not have known of the poet of humanity, of the soul capable of a world-poem! Great though the loss, we might do without The Progress of Poesy, and The Bard; but imagine, if imagination can, the English race without Gray's Elegy! I do not wonder at Wolfe's exclamation. British history could less well spare the poem than the victory on the Heights of Abraham.

The Elegy was the protest of the natural in Gray against the pedantry of his age, its affectation of a stilted reasonableness, allied with an unwholesome appetite for rhetoric, its as unhealthy cynicism, its insensibility to simple emotions—against, perhaps, strong tendencies in himself. It is a revelation to posterity, perhaps to its writer as well, of an opposing ingredient in his own inner being of common, unbrocaded human kindliness and pathos. I have tried to resist—but cannot—the temptation to quote in proof, though I feel that, if I quote for that purpose at all, I ought to quote the whole :

> Now fades the glimmering landscape on the sight;
>   And all the air a solemn stillness holds,
> Save where the beetle wheels his droning flight,
>   And drowsy tinklings lull the distant folds.
>
> Beneath those rugged elms, that yew-tree's shade,
>   Where heaves the turf in many a mould'ring heap,
> Each in his narrow cell for ever laid,
>   The rude forefathers of the hamlet sleep.
>
> Perhaps, in this neglected spot, is laid
>   Some heart once pregnant with celestial fire;
> Hands that the rod of empire might have sway'd,
>   Or wak'd to extasy the living lyre;

> Full many a gem of purest ray serene,
>   The dark unfathom'd caves of ocean bear ;
> Full many a flower is born to blush unseen,
>   And waste its sweetness on the desert air.
>
> Some village-Hampden, that, with dauntless breast,
>   The little tyrant of his fields withstood,
> Some mute inglorious Milton here may rest,
>   Some Cromwell guiltless of his country's blood.
>
> Th' applause of list'ning senates to command,
>   The threats of pain and ruin to despise,
> To scatter plenty o'er a smiling land,
>   And read their history in a nation's eyes,
>
> Their lot forbad ; nor circumscrib'd alone
>   Their growing virtues, but their crimes confin'd ;
> Forbad to wade thro' slaughter to a throne,
>   And shut the gates of mercy on mankind.
>
> Their name, their years, spelt by th' unletter'd Muse,
>   The place of fame and elegy supply ;
> And many a holy text around she strews,
>   That teach the rustic moralist to die.
>
> For who, to dumb forgetfulness a prey,
>   This pleasing anxious being o'er resign'd,
> Left the warm precincts of the cheerful day,
>   Nor cast one longing ling'ring look behind ?
>
> On some fond breast the parting soul relies,
>   Some pious drops the closing eye requires ;
> E'en from the tomb the voice of nature cries,
>   E'en in our ashes live their wonted fires.[9]

But in truth evidence is superfluous. An exquisite simplicity exhales from every line. The miracle is the invisible art, which is as ubiquitous. Admirable as the piece is from every point of view, from that it is incomparable. To say that there is art in the Elegy will seem to many like accusing a rainbow, an afterglow, a daffodil, of being machine-made. Yet no student can doubt but that, as it is, the whole is as much an artificial product as ever were

> Thoughts that breathe, and words that burn.

If the art works unseen, it is that the poet understood how to unseal sources of sympathetic emotion in his readers. The waters gush out in a flood, deafening, blinding us to the artist in the singer. It has consecrated anew every village churchyard. Who can say that an English summer or autumn evening would be the same, were it not that, as the twilight descends, for him still—

> The curfew tolls the knell of parting day,
> The lowing herd winds slowly o'er the lea,
> The ploughman homeward plods his weary way,
> And leaves the world to darkness and to me.[10]

We take the Elegy to our hearts. But let us not, therefore, from where we stand, farther off, fail to recognize the grandeur of the Odes, and honour the author of them all. Out of one spirit the whole alike emanated; and an amazing furnace it must have been. The strength, the grace, the refusal to be content with anything short of perfection! A laborious life, and one tiny casket of jewels to show for it! I may be thought by readers remembering other poets to have exaggerated. Each, however, has a right to be viewed as within the circle of his own light; and the circle in which Gray stands dazzles!

The Poetical Works of Thomas Gray. One vol. William Pickering, 1853.

[1] The Progress of Poetry: a Pindaric Ode, vv. 112-23.
[2] Ibid., vv. 33-41.   [3] Ibid., vv. 63-5.
[4] Ibid., vv. 95-111.   [5] The Bard, vv. 17-22.
[6] Ibid., vv. 49-62.   [7] Hymn to Adversity, vv. 9-16.
[8] Ode on the Pleasure Arising from Vicissitude (Posthumous Poems), vv. 53-6.
[9] Elegy written in a Country Churchyard, stanzas 2, 4, 12, 14, 15, 16, 17, 21, 22, 23.   [10] Ibid., st. 1.

WILLIAM COLLINS
1721—1759

Hapless Collins! Never was poet visited by misfortunes more continuous, various, undeserved, pitiless, and, at the long end, incurably tragic. Family calamities threw him, an orphan, on the charity of a relative for his education. By an accident he lost the reward of his proficiency at school. He was as unlucky at Oxford. London, on which he had cast himself for support by literature, recognized his wit at coffee-houses, but would not give him bread. So few copies of his Odes found purchasers that he had to burn a large remainder. Think of the Passions expiring in smoke up a Grub Street garret chimney! Then, at scarce thirty, when fortune was beginning to smile, a pall drawn over all by madness!

Wordsworth has sung of

> mighty poets in their misery dead.

If Collins cannot be called a mighty poet, at all events he produced mighty poetry. As the echo of it passes over the mind, the blood courses faster through the veins. After a century and a half have done their utmost to wear the freshness out of the chorus of the Passions, with what imperishable grace the forms move still across the stage— how exquisitely graduated the strains they utter! A little volume includes his entire life's work; and it contains almost as many masterpieces as there are pages.

He is picturesque and dignified when, in the Ode on Highland Superstitions, he tells of wizard seers and frolicsome or malicious elves. His sympathy invests the memory of the poet of the Seasons with a tenderness we do not commonly find in the dead bard's own verse :

> Remembrance oft shall haunt the shore
>   When Thames in summer wreaths is drest,
> And oft suspend the dashing oar,
>   To bid his gentle spirit rest ![1]

What a delicately fragrant wreath, if, in its sentiment, an anachronism perhaps for Cymbeline, he lays as a tribute at Shakespeare's feet in the Dirge for Fidele !

> The redbreast oft, at evening hours,
>   Shall kindly lend his little aid,
> With hoary moss, and gather'd flowers,
>   To deck the ground where thou art laid.
>
> When howling winds and beating rain
>   In tempests shake the sylvan cell ;
> Or 'midst the chase, on every plain,
>   The tender thought on thee shall dwell ;
>
> Each lovely scene shall thee restore ;
>   For thee the tear be duly shed ;
> Beloved till life can charm no more,
>   And mourn'd till Pity's self be dead.[2]

When least inspired he does not miss, even in the Oriental Eclogues of his boyhood, being refined and interesting. In his loftier, his more habitual, mood, he becomes impetuous, august, sublime. A grand image is that picturing Fear as unable to shake off the companionship of Danger :

> Who stalks his round, an hideous form,
> Howling amidst the midnight storm ;
> Or throws him on the ridgy steep
> Of some loose hanging rock to sleep.[3]

Amidst the wild visions haunting him of civil strife threatening our isle, how gracefully he pours out blessings on Pity, with eyes of dewy light, for intervening :

> the friend of man, assign'd
> With balmy hands his wounds to bind ; [4]

and on Mercy, who, when the enemy of peace was on his way :

> from out thy sweet abode,
> O'ertook him on his blasted road,
> And stopp'd his wheels, and look'd his rage away ! [5]

Abstractions, such as these, on Peace, the Manners, Simplicity, Liberty—the manacles of Grecian epode, strophe, and antistrophe notwithstanding—at his appeal assume statuesque form and substance, till finally they are gathered by all the powers of a poet-soul into the gorgeous pageant of the Passions ! Wonderful throughout, the great Ode touches ecstasy in the musical rivalry of Fear, Anger, Despair, Hope, Revenge, Pity, and Jealousy :

> First Fear his hand, its skill to try,
>   Amid the chords bewilder'd laid,
> And back recoil'd, he knew not why,
>   E'en at the sound himself had made.
> Next Anger rush'd ; his eyes on fire,
>   In lightnings own'd his secret stings ;
> In one rude clash he struck the lyre,
>   And swept with hurried hand the strings.
> With woful measures wan Despair,
>   Low, sullen sounds, his grief beguiled ;
> A solemn, strange, and mingled air ;
>   'Twas sad by fits, by starts 'twas wild.
> But thou, O Hope, with eyes so fair,
> What was thy delighted measure ?
> Still it whisper'd promised pleasure,
>   And bade the lovely scenes at distance hail !
> Still would her touch the strain prolong ;
>   And from the rocks, the woods, the vale,
> She call'd on Echo still, through all the song ;
>   And where her sweetest theme she chose,
> A soft responsive voice was heard at every close,
> And Hope enchanted smiled, and waved her golden hair.

And longer had she sung;—but with a frown,
　Revenge impatient rose;
He threw his blood-stain'd sword in thunder down;
　And with a withering look,
　The war-denouncing trumpet took,
And blew a blast so loud and dread,
Were ne'er prophetic sounds so full of woe!
　And, ever and anon, he beat
　The doubling drum with furious heat;
And though sometimes, each dreary pause between,
　Dejected Pity, at his side,
　Her soul-subduing voice applied,
Yet still he kept his wild unalter'd mien,
While each strain'd ball of sight seem'd bursting from his head.
Thy numbers, Jealousy, to nought were fix'd;
　Sad proof of thy distressful state;
Of differing themes the veering song was mix'd;
　And now it courted Love, now raving call'd on Hate.[6]

The publication of the Odes in 1747 is an epoch in English literature. The volume preceded by a year Gray's Ode on Eton. It was the first distinct break in the weary interregnum of dullness which assumed that the essential difference of poetry from moralizing is metre. Its music sounded in the deepest darkness just before the dawn. To have proclaimed that it is the poet's duty to sing would have entitled Collins to warm gratitude, had he no other title. Any one of a dozen lovely lyrics establishes an independent right. He has his defect; and he could not well have escaped it. Books, in conformity with his training, gave the impulse to his inspiration. When he desired to improve, or correct, still to books he went. A ripe scholar, he consulted primarily the Greek or Latin classics. In default of the Ancients he sat at the feet of illustrious Moderns. 'Unrivalled' Shakespeare, who
　　　scorn'd the trifling rules of art,
　But knew to conquer and surprise the heart,[7]

'gifted' Spenser, 'critic' Jonson, 'gentle' Fletcher, 'Roman' Corneille, and 'sweet' Racine, were his teachers. But his school was still a library. The result doubtless is a certain unreality. The characters move as on the Attic stage, with gestures too elaborately studied. Their life, actual life for the time being, is of the sort communicated to Pygmalion's statue. The action in general is that of the theatre. We may be sure from the incidents of his life, with its hardships and disappointments, that he had opened many pages of the book of Man. The sad close of his career indicates even an excess of introspection. But we are as conscious in him, as in Gray, that his habit was to view humanity through dead eyes, and much less conscious than in Gray, that observation at first hand had preceded.

Yet, without using experience or social intercourse to stir or feed inspiration, Collins was inspired. I have heard a nightingale in January sing in the dining-room of a Turin hotel. It mistook the lights and warmth for the chequered shades of a sunset in May. Collins was such a nightingale. He was set singing mainly by borrowed light from Sophocles, Pindar, Virgil, Horace. From dead tongues, however, the inspiration for him was vital and vitalizing. The answering flame it kindled in his breast was quick and pure. No sordid calculations of patronage fanned it; and in dismal truth it brought him no reward in money, or even praise. With a public requiring of poetry that, to be popular, it should retail the gossip of a tavern or drawing-room, versify a sermon, or flatter, if it did not libel, a Minister, I do not suppose he could have done better than imagine himself back into a living Greece. His Muse was more worthily employed in dreaming of Harmodius and Aristogeiton than, as once in a fit of angry Whig panic, in travestying the Butcher of Culloden as a hero. If the music has always a far-off, and sometimes a thin and reedy, cadence, the fault is in the period, not in the singer. He could not freely breathe the air about him. The soil he trod could not nourish his genius.

It would have been different half a century later, when the sluggish vapours of a self-satisfied age were rolling away. I account it a strange and happy accident, that for one song, as it was, they lifted enough for him to catch no mere refraction from his books of green fields and blue sky, but to breathe real air, and to see the actual heavens above him. The volume of 1747 contained, together with the several Odes to the Passions, that To Evening; and, all but perfect though it is, it shared in the general neglect. Never was there in a single body of verse a more entire contrast to the mass. It is pervaded by a quality—self-restraint—rare in all poets, rarest in the young: perhaps least to be expected of one like its writer. It has so much more to say than it says. With a soft hand it seems to cool life's fever, to still the stir of wakeful Nature herself; to hush the throbs also of the restless fancy, from which more brilliant, but not more beautiful, creatures of song had emerged into being:

If aught of oaten stop, or pastoral song,
May hope, chaste Eve, to soothe thy modest ear,
    Like thy own brawling springs,
    Thy springs, and dying gales;

O nymph reserved, while now the bright-hair'd sun
Sits in yon western tent, whose cloudy skirts,
    With brede ethereal wove,
    O'erhang his wavy bed;

Now air is hush'd, save where the weak-eyed bat
With short shrill shriek flits by on leathern wing;
    Or where the beetle winds
    His small but sullen horn,

As oft he rises 'midst the twilight path,
Against the pilgrim borne in heedless hum;
   Now teach me, maid composed,
   To breathe some soften'd strain,

Whose numbers, stealing through thy darkening vale,
May not unseemly with its stillness suit;
   As, musing slow, I hail
   Thy genial lov'd return!

For when thy folding star arising shows
His paly circlet, at his warning lamp
   The fragrant Hours, and Elves
   Who slept in buds the day,

And many a Nymph who wreathes her brows with sedge,
And sheds the freshening dew, and, lovelier still,
   The pensive Pleasures sweet,
   Prepare thy shadowy car.

Then let me rove some wild and heathy scene;
Or find some ruin, 'midst its dreary dells,
   Whose walls more awful nod
   By thy religious gleams.

Or, if chill blustering winds, or driving rain,
Prevent my willing feet, be mine the hut,
   That from the mountain's side,
   Views wilds, and swelling floods,

And hamlets brown, and dim-discover'd spires;
And hears their simple bell, and marks o'er all
   Thy dewy fingers draw
   The gradual dusky veil.

While Spring shall pour his showers, as oft he wont,
And bathe thy breathing tresses, meekest Eve!
   While Summer loves to sport
   Beneath thy lingering light;

While sallow Autumn fills thy lap with leaves;
Or winter, yelling through the troublous air,
　　Affrights thy shrinking train,
　　And rudely rends thy robes;

So long, regardful of thy quiet rule,
Shall Fancy, Friendship, Science, smiling Peace,
　　Thy gentlest influence own,
　　And love thy favourite name! [8]

No comet this, flaming from a youthful, teeming brain, but a luminous shadow from a large soul. It is impossible to assign limits to poetic capabilities such as it indicates.

On students of literature coming suddenly, in the mid-eighteenth-century wilderness, upon the poetry of Collins, of whichever class, the effect is startling. The light of a star suddenly flashes upon them, and as suddenly goes out. His contemporaries, unless a few acquaintances like Samuel Johnson, and he but partially, could not see Heaven as it opened to him. They were as careless of one offer by him to labour for them as of another, of a History of the Revival of Learning, as of an Ode to the Passions. They let him, with the great songs he had sung, with the as great, if not greater, he might have sung, beat his starved wings against the cage bars of crass indifference—until the tragic end—a monomaniac moaning year after year up and down the cathedral cloisters of his birthplace.

The Poetical Works of William Collins (Aldine Edition of the British Poets). William Pickering, 1853.

[1] Ode on the Death of Thomson, vv. 13-16.

[2] Dirge in Cymbeline; Sung by Guiderus and Arviragus over Fidele, supposed to be dead, vv. 13-24.

[3] Ode to Fear, vv. 12-15.　　[4] Ode to Pity, vv. 1-2.
[5] Ode to Mercy, vv. 17-19.　　[6] The Passions, vv. 17-56.
[7] On our last Taste in Music, vv. 65-6.　　[8] Ode to Evening.

MARK AKENSIDE

1721—1770

A GHOST!

Who reads Pleasures of Imagination, Odes on Several Subjects, Hymn to the Naiads, Inscriptions? Who did not pretend to have studied them down to the middle of the nineteenth century? Mark Akenside came to London from the North a young medical student, without position or money, possessed of a single friend—a jewel—and of a manuscript poem. For the poem he asked £120 of astounded Dodsley, the publisher. Pope, dying, had approved; and positively he got his price. The Town welcomed the volume rapturously. Nobody, not even captious Tory Johnson, disputed its Whig author's claim to a place among the poets. For half a century his title to it was unanimously allowed. 'Great work', 'splendid production', are among the most moderate expressions of admiration lavished upon The Pleasures. His Odes were described so late as 1835, as 'a valuable accession to the lyric poetry of England'! Then gradually his works ceased to be of those with which the educated public is expected to be familiar. Many well-read persons would now confess without shame, if not boast, that they had never seen a line of them.

The saddest evidence of the decay of sensibility in the eighteenth century would be that it rejoiced at the advent of a versifier like Akenside but for one consideration. There is comfort at least in the evidence it affords that the period could not dispense with fresh supplies of poetry.

In its extremity, before Collins, Gray, Goldsmith, Cowper, had made themselves audible, it had to listen to Akenside. The poor thirsty age! It goes much against the grain with me to attribute his acceptance to the accident of such impoverishment, and deny personal merit to the man. That axiom of mine that the applause of educated contemporaries testifies to the existence of a justification for it, is thereby rudely overridden. But I have sought patiently, honestly, and in vain, for a real root of poetry here.

Occasionally I recognize melody in the Pleasures of Imagination ; the writer marshals his topics carefully ; and his reasoning in general is, though never subtle, judicious :

> The sweets of sense,
> Do they not oft with kind accession flow,
> To raise harmonious Fancy's native charm ?
> So while we taste the fragrance of the rose,
> Glows not her blush the fairer ? While we view
> Amid the noontide walk a limpid rill
> Gush through the trickling herbage, to the thirst
> Of summer yielding the delicious draught
> Of cool refreshment ; o'er the mossy brink
> Shines not the surface clearer, and the waves
> With sweeter music murmur as they flow ?[1]

Vigorous passages occur in the Odes ; and they contain some good descriptions of natural scenery. That to the Evening Star contributes several pretty stanzas to the vast Nightingale anthology ; as, for example :

> See the green space ; on either hand
>   Enlarg'd it spreads around ;
> See in the midst she takes her stand,
> Where one old oak his awful shade
> Extends o'er half the level mead
>   Inclos'd in woods profound.

> Hark, how through many a melting note
>   She now prolongs her lays;
> How sweetly down the void they float!
> The breeze their magic path attends;
> The stars shine out; the forest bends;
>   The wakeful heifers gaze.[2]

The address To the Country Gentlemen of England, in 1758, is spirited and picturesque, if not 'rising to a gnomic grandeur which cannot be surpassed'.[3] He can be righteously indignant at the barbarities of the Inquisition, even, it was reported, to British captives. His wrath at the Leader of the Opposition for presumed apostasy from the cause of freedom, though probably in the particular case without any proper foundation, appears to be sincere. The Hymn to the Naiads is illustrated agreeably from history, mythology, and nature itself. The Virtuoso—one with a most miscellaneous inquisitiveness—has genuine humour and variety.

> He many a creature did anatomize,
>   Almost unpeopling water, air, and land;
> Beasts, fishes, birds, snails, caterpillars, flies,
> Were laid full low by his relentless hand,
> That oft with gory crimson was distain'd:
>   He many a dog destroy'd, and many a cat;
> Of fleas his bed, of frogs the marshes drain'd,
>   Could tellen if a mite were lean or fat,
> And read a lecture o'er the entrails of a gnat.[4]

I recognize the graces of dignity and repose in the verses to Chaucer,

>   who, in times
> Dark and untaught, began with charming verse
> To tame the rudeness of his native land.[5]

Even though love's ardour is kept well under, I have read worse amatory songs than that to Arpasia.[6]

I can go so far in the way of commendation, without

straining my conscience; and the praise is the most damnatory of indictments. The just a spark here and there of fire, as when he gives voice to calumnies against weary Pulteney of treason to liberty for the poor bribe of an earldom, or to a silly legend, as of Jenkins's Ears, only throws into drearier relief the prevailing negation of poetic glow. One never falls into a rapture at images he has conjured up. Not a verse he ever wrote has the power of calling tears into the eyes. We experience no sense of mystery or magic as we read; no strange feeling of affinity between rhythm and thought, as if the one had naturally clothed itself with the other. The only discernible relationship of the two is that both are equally commonplace.

It is hard to restrain an emotion of resentment at the juvenile audacity which took Imagination for theme where none is forthcoming for its handling. Dexterity in reasoning is as absent as sweetness and sympathy. When an idea is touched, it quickly runs itself upon a sand bank. Frequently the sole result of an attempt at literary criticism is an exhibition of sheer ignorance, or of inability to distinguish contrary qualities. Thus Petrarch's Muse is travestied as 'wildly warbling';[7] while a poet, who was nothing if not artificial,

> Waller, longs,
> All on the margin of some flowery stream
> To spread his careless limbs amid the cool
> Of plantane shades, and to the listening deer
> The tale of slighted vows and love's disdain
> Resound soft-warbling all the livelong day.[8]

In the desperate struggle to make a point contrasts are alleged where no comparison is possible. How, for example, answer the ridiculous question:

> In Nature's fairest forms, is aught so fair
> As virtuous friendship?[9]

The rhetoric itself is so sluggish and trite that one is tempted to cry out for the false, turgid strength of Night Thoughts. Anything to stimulate, divert, interest! In search of an emotion I go yawning from Imagination to Inscription, from Inscription to Song, from Song to Ode, where

> Eurus waves his murky wings
> To damp the seats of life;[10]

or Cheerfulness, in intervals between listening to

> winter's voice, that storms around,
> And yon deep death-bell's groaning sound,

orders somebody to

> Haste, light the tapers, urge the fire,
> And bid the joyless day retire.[11]

Well might Horace Walpole rank Akenside among the 'tame geniuses'![12] Everywhere, whether Pindar or Pope be the model, we find the same dead level, the same didactic tedium. Not that to be didactic means of necessity to be dull. Lucretius, Virgil in the Georgics, Horace in the Epistles, the Essay on Man, The Traveller, The Task, The Pleasures of Memory, and of Hope, The Excursion, all are didactic, and poetry also. Still, it always is uphill work for a didactic poet; and what then must it have been for Akenside! Fancy in a red-heat may roll philosophy boiling along; or, under cover of it, the poet may play music of his own. Akenside's imagination could heat neither science nor itself. It is absolutely cold, absolutely uncreative. I pity the generation which crowned him, the generations upon which he was imposed as a poet. I pity them less than I pity himself. Rarely has there been a writer of an unhappier temperament, more continually jangling, alike with society, and with himself. He was angry with fate for having brought him into the world as a Dissenting butcher's son; which had provided neither rank, nor fortune, nor medical practice, and perhaps skill, sufficient to render him independent of Jeremiah Dyson's generosity. He was angry with his hospital patients, against whom, and their objectionable liability to infect their physician, he protected himself by a bodyguard of certificated convalescents. He was angry with his professional brethren, with the men of letters, and men of none, whom he met at coffee-houses. He was angry even with his poems, which he proceeded to re-write.

Therein at last I perceive some signs of grace. It is a horrid thing to have nightmare-ridden English poetry with shallow yet heavy versified treatises, with leaden Odes which will not burn, and object to being buried. But at all events, though he had originally the folly to believe himself a born poet, to whom the Muses

> In early days did to my wondering sense
> Their secrets oft reveal,[13]

he has a right to plead that he did not remain satisfied with his primary experiments as interpreter; that finally, in a fit of despair, I could suppose, at the discovery of his inability to coax the embers of sulky fancy into a flame, he declared, it is reported, poetry to be only 'eloquence in metre'![14] The fact that, so far from bettering his compositions by elaborate revision or reconstruction, he spoilt irretrievably the solitary exception to their pervading mediocrity, the Epistle to Curio, deepens my compassion for a poet manqué. Let any one who thinks such a measure of critical leniency parsimonious, do penance with me by reading for himself, and try to be as indulgent!

The Poetical Works of Mark Akenside (Aldine Edition of the British Poets). William Pickering, 1835.

[1] The Pleasures of Imagination, Book II, vv. 73-83.
[2] To the Evening Star (Odes on Several Subjects), Book I, Ode xv, stanzas 9-10.
[3] Life: by Alexander Dyce, p. xc.
[4] The Virtuoso—in imitation of Spenser's Style and Stanza, st. 2.
[5] Inscription for a Statue of Chaucer at Woodstock.
[6] Song.
[7] The Pleasures of Imagination, Book II, v. 20.
[8] Ibid., Book III, vv. 558-63.
[9] Ibid., Book I, vv. 503-4.
[10] Ode v, Against Suspicion, st. 6.
[11] Ode vi, To Cheerfulness, vv. 3-4 and 9-10.
[12] To Sir Horace Mann, March 29, 1745.
[13] Hymn to the Naiads, vv. 243-4.
[14] Mason: Memoirs of Gray, p. 261, edition 1775.

OLIVER GOLDSMITH

1728—1774

NATURE meant Goldsmith for a poet, and overdid her work. She gave a heart to sympathize with joy and sorrow, with every virtue and every weakness. To it she added a brain of versatility almost boundless, which, as Johnson has truly pronounced, could touch nothing without leaving a new beauty behind. She mixed sensibility to absurdities in others with insensibility to his own; a habit of impecuniosity with another of prodigality, in large doses; thirst for posthumous fame with a propensity for mortgaging it for present cash; rare delight in the exercise of heaven-born faculties with a less unusual appreciation of their market value; the dainty taste of a Gray with the indiscriminateness of a booksellers' hack. None of his gifts or foibles, except perhaps the last, were out of place in a poet. He himself always recognized the composition of poetry as his legitimate profession. But together they inclined to jostle him from its practice. With less wit and humour, less generosity and compassion, something less even of intelligence, he must have been more definitely a poet, and nothing else or lower.

He knew it himself, though ungrateful in imputing to poetry his poverty as well as his bliss. He had, as he was fully conscious, an ear exactly true for rhythm. His instinct discerned just what in a subject was poetical. His pen could paint a scene both delicately and broadly, with human life, its pleasures and troubles, to animate the landscape. A suggestion of heroism or tyranny roused in him a storm of enthusiasm or indignation. Wit, cutting like a razor, and leaving no poison or taint behind, worked in him in alliance with an insight into character of extraordinary subtlety. Between them they opened on an instant for posterity in Retaliation a gallery of etched portraits, in its own way incomparable. With such qualities, all was constantly being prepared to make him the poet of his age, and eliminate, perhaps, in consequence, from the museum of literature an adorable curiosity. Wreath after wreath was twined, when the laureate-elect was ever finding that he could not exist without a peach-coloured velvet coat, or that his ragged regiment of vagabond clients were without shoes to their feet. An over-ready brain wandered off to supply the double want; and the Muse had to plait another crown. The sole comfort is that, if poetry suffered a loss in quantity, there was none in quality. At it he always, or with one or two exceptions—a Threnodia Augustalis, or an equally worthless Oratorio—insisted upon working with no regard for pay. On his poems he bestowed his best of heart and head without question of the proportion of labour to its pecuniary value.

Fortunately for us; for it was at the high tide of his ascendancy with publishers, when histories, biographies, plays, moral essays, scientific treatises, and manuals poured from his complaisant fancy. Gold rained—at any rate, freely trickled—yet never filled his purse. While the thirst increased with the supply, he jealously held back one jewel of price for a couple of years' unwearied revision. In his poems literature is put off with no drudge's work, though his genius could illuminate penny-a-lining itself. The reward is that his verse remains eternally young. In the spirit it is true of all, even of The Traveller. I do not suppose that this, with its mannered eloquence, and rather insular patriotism, appeals as a whole to modern sympathies. But it contains many noble passages, though indeed the charm of the score or so of opening lines would itself have preserved a worse poem fresh and fragrant. No Johnsonian pomp clogs his thought of brother and home :

>Remote, unfriended, melancholy, slow,
>Or by the lazy Scheld, or wandering Po ;
>Or onward, where the rude Carinthian boor
>Against the houseless stranger shuts the door ;
>Or where Campania's plain forsaken lies,
>A weary waste expanding to the skies ;
>Where'er I roam, whatever realms to see,
>My heart untravell'd fondly turns to thee ;
>Still to my brother turns, with ceaseless pain,
>And drags at each remove a lengthening chain.
>Eternal blessings crown my earliest friend,
>And round his dwelling guardian saints attend ;
>Blest be that spot, where cheerful guests retire
>To pause from toil, and trim their evening fire ;
>Blest that abode, where want and pain repair,
>And every stranger finds a ready chair ;
>Blest be those feasts with simple plenty crown'd,
>Where all the ruddy family around
>Laugh at the jests or pranks that never fail,
>Or sigh with pity at some mournful tale ;
>Or press the bashful stranger to his food,
>And learn the luxury of doing good.[1]

For the second of the only two compositions of any length no qualification is needed. I cannot deny that, like The Traveller, it is weighted with a strong didactic element. The reasoning is not very cogent, and often is not very fair. But the whole is set in a framework of tender homeliness irresistibly captivating and absorbing. A reader forgets that verse is capable of anything beyond. English poetry may boast of much grander things than The Deserted

Village; of none better loved. Of the triumphs of verse I have been accustomed to say to myself that I do not understand whence they come. They are there; not more the birth of the singer's brain than of the reader's. That is direct and ordinary inspiration; and I must allow that, in its structure, The Deserted Village is not thus inspired. Absolutely nothing is in it which conceivably might not have been seen, known, heard, by the narrator, or by any other dweller in his birthplace. The representation is so complete, so manifestly precise, that it requires no painful effort of fancy to live in the scene. The reflections themselves are such as necessarily rise from the contrast between the happy past and its dreary ruins. Yet every reader is aware that, had he succeeded in identifying Auburn with Pallas, or with any other spot, he would have recognized in the reality a body without its soul. The disenchantment would be no fault of the poet. He delineated but what he saw, and intended to be a faithful copyist, a faithful moralist. Memory, if it played him false, had meant to be honest also. While it slept, native sweetness of heart had worked upon its canvas. Without a suspicion of the transfiguration, Goldsmith reproduced in verse the picture he saw. Amidst the toils, revelries, mortifications, and flatteries, debts and sickness, in wearing, tearing Fleet Street, the modest habitation of his childhood reappeared, true in all the outlines; only, with the angles softened, and the rude colours toned by a fond, sunny haze.

The vision is delightful, but never impossibly perfect:

    Sweet was the sound, when oft at evening's close
    Up yonder hill the village murmur rose;
    There as I past with careless steps and slow,
    The mingling notes came soften'd from below;
    The swain responsive as the milkmaid sung,
    The sober herd that low'd to meet their young;

> The noisy geese that gabbled o'er the pool,
> The playful children just let loose from school;
> The watch-dog's voice that bay'd the whispering wind,
> And the loud laugh that spoke the vacant mind;
> These all in sweet confusion sought the shade,
> And fill'd each pause the nightingale had made.[2]

To reward for the labours of the day, and provide for social converse, and the sessions of the rustic parliament, there was the house,

> where nut-brown draughts inspir'd,
> Where gray-beard mirth, and smiling toil retir'd,
> Where village statesmen talk'd with looks profound,
> And news much older than their ale went round.
> Imagination fondly stoops to trace
> The parlour splendours of that festive place;
> The whitewash'd wall, the nicely sanded floor,
> The varnish'd clock that click'd behind the door:
> The chest contriv'd a double debt to pay,
> A bed by night, a chest of drawers by day;
> The pictures plac'd for ornament and use,
> The twelve good rules, the royal game of goose;
> The hearth, except when winter chill'd the day,
> With aspen boughs, and flowers, and fennel gay;
> While broken teacups, wisely kept for show,
> Rang'd o'er the chimney, glisten'd in a row.[3]

Culture, not inadequately, was supplied by the school, with its master:

> A man severe he was, and stern to view;
> I knew him well, and every truant knew;
> Well had the boding tremblers learn'd to trace
> The day's disasters in his morning face;
> Full well they laughed with counterfeited glee
> At all his jokes, for many a joke had he;
> Full well the busy whisper, circling round,
> Convey'd the dismal tidings when he frown'd.
> Yet he was kind, or, if severe in aught,
> The love he bore to learning was in fault;

> The village all declar'd how much he knew;
> 'Twas certain he could write and cipher too;
> Lands he could measure, terms and tides presage,
> And e'en the story ran that he could gauge;
> In arguing too the parson own'd his skill,
> For e'en though vanquish'd he could argue still.[4]

And for souls—were they ever better nursed and cherished than by the village pastor?

> A man he was to all the country dear,
> And passing rich with forty pounds a year;
> Remote from towns he ran his godly race,
> Nor e'er had changed, nor wish'd to change his place.
> His house was known to all the vagrant train,
> He chid their wanderings, but reliev'd their pain.
> The long remember'd beggar was his guest,
> Whose beard descending swept his aged breast;
> The ruin'd spendthrift, now no longer proud,
> Claim'd kindred there, and had his claims allow'd;
> The broken soldier, kindly bade to stay,
> Sate by his fire, and talk'd the night away;
> Wept o'er his wounds, or tales of sorrow done,
> Shoulder'd his crutch, and show'd how fields were won.
> Pleas'd with his guests, the good man learn'd to glow,
> And quite forgot their vices in their woe;
> Careless their merits, or their faults to scan,
> His pity gave ere charity began.
> Thus to relieve the wretched was his pride,
> And e'en his failings lean'd to virtue's side;
> But in his duty prompt at every call,
> He watch'd and wept, he pray'd and felt for all.
> And, as a bird each fond endearment tries
> To tempt its new-fledg'd offspring to the skies,
> He tried each art, reprov'd each dull delay,
> Allur'd to brighter worlds, and led the way.[5]

It is bewitching scene-painting—an idyll conjured up out of the humblest materials by the deftest of fancies, and the kindest of hearts. I verily believe that it deceived its maker; that, in his beautiful simplicity, he actually had dreamt of retracing his steps to what he supposed was home ; and of finding a Paradise where he had left slovenly farm-land :

> In all my wanderings round this world of care,
> In all my griefs—and God has given my share—
> I still had hopes my latest hours to crown,
> Amidst these humble bowers to lay me down ;
> To husband out life's taper at the close,
> And keep the flame from wasting by repose ;
> I still had hopes, for pride attends us still,
> Amidst the swains to show my book-learn'd skill,
> Around my fire an evening group to draw,
> And tell of all I felt, and all I saw ;
> And as a hare, whom hounds and horns pursue,
> Pants to the place from whence at first he flew,
> I still had hopes, my long vexations past,
> Here to return—and die at home at last.[6]

The metamorphosis was the work of sympathetic imagination ; essentially as much an inspiration as an Ode by Collins or Gray. Whether it be a magical chorus of the Passions, a prophet-harper's wrathful panorama of history, or a

> Sweet, smiling village, loveliest of the lawn,

transplanted from Arcadia into Roscommon, or Longford, the whole is still the plaything of the same enchantress. But the order of procedure has varied, and the results likewise. Collins and Gray built their fairy palaces on the clouds. Goldsmith's always have the air of being founded on solid earth. His painting, gay or serious, is portraiture. He was the friend, son, or brother, of the preacher,

> to all the country dear.

He had sat in the alehouse. Doubtless well he had known the schoolmaster ; for

> every truant knew.

He was acquainted no less with the man so good, whom the dog, to gain some private ends, in a fit of madness imprudently bit. He had been among charitable Mrs. Mary Blaize's admirers. He had wept over the heart-break in Olivia's song. Probably he felt himself, before he had finished the pretty ballad, Angelina's Edwin.

That his vehicle of expression changed made little difference so far in the writer's spirit. As the charm of The Deserted Village is in the conviction that the writer saw it all as he rhymed, so it is with the Vicar in the perfect prose-poem. Always there is an inherent persuasion of good faith. The author expects his readers to believe nothing of which he has not first convinced himself. It was the secret of his almost suicidal successes as Prince of Grub Street. As I myself experienced when a child, it lent a nobility as of original research to a mere piece of bookmaking, which was my introduction to Roman History. It lighted the lamp which would hold him in the purest fiction of humorousness fluttering over the sepulchre of a dead joke. More even than his splendid genius—if the two can be separated—it endeared the charming, blundering egotist to a Johnson, a Burke, a Reynolds, and keeps him the friend of all who at any time have read one of his evergreen books.

The Poetical Works of Oliver Goldsmith (Aldine Edition of the British Poets). William Pickering, 1835.
[1] The Traveller. [2] The Deserted Village.
[3] Ibid. [4] Ibid.
[5] Ibid. [6] Ibid.

CHARLES CHURCHILL

1731—1764

An eminent instance of the not uncommon phenomenon in life, and especially in literature, of popularity quickly won, and as quickly lost. The world, from its own point of view, I do not suppose was wrong in either case. Churchill packed into the three years and a half of his poetical career enough to storm the interest of a single generation, and no more. In a play-going age the Rosciad was like a spark in a heap of shavings. His subsequent treatment of social and political scandals kept at fever-heat public curiosity about the self-unfrocked priest, the confidant and mouthpiece of Wilkes. He hated whatever and whoever happened to be the especial bugbear of the hour. Fiery revilings of Bute and Scottish office-mongers, Ministerial and Legislative usurpations, and the shamelessness of vice in high places were sure to be read. The fearlessness of his onslaughts, against a mitred Warburton, or a thinly disguised 'Lothario', the unbridled recklessness always of his rage, worked like a spell. Whether it were generous indignation at the vulgar grossness of eighteenth-century sensuality, spite at fate for having deferred for thirty poverty-stricken years his personal wallowing in its joys, or resentment of the reproaches of his conscience for present indulgence—perhaps exaggerated by scandal—or a medley of all three, mattered nothing. The doubts and the controversies about the private character of the executioner simply added a zest to coffee-house gossip as it diverted itself with the contortions of his victims.

Not that a tempest of vindictiveness against circumstances, despotism, imposture, effrontery, lust, fortune, and self, would have been sufficient to explain the fascination of public opinion, had there been nothing besides. Real greatness there was not. Such could not have sold itself for a mess of pottage, for the coarse tribute of a mob's wonder and applause. But, at the back of all, a particle of genius, not too pure to admit of base companionship, must have been present.

In his earliest publication he manifested, along with not a little brutality, some insight, and much epigrammatic smartness. He sums up admirably the respective merits of the two chief rival actors. There is Quin, too invariably himself for true impersonation ; ' happy in art ', and

        In all the labour'd artifice of speech ;

but apt to

        Neglect the heart to compliment the head ;

forgetful that :

      spite of all the criticizing elves,
Those who would make us feel, must feel themselves.
His eyes, in gloomy socket taught to roll,
Proclaim'd the sullen habit of his soul.
Heavy and phlegmatic he trod the stage,
Too proud for tenderness, too dull for rage.
When Hector's lovely widow shines in tears,
Or Rowe's gay rake dependent virtue jeers,
With the same cast of features he is seen
To chide the libertine, and court the queen.
From the tame scene, which without passion flows,
With just desert his reputation rose ;
Nor less he pleas'd, when, on some surly plan,
He was at once the actor, and the man.[1]

Between him and one in whom the characters were always united, real competition was impossible. Such was

Garrick; and to him Shakespeare as judge awards, of right, the succession to Roscius:

> 'If manly sense, if Nature link'd with Art;
> If thorough knowledge of the human heart;
> If pow'rs of acting vast and unconfin'd;
> If fewest faults with greatest beauties join'd;
> If strong expression, and strange pow'rs, which lie
> Within the magic circle of the eye;
> If feelings which few hearts, like his, can know,
> And which no face so well as his can shew;
> Deserve the pref'rence—Garrick, take the chair;
> Nor quit it—till thou place an equal there.' [2]

He was less judicial in his political satires, and far more violent; though occasionally there also he was right in his censures. Imagining himself a Sovereign, the Ruler of Gotham, in a spirit which has a show of nobility, notwithstanding the acrid innuendo at Bute and the Princess his Patroness, he prescribes and accepts the obligations of his Royalty:

> To prevent
> The course of justice from her fair intent,
> In vain my nearest, dearest friend shall plead,
> In vain my mother kneel—my soul may bleed,
> But must not change.—When Justice draws the dart,
> Tho' it is doom'd to pierce a favourite's heart,
> 'Tis mine to give it force, to give it aim—
> I know it duty, and I feel it Fame.[3]

Much more habitually he was satisfied to dispense with any pretence of argument, to wield no instruments of fancy but the bludgeon and the sledge-hammer. Passionateness is a primary attribute of poetry. A poet ought to have it at command. It was a quality of Churchill's; only it had him at command, not he it. He was perpetually in a passion, boiling over with it. The temper suited his readers who were eager for a summons to boil over in unison. His verses were battle-songs like Tyrtaeus's. Had they passed away like those with the struggles which gave them birth, the tradition of them might have preserved his memory fresh as Tyrtaeus's has been kept through a legend of fire in his melodies which extant fragments do not justify. It was Churchill's misfortune that productions naturally ephemeral should survive for posterity coldly to scrutinize, and wonder why the writer was extolled for matter stale and dead.

The measurement, indeed, whether of his influence, or of his fame, by a reference to posterity is, I am aware, far too complimentary to either. His writings were never anything but a display of fireworks. Their discharge had in his lifetime scared none from their lusts or knaveries. No Parliament or Prince was cured by his invectives of plotting against the liberty of the subject. His voice was not likely to be more effectively audible posthumously. Wilkes himself, whose name he was so sure that

> future ages shall adore,
> When he can act, and I can write no more,[4]

desired to forget the extravagances in which they had been allies. No friends of the Protestant Succession remembered to set in the scales against denunciations of the young king's early advisers the satirist's equally vehement indictment of the exiled Stuarts.[5] The curtain fell upon the whole stage of his glory or notoriety before admirers or enemies were really aware that he was dead. It was not necessary for the Muse of a contemporary versifier to goad herself into something a little beyond her customary gentle dullness in protest against the erection of a monument to him in Westminster Abbey.[6] He was all but forgotten before a sculptor could have carved the stone. He had chosen to be 'the comet of a day';[7] to hurry a life into three years; and his reputation was as casual and fleeting.

It surprises, though it should not, that he himself had cherished very different anticipations. Few estimates of posthumous renown read more pathetically than this penned by himself in the year he died:

> Let one poor sprig of bay around my head
> Bloom whilst I live, and point me out when dead;
> Let it—may Heav'n indulgent grant that pray'r—
> Be planted on my grave, nor wither there;
> And when, on travel bound, some rhyming guest
> Roams thro' the church-yard whilst his dinner's dress'd,
> Let it hold up this comment to his eyes;
> 'Life to the last enjoy'd, here Churchill lies';
> Whilst—O, what joy that pleasing flatt'ry gives—
> Reading my Works, he cries—'Here Churchill lives'. [8]

Alas for his memory, and his hope! Who reads those Works! Yet Nature meant their writer, if not for a Persius, or a Dryden, at all events for a Poet!

The Poems of Charles Churchill (Johnson's Poets, vols. lxvi and lxvii). London, 1790.

[1] The Rosciad. [2] Ibid.
[3] Gotham, Book III.
[4] The Candidate.
[5] Gotham.
[6] Beattie's Poems. Report of a monument to be erected.
[7] Byron: Churchill's Grave (1816). Occasional Pieces.
[8] The Candidate.

WILLIAM COWPER

1731—1800

The general impression of Cowper as a serious and secular poet is, I should say, that of an early autumn afternoon; soft, hazy, tempered sunshine, hinted tints, half-lights, sombre stillness; nothing of stormy passionateness, or the summer solstice.

Read, and a very different being presents himself. At the thought of ambitious potentates desolating eighteenth-century Europe a torrent of anger, red-hot lava, rushes forth. He sees in subject nations a scattered flock, and in a martial King,

> Some royal mastiff panting at their heels,
> With all the savage thirst a tiger feels.[1]

He has none of Carlyle's admiration for the War-Lord,

> self-proclaim'd in a gazette
> Chief monster that has plagued the nations yet.[2]

His wrath burns as fiercely against civil tyranny. He hopes against hope, not forecasting a near future, to hear of the fall of the Bastille:

> Ye horrid towers, the abode of broken hearts,
> Ye dungeons, and ye cages of despair,
> That monarchs have supplied from age to age
> With music, such as suits their sovereign ears.[3]

If other States have earned reprobation, much more has his own 'far guiltier England' with her exceptional opportunities.[4] He condemns the sinful luxury of the rich, the intolerance to a Saint like Whitefield, the toleration of a priesthood like Baal's, and a Petronius-Chesterfield:

> Graybeard corrupter of our listening youth;[5]

the deafness of parochial officials to suppliants, who

> ask with painful shyness, and refused
> Because deserving, silently retire ; [6]

and their indulgence to the lazy sot who drinks away his children's food :

> O for a law to noose the villain's neck ! [7]

Wilberforce never rose to his passion of self-sacrifice against negro bondage :

> I had much rather be myself the slave,
> And wear the bonds than fasten them on him ! [8]

Not permitted thus to sacrifice himself—unable by act or word to redress the cruel, inhuman wrongs suffered by man at the hands of man, he would fain bury himself in a hermitage :

> Oh for a lodge in some vast wilderness,
> Some boundless contiguity of shade,
> Where rumour of oppression and deceit,
> Of unsuccessful or successful war,
> Might never reach me more ! [9]

Seldom has there been a more vehement, even a more vindictive, satirist. Only, the anger never had aught in it of selfishness, aught of a personal element. That he reserved for the stabbing of his own innocent heart.

He was incapable of malignity ; not of malice. A spice of that is inseparable from wit and humour ; and he possessed both. Tithing time, Nose v. Eyes, the dilemma of casuistical Tom, the Colubriad, not to speak of immortal John Gilpin, are proof demonstrative. To wing his pleasant arrows he had an unfailing neatness of diction. He was not at his best in dealing with the dignity of Milton's Latin, or Madame Guyon's French ; and he failed to represent either the liquid sweetness, or the rush, of Homer ; but, in general, his gift for thinking into English an ancient author, or making his author by anticipation think him, must be acknowledged to be wonderful. He was especially happy in his versions of Vincent Bourne, who might almost have envied the Classical crispness, though in English, of his disciple's complaint by the poor goldfinch against its barbarous jailer, that

>Caught and caged, and starved to death,
>In dying sighs my little breath
>Soon pass'd the wiry grate.[10]

Greek epigrams in particular attracted him, from recollections, in a mellowing afterglow, of old Westminster days. He rendered many into admirable English. Apart from the accident of acquaintance with the fact, it would be difficult, for instance, to decide whether the Cricket and Grasshopper lyrics were originals or not. The grasshopper's joyous carol, in which Cowper vied with Cowley's delightful paraphrase, is like a bird's singing :

>Earth-born, bloodless, undecaying,
>Ever singing, sporting, playing,
>What has nature else to show
>Godlike in its kind as thou ?[11]

He had, indeed, in such things the ease and facility of Matthew Prior to a degree which actually involves his literary rank ; for Prior's claim to be a poet, as resting on them, has been questioned ; can Cowper's be? There have been times when I doubted, when I have felt that he was not inspired, but heard the wind of inspiration rushing by him. There are times, on the other hand, when I have been unwilling to assign him a place below the highest. He could be desperately prosaic ; and often, when in earnest, most of all. His half-dozen sets of verses on the Northampton yearly bills of mortality might have been penned by the parish clerk, who, I hope, signed them. The sixty-six

Hymns are as sterile as even hymns are licensed to be, with the exception of the famous eighteenth, the work of a poet:

> Can a woman's tender care
> Cease towards the child she bare?
> Yes, she may forgetful be,
> Yet will I remember thee.[12]

Not rarely he is distressingly pointless in his orthodoxy, as in the tale of Misagathus. Sometimes his fanaticism, to the verge of sheer stolidity, in tilting against scientific progress, is such as, had he foreseen the grandson, might have cost the author of The Botanic Garden his panegyric.

Then suddenly the clouds break, and the Heavens open!

At his mild call everyday scenes and circumstances discover an intimate charm. Never poet before him—Thomson not excepted—had watched skies, woods, fields, and streams, and the life in them, so sympathetically. In company with Spenser, and more consistently, he was aware of the sex of the songster nightingale. From his pen the Ouse flows before our eyes through a variegated landscape of meads, groves, heaths, spires, and villages, to the music of mighty winds. What a lulling requiem he can sing over trees he loved:

> The poplars are fell'd, farewell to the shade,
> And the whispering sound of the cool colonnade![13]

He approaches sublimity, a sublime simplicity, in the Loss of the Royal George.

> Toll for the brave!
>   The brave that are no more!
> All sunk beneath the wave,
>   Fast by their native shore!
>   . . . . .
> Her timbers yet are sound,
>   And she may float again
> Full charged with England's thunder,
>   And plough the distant main.

> But Kempenfelt is gone;
> His victories are o'er;
> And he and his eight hundred
> Shall plough the wave no more.[14]

Never has ship—not even the Revenge—had a longer-echoing knell rung for her. In his Mother's Picture he pierces to a spring of tender regret deeper than tears. His farewell to dying Mary Unwin is an agony of affection—almost, remorse:

> The twentieth year is well nigh past
> Since first our sky was overcast;
> Ah would that this might be the last!
> My Mary!
>
> Thy spirits have a fainter flow,
> I see thee daily weaker grow—
> 'Twas my distress that brought thee low,
> My Mary!
>
> Thy indistinct expressions seem
> Like language utter'd in a dream;
> Yet me they charm, whate'er the theme,
> My Mary!
>
> Thy silver locks, once auburn bright,
> Are still more lovely in my sight
> Than golden beams of orient light,
> My Mary!
>
> Such feebleness of limbs thou provest,
> That now at every step thou movest
> Upheld by two; yet still thou lovest,
> My Mary!
>
> And still to love, though press'd with ill,
> In wintry age to feel no chill,
> With me is to be lovely still,
> My Mary!
>
> But ah! by constant heed I know,
> How oft the sadness that I show
> Transforms thy smiles to looks of woe,
> My Mary!

> And should my future lot be cast
> With much resemblance of the past,
> Thy worn-out heart will break at last,
> My Mary! [15]

None but a master hand could have painted the penury of a brave peasant's cottage in hard midwinter:

> Warm'd, while it lasts, by labour, all day long
> They brave the season, and yet find at eve,
> Ill clad, and fed but sparely, time to cool.
> The frugal housewife trembles when she lights
> Her scanty stock of brushwood, blazing clear,
> But dying soon, like all terrestrial joys.
> The few small embers left she nurses well;
> And, while her infant race, with outspread hands,
> And crowded knees, sit cowering o'er the sparks,
> Retires, content to quake, so they be warm'd.
> The taper soon extinguish'd, which I saw
> Dangled along at the cold finger's end
> Just when the day declined; and the brown loaf
> Lodged on the shelf, half eaten without sauce
> Of savoury cheese, or butter, costlier still;
> Sleep seems their only refuge; for, alas,
> Where penury is felt the thought is changed,
> And sweet colloquial pleasures are but few!
> With all this thrift they thrive not. All the care
> Ingenious Parsimony takes, but just
> Saves the small inventory, bed, and stool,
> Skillet, and old carved chest, from public sale.
> They live, and live without extorted alms
> From grudging hands; but other boast have none
> To soothe their honest pride, that scorns to beg,
> Nor comfort else, but in their mutual love. [16]

Though a grim picture—how steeped in tenderness! But a reader new to Cowper must not expect to find in his peasants the happy villagers of sunny Auburn. Life is hard to them. The compensatory rays of patience, honesty, dignity, self-sacrifice, have to struggle, few and far between, through gross clouds, themselves of human origin ; for Cowper saw man very hard to man.

If we wish for fullness of beauty, as visible to his eyes, we have to follow him to his solitude—to Nature, and Nature's God :

      One spirit, His
Who wore the platted thorns with bleeding brows,
Rules universal nature. Not a flower
But shows some touch, in freckle, streak, or stain,
Of His unrival'd pencil. He inspires
Their balmy odours, and imparts their hues,
And bathes their eyes with nectar, and includes,
In grains as countless as the seaside sands,
The forms with which He sprinkles all the earth.[17]

The poet rejoices with the Maker. It is for him, pacing the woodlands, an act of worship to note, and marvel at, the feast of colour as each wild bloom emerges in its hour.[18] Each successive season has its several beauties, and high thoughts, and companionships, for him—just for him :

  E'en in the spring and playtime of the year,
  That calls the unwonted villager abroad
  With all her little ones, a sportive train,
  To gather kingcups in the yellow mead,
  These shades are all my own. The timorous hare,
  Grown so familiar with her frequent guest,
  Scarce shuns me ; and the stockdove unalarm'd
  Sits cooing in the pine tree, nor suspends
  His long love-ditty for my near approach.
  Drawn from his refuge in some lonely elm,
  That age or injury has hollow'd deep,
  Where, on his bed of wool and matted leaves,
  He has outslept the winter, ventures forth
  To frisk awhile, and bask in the warm sun,
  The squirrel, flippant, pert, and full of play ;
  He sees me, and at once, swift as a bird,

> Ascends the neighbouring beech; there whisks his brush,
> And perks his ears, and stamps, and cries aloud,
> With all the prettiness of feign'd alarm,
> And anger insignificantly fierce.[19]

In winter, so long as his narrow circle does not widen, perhaps he joys most of all. The chilly Power warms and kindles at his neighbourly touch. Abroad it has many a charm, and still more within:

> I love thee, all unlovely as thou seemst;
> I crown thee king of intimate delights,
> Fireside enjoyments, home-born happiness.
> Now stir the fire, and close the shutters fast,
> Let fall the curtains, wheel the sofa round,
> And while the bubbling and loud hissing urn
> Throws up a steamy column, and the cups,
> That cheer but not inebriate, wait on each,
> So let us welcome peaceful evening in.[20]

His it was, and ours, through him, it is, to evoke the beauty innate in the most modest materials, when the soul informs the eyes; to obey a universal summons to be gay:

> An ecstasy too big to be suppressed.

The delight in dancing to his exulting music is not the less vivid that all the time we feel a conflict is proceeding in him between his instinct of pious orderliness, and a rapture of the free wilderness. While condemning, he is admiring, perhaps envying, even the gipsy vagrants, as they frolic in the intervals between their mendicant whinings:

> Such health and gaiety of heart enjoy
> The houseless rovers of the sylvan world![21]

Verse so steeped in the spirit of nature would be enough by itself to establish his poetic title. It permits, even compels, us to admire, without regard to carping criticisms upon his Alexander Selkirk, Rose, and Boadicea, though something might be said too for these friends of our childhood. But the English people, more than the critics— even when poets,—settled the question long since. It adopted Cowper, and his moods, his phrases, his thoughts.

Never poet less with intention than he stormed the citadel of Parnassus. As a man he had long been dead to society. He came back to life as a poet. With an infusion of arrogance he might possibly have been more continuously admirable; for pride would have saved him from being slovenly, as he often was. But he would not have been the Cowper that a race has taken to its heart. Not till the age of forty-nine did he become, or, rather, was made, conscious that he could write. When already his gift was recognized in the world, he had difficulty in recognizing it himself. Thenceforward, while a hypochondriac always, a lost sinner by profession, ever and anon mad, he produced volume after volume. He sang, now, as commissioned from on High, now, with the careless gaiety of a Charles Lamb, his analogue in humour and half in fate. Meanwhile, it remained his abiding creed that Hell waited yawning for him. Very gradually his countrymen had accepted the new poet; and with the poet they accepted the man. They learned to dwell with affection on the

> stricken deer, that left the herd
> Long since; with many an arrow deep infix'd
> My panting side was charged, when I withdrew,
> To seek a tranquil death in distant shades.[22]

Some authors become friends of their readers—incorporate in them—even more than teachers and guides. That has been Cowper's lot. We could spare far less impatiently divers self-assertive and tempestuous bards from the magic circle of our poets than the true eye for a landscape, the wise simplicity, the panorama, narrow, and narrowed, as was its area, of human life, the cropped water-lilies on creeping Ouse, the hares, the gentle moralizing over a superabundantly watered rose, of William Cowper.

The Poetical Works of William Cowper (Aldine Edition of the British Poets). Three vols. William Pickering, 1830.

[1] Table-Talk.   [2] Ibid.
[3] The Task, Book V.
[4] Ibid., Book II, The Time-piece.
[5] The Progress of Error.
[6] The Task, Book IV, The Winter Evening.
[7] Ibid.   [8] Ibid., Book II, The Time-piece.   [9] Ibid.
[10] On a Goldfinch starved to Death in his Cage, st. 2.
[11] On the Grasshopper (Translations of Greek Verses).
[12] Hymns, XVIII.   [13] The Poplar Field.
[14] On the Loss of the Royal George, Sept. 1782.
[15] To Mary, stanzas 1, 2, 6, 7, 10, 11, 12, 13.
[16] The Task, Book IV, The Winter Evening.
[17] Ibid., Book VI, The Winter Walk at Noon.
[18] Ibid.   [19] Ibid.
[20] Ibid., Book IV, The Winter Evening.
[21] Ibid., Book I, The Sofa.
[22] Ibid., Book III, The Garden.

JAMES BEATTIE

1735—1803

Any one who wishes to have a favourable opinion of Beattie had better read the ninth, thirty-eighth, and thirty-ninth stanzas in the first Book of The Minstrel, and the seventeenth and eighteenth in the second; in The Hermit the first and fourth; the fifty-third in the aptly-christened Triumph of Melancholy; and the seventh in Retirement. If it be not indiscreet to interfere between a parent and his literary offspring, I should further recommend the fifteenth to twentieth, describing the apparition of the three goddesses to the shepherd Prince, in The Judgement of Paris, which the decorous author discarded from later collected editions. Outside the domain of pure poetry there might be added a couple of fables, The Hares and The Wolf, sufficiently agreeable to excuse a regret that others in the same easy vein were not written; a pleasant translation from Addison's Greek of the Battle of the Pigmies and Cranes; and, for tougher digestions, a spirited, if not very chivalrous, protest against a proposed monument to Churchill in Poets' Corner.[1]

My selection comprises, I sincerely believe, the whole flower of Beattie's poetical work. What then? The fragments may be admitted to possess merit adequate to the justification of their own existence as verse. The question is how far their worth stretches to establish their author's claim to inspiration. That they are, in quality, exceptions, not samples, is not conclusive against it. It is as immaterial that, with the omission of the fables, and translation, the total, eighty-nine lines, bears an insignificant proportion to the residuary fifteen hundred and sixty-three. Had the eighty-nine evinced among them symptoms of greatness, lack of bulk would have been readily condoned. The narrowness of the margin by which they prove their own title is fatal to the writer's. It is an insuperable impediment to an individual's entrance into the poetical hierarchy that, with varieties in degree, good and indifferent among an aspirant's verses belong essentially to the same class. From the one piece by which Beattie himself was prepared to stand or fall—the minstrel without a harp, the metre without the fairy Queen—down to The Triumph of Melancholy, all alike suffer from the incurable taint of mediocrity.

A true poet is liable to episodes of disastrous failure; he will never rest complacently at a dead level of mere respectability. Mediocrity for poetry, if not for other things, means absence of the breath of life. For a poem to deserve the name it is indispensable that it should have a life of its own. It must be capable of doing and suffering, and of multiplying itself in thought and spirit. The marvel is that, when an age has provided store, never a superabundance, of genuine poetry fulfilling the conditions, counterfeits with no vitality, or none which outlasts a day, have continually been planted upon its patient public. Society in 1771 still was served by Gray, Goldsmith, Cowper. It was beginning to recollect that it might have had Collins. Nevertheless, as it had been deceived, or had deceived itself, when at the Restoration it admired Davenant and Denham, and, under George the Second, Akenside, so, in the following reign, it cheated itself more flagrantly into imagining inspiration, which had never been there, in the most innocent of impostors, the virtuous, learned, intelligent, and sympathetic Beattie.

I think no lover of poetry can now read through the volume of Beattie's verse, and assert that the man able to produce no better than its best was, if a poet at all, more than a confirmed minor one.

Let him read, or re-read, the description in The Minstrel of opening day. It has always pleased me:

> But who the melodies of morn can tell?
> The wild brook babbling down the mountain side;
> The lowing herd; the sheepfold's simple bell;
> The pipe of early shepherd dim descried
> In the lone valley; echoing far and wide
> The clamorous horn along the cliffs above;
> The hollow murmur of the ocean-tide;
> The hum of bees, the linnet's lay of love,
> And the full choir that wakes the universal grove.
> The cottage curs at early pilgrim bark;
> Crown'd with her pail the tripping milk-maid sings;
> The whistling plough-man stalks afield; and, hark!
> Down the rough slope the ponderous waggon rings;
> Thro' rustling corn the hare astonish'd springs;
> Slow tolls the village clock the drowsy hour;
> The partridge bursts away on whirring wings;
> Deep mourns the turtle in sequester'd bower,
> And shrill lark carols clear from her aerial tour.[2]

A greater writer might easily have composed, without a permanent slur on his dignity, much less agreeable lines than these—much less melodious—less a succession of delightful scenes. Only when uninspired could he have compiled and shot out upon literature a miscellany of rustic facts for his readers to bind together, or not, without one illuminating thought.

Again, The Hermit—how soft the cadences; how soothing it all is; and how absolutely unideaed! A philosopher, a Wordsworthian Solitary—and with nothing to show for it but petty, painless musings, welling up from quite fathomable depths, and rippling across the surface, on Nature's unconcern at the mutability of all things human! So valuable a being as a Sage need not have risked bronchitis by venting on his symphonious harp outside a cave soliloquies not in the least above ordinary drawing-room pitch:

> At the close of the day, when the hamlet is still,
> And mortals the sweets of forgetfulness prove,
> When nought but the torrent is heard on the hill,
> And nought but the nightingale's song in the grove;
> 'Twas thus, by the cave of the mountain afar,
> While his harp rung symphonious, a hermit began;
> No more with himself or with nature at war,
> He thought as a sage, though he felt as a man.
>
> '' 'Tis night, and the landscape is lovely no more;
> I mourn, but, ye woodlands, I mourn not for you;
> For morn is approaching, your charms to restore,
> Perfum'd with fresh fragrance, and glittering with dew;
> Nor yet for the ravage of winter I mourn;
> Kind Nature the embryo blossom will save;
> But when shall spring visit the mouldering urn!
> Or when shall it dawn on the night of the grave!' [3]

Once or twice, scarcely oftener, a fine image sets the sensibilities pulsating: for instance in The Triumph of Melancholy:

> The traveller thus, that o'er the midnight waste
>   Through many a lonesome path is doom'd to roam,
> Wilder'd and weary sits him down at last;
>   For long the night, and distant far his home.[4]

Unfortunately it is the closing stanza of fifty-three, otherwise excruciatingly tedious. Similarly, but as disappointingly, a passing illustration will start a hope of power in reserve; as when, at the tread of human footsteps on the beetling cliff, with its solitary pine:

> the scar'd owl on pinions gray
> Breaks from the rustling boughs,
> And down the lone vale sails away
> To more profound repose.[5]

A casual, benevolent doubt will intermittently arise whether the frequent catalogues of scenic amenities and upholsteries, with their pretty prattle, may not, after all, have been compiled by an owner, instead of a house-agent; by a creative fancy, not out of reminiscences of school classics. All such kindly illusions speedily die, however, under an overwhelming sense of a dearth of spiritual emotion, of the rapture which poets feel. Reason and information, nothing else, have clearly been exerting their utmost energy. We seem to surprise a smirk upon the versifier's face; an assurance to himself that his labours and lamp-oil have not been wasted, that the products are being wheeled fast up Parnassus. Somehow, I dare say, he had caught a distant view of the peak. He may have honestly supposed that he and his were scaling the giddy heights, when in reality an impassable abyss yawned between.

Not that he was alone in his misconception. Whether for good or ill, he appears not to have been blinder than his contemporaries. They accepted him at an estimate even more flattering than his own. Gray and Goldsmith had scarcely been more praised for the Elegy and the Deserted Village, and Collins far less for the Passions. Johnson's churlish correctness of literary instinct softened or slept in favour of a Scottish Presbyterian Professor! A supreme arbitress of taste courted him for her salon. A peer of intellect and refinement, Lyttelton, fell into ecstasies over strains which he described as angelic. How explain the general outburst of panegyric in consistency either with common sense, or with common conscience?

A prejudice for verse by the author of the Essay on Truth, now also forgotten, may have contributed to its popularity with the orthodox. A public, too, a little weary of the school of Pope, probably was beguiled by the assumption of familiarity with unsophisticated nature, which a born and bred countryman, as was Beattie, might have had, but does not show. At any rate, not the most timorous instructress of youth could doubt the absolute innocence of such an exercise of the gift of fancy. That, indeed, must be the real clue to the oddity of a mere versifier's acceptance as a classic. The Minstrel and The Hermit kept favour for half a century or longer through their negative, rather than their positive, characteristics. It was something, while a Churchill, and soon a Burns, were running rampant in metre, to have at call this self-satisfied, moral minstrel of the North Countrie, who chases rainbows as if they were butterflies. The Twa Corbies would have picked little marrow from the poetic cells of his brain, but also not a particle of indecorum.

My copy of the Aldine Beattie seems to have been presented to a boarding-school young lady for 'uniform good conduct' fifty years ago. No more eloquent testimony could be found to the docility in modern antiquity of the juvenile feminine intelligence, or, at all events, of its professional guides. Yet their literary standard itself was merely a survival from that of the average well-conducted family circle in the early days of George the Third. As my imagination recalls the period, I am disposed to temper my judgement of this its typical poet both for good and for ill. While I have been deriding his verse I have admired the valour of the man in proclaiming himself inspired on credentials so equivocal. When I conjure up his period before my mind the lustre of heroic audacity fades from off his enterprise. I can hear Miss Burney's Princesses reading aloud The Minstrel, and their Royal parents in full faith applauding its respectable bald platitudes. Its ready acceptance is pitiable in the land of Shakespeare, Milton, Dryden, Pope. At the same time, in view of the tendency of the age, I cease to be surprised. The period was one of a meeting of the ways. Below a surface of decorum and system, an underworld was murmuring, sneering, questioning, growling, dreaming. Poetical passion alarmed the classes in possession. If people must feel thirst, they could not take a milder draught than was supplied by Beattie's blend of douce Presbyterianism with a dash of tempered Scottish metaphysics. His enthusiasm never exceeded the modest level to which the important middle-class sentiment of his public, whether behind a counter, or in a Palace, could attain. It flowed in a stream clear, if thin. The entire beverage he provided could be warranted absolutely unalcoholic!

The Poetical Works of James Beattie (Aldine Edition of the British Poets). William Pickering, 1831.
[1] On the Report of a Monument to be erected in Westminster Abbey, to the memory of a late Author.
[2] The Minstrel; or, The Progress of Genius, Canto i, stanzas 38-39.
[3] The Hermit, stanzas 1 and 4.
[4] The Triumph of Melancholy, st. 53.
[5] Retirement, st. 7.

THOMAS CHATTERTON

1752—1770

PUT it how you will; either, one year and a half spent on fair Plantagenet imaginings, and four months on grimy Georgian actualities; then a draught of poison, and a pauper's grave in Shoe Lane; or, a whole life—of brief babyhood, hard studying, musing, writing, forging, and heart-gnawing—comprised in seventeen years and three-quarters. Other poets have known grinding poverty, but not a poverty which denied them all sympathy, all recognition. Others have died before old or middle age, but not in boyhood. Where there has been youth, though not green as his, literature can point to promise, scarcely to performance. Chatterton was formed to be great, and executed greatly; writings of his are monumental. The mere vehicle of his thoughts is a wonder. Spenser was remarkable for reverting in language, not very learnedly, a century or less. Chatterton handled a diction three centuries old, if not accurately, or consistently, as fluently as if it had been his birthright. Altogether history may suggest comparisons; it can offer no adequate parallel.

Admirers of precocious genius are not always as jealous as they ought to be of allusions to age. I am, on Chatterton's behalf. I do not deny that the works imputed by him to Thomas Rowley, priest, and William Canynge's friend, vary in merit, and, it may be, with the years of their author. The difference is in degree, not in spirit. All are interesting; and few are wanting in formed poetic feeling. The Moral of Our Ladies Chyrche can never grow old. The Balade of Charitie could fitly have been recited to the Pilgrims by Chaucer's Parson, though the Samaritan's part would not have been assigned to a Limitoure :

We are Goddes stewards all, nete of oure owne we bare.[1]

There would, with allowance, as always, made for occasional anachronisms, have been no glaring incongruity in the production by a real Rowley of The Parlyamente of Sprytes for the glorifying of a real Canynge and his grand new Church of St. Mary of Redcliffe. The Tournament is rich throughout in mediaeval colour and picturesqueness ; and it contains fine poetic passages ; for instance, the minstrel's song of the royal hunt.[2] The whole conception of the dialogue between Elinoure and Juga, awaiting the issue of the bloody Battle of St. Albans—sure, each, that one or other, Yorkist or Lancastrian, would be a mourner for her knight and lover—is full of pathos, with its heart-breaking climax :

Theie moved gentle oere the dewie mees
To where Seyncte Albon's holie shrynes remayne.
There dyd theye fynde that bothe their knyghtes were slayne.[3]

In Goddwyn, the noble prelude to the two spirited but youthfully gory versions of the Battle of Hastings, a lad's imagination has succeeded in voicing the accumulated indignation of a couple of centuries against Norman usurpation. At the close it bursts into a cry of Freedom—alas ! a torso—such as no contemporary of his but Gray could have surpassed. I have ventured to brush off, except here and there, the imputed rust, or patina,—for the most part, mere spelling—of antiquity :

When Freedom, dressed in blood-stained vest,
  To every knight her war-song sung,
Upon her head wild weeds were spread ;
  A gory falchion by her hung.
    She danced on the heath ;
    She heard the voice of death ;

Pale-eyed Affright, his heart of silver hue,
All vainly strove her bosom to congeal;
Fearless she heard unmoved the shrieking voice of woe,
And th' owlet's mournful hooting in the dale.
    She shook the pointed spear,
    On high she raised her shield.
    Her foemen all have fear,
    And flee along the field.
Force, with his head stretched forth into the skies,
His spear a sunbeam, and his shield a star,
Like to two flaming meteors rolls his eyes,
Stamps with his iron feet, and sounds to war.
    She sits upon a rock,
    She bends before his spear,
    She rises from the shock,
    Wielding her own in air.
Hard as the thunder doth she drive it on,
Craft closely hidden guides it to his crown—
His long sharp spear, his spreading shield is gone.
He falls, and falling rolleth thousands down.[4]

Rowley is made by his audacious creator to say:

Vearse maie be goode, botte poesie wantes more.[5]

Had we received nothing more from him than Freedom's battle-cry, he would have been entitled to rank above mere versifiers. But, over and above all else, there is Ælla, drama and epic in one; and by that he may claim to be finally judged.

Many keys are touched in it, and all with the hand of a master. There is the love of Bristowe's lord for Birtha, with their marriage. On their wedding night an entreaty comes from Wedecesterre for succour from a Danish foray led by Magnus and Hurra. The Chief tears himself from his bride, and fights, and conquers, at the cost of a wound. Celmonde, an old lover of Birtha, brings false news that he is dying, and would bid her adieu. Telling none of her departure she instantly accompanies him. On their way he seeks to ravish her. She is rescued, and he slain, by a body of Danes escaped under the leadership of Hurra from the fatal field. In requital for the remembered magnanimity of Ælla, who once before had vanquished, captured, and spared them, they conduct her to Bristowe. Meanwhile, Ælla, disdaining his hurt, and impatient to rejoin her, had returned thither, to be overwhelmed by the tidings that she had fled. Believing her faithless, he stabs himself, living just long enough to discover, on her arrival with the Danes, her innocence, and to die happy in her loyal love.

Seldom has suitor exaggerated with a finer grace than Ælla in his wooing:

> Layde the whol worlde a falldstole atte thie feete,
> One smyle would be suffycyll mede for mee.[6]

As seldom has the agony of parting of bride and bridegroom been more tenderly described—the struggle between fondness and a Chieftain's sense of duty to his people bleeding from a

> scolle of locusts caste oppe bie the sea.[7]

Sublimity and pathos interchange and blend throughout. The bitterness to the Saxon champion is sharpened by the young wife's inability to reconcile herself. He pleads the imperative call of honour:

> My country waits my march: I must away;
> Albeit I should go to meet the dart
> Of certain death, yet here I would not stay.
> My torturing pain cannot be told by tongue.
> Rouse then thy courage up, and hope the day
> When round about they sing the victor's song.
> O Birtha, strive my misery to allay,
> And joyous see my arms dight out in war's array.

For a moment his Birtha resigns herself. She feels herself a warrior's consort :

> Difficult is the penance, yet I'll strive
> To keep my woe deep hidden in my breast,
> Though nothing can to me a pleasure give,
> Like thee, I'll strive to set my mind at rest.
> And oh ! forgive, if I have thee distressed !
> Love, jealous love, will bear no other's sway.
> Just as I was with Ælla to be blest,
> Fate foully thus is snatching him away.
> It was an ache too mastering to be borne,
> Without a flood of tears, and breast with sighing torn.

Then again the grief overpowers. She appeals against his care for honour above love. In vain ; he bids a last adieu :

> I may not here abide ;
> I fly myself in flying from thy side.

And she, in agony :

> O Ælla, friend, and lord, and husband, stay !—
> He's gone, he's gone ; alas ! what if he's gone for aye ! [8]

A willow song, with its keynote from Shakespeare who himself had adapted it, at once foreshadows, and sweetens the doom impending over them and their brief wedded love :

> O ! sing unto my roundelay,
> O ! drop the briny tear with me,
> Dance no more at holiday,
> Like a running river be ;
>   My love is dead,
>   Gone to his death-bed,
>   All under the willow tree.

> Black eyes as the winter night,
> White his neck as the summer snow,
> Ruddy his face as the morning light,
> Cold he lies in the grave below.
>   My love is dead.

Sweet his tongue as the throstle's note,
Quick in dance as thought can be,
Deft his tabor, cudgel stout,
O! he lies by the willow tree;
   My love is dead.

Hark! the raven flaps his wing,
In the briered dell below;
Hark! the death-owl loud doth sing,
To the night-hags as they go;
   My love is dead,
   Gone to his death-bed,
   All under the willow tree.[9]

Even in death Ælla's spirit is dominant in Bristol. Rowley appeals to it to continue to be the city's tutelary genius; as

When Dacia's sons, whose hair of blood-red hue,
Like king-cups bursting with the morning dew,
   All ranged in dread array
   Upon the deadly day,
Spread far and wide on Watchet's shore,
   Then didst thou furious stand,
   And by thy valiant hand,
Besprinkledst all the mead with gore.

   Dragged by thy falchion fell,
   Down to the depth of hell
   Thousands of Dacians sped;
   Bristowans, men of might,
   They dared the bloody fight,
   And wrought their deeds of dread.

Oh thou where'er—thy bones at rest—
Thy spirit to haunt delighteth best,
Whether upon the blood-imbruèd plain,
   Or where thou ken'st from far
   The dismal cry of war,
Or see'st some mountain made of corpses slain,

> Or viewst th' emblazoned steed,
> High prancing o'er the mead,
> Neighing to be among the pointed spears,
> Or in black armour stalk'st around
> Embattled Bristol, once thy ground,
> Where the stark Castle aye thy scutcheon wears;
>
> Or rangest round our minster fair—
> Let Bristol still be made thy care;
> Guard it from foeman and consuming fire;
> Like Avon's stream circle it round,
> And let no spark harm hallowed ground,
> Till in one flame the whole wide world expire! [10]

It is a fine whole, in which the 'swetie moonthe of Maie' variegates battles, treachery, heartache, and heartbreak, with singing of ouzle and 'greie morn lark', and the soft verdure of meadows starred with spring flowers. Only the superficial archaic form accounts for the general ignorance still of a poem like Ælla. Rendered into modern spelling, it must have delighted a thousand readers where now it counts hardly ten. Its fame, were it fairly spread, would have lit up the rest of the so-called Rowley Poems. Even as it is, the popular neglect of a dirge like the brave ballad on the execution for high treason of Sir Baldwin Fulford, here styled Sir John Bawdin, is inexcusable. How grand a touch is ruthless King Edward's own testimony to the Lancastrian's dauntlessness:

> 'To hym that soe much dreaded dethe
> Ne ghastlie terrors brynge.
> Behold the manne! hee spake the truthe,
> Hee's greater thanne a kynge!' [11]

To pass from Chatterton in the priestly robe of Rowley to the eighteenth-century satirist conscious that he was versifying for bread, is like stepping from an illuminated ballroom into the grey London dawn. It is not that genius has failed the writer; the failure is in the motive. A commonplace of criticism has been the assumption of so entire a want of merit in the Acknowledged Poems as to argue the absence of all remarkable gifts in their author. I do not myself recognize any such poverty in the modern verse as reflects upon the intellect of Chatterton. For me, unsympathetic, even repulsive and tedious, as most of the modern pieces are, they show extraordinarily mature force of declamation, and imaginativeness also. Considered as by one absolutely unacquainted with the proper scenery and conditions of an African Eclogue, The Death of Nicon is a fine rhetorical exercise. Political satire paid, particularly if directed against the Government. It harmonized with the poor starveling's rage; with 'the unlucky way of raillery', to which, ' sparing neither friend nor foe, when the strong fit of satire is upon me,' he penitently confesses in the strange Will of April 14, 1770. For some time before his four months' raid from Bristol upon Grub Street it was the principal occupation of his pen. Already he had hurled his Kew Gardens against his unsympathetic native town. I do not understand how it can be disputed that the piece is as full of vigour as it is of exasperation against ' my prudent neighbours ', who, contemptuous of the ' attorney's clerk ', never sought to brighten a sombre life :

Few are the pleasures Chatterton e'er knew.[12]

He fancied, not very unreasonably, had Bristol not been anticipated by London, that it would have gone far towards preparing for the self-willed youngster the fate of

Another Savage to be starved in me.[13]

From Bristol still he had followed Kew Gardens up with

THOMAS CHATTERTON

the yet more scurrilous, but equally strong, Consuliad. In Shoreditch and in Brook Street he was always ready to work the same vein. Indiscriminately he attacked Bute, marking 'poor Freedom for sacrifice', and 'selling the peace' for Gallic millions; [14] Grafton's

> insignificance of face,
> Which dignifies you more than power or place; [15]

the iron soul of Charles James Fox's father, Lord Holland, 'infernal wretch',

> a name
> Which bids defiance to all sense of shame; [16]

the 'heavy head' of Samuel Johnson, maintained, 'hapless' hireling, by the Scotch minion 'in his list of slaves'; [17] and the booksellers, because—I grieve to have to quote:

> they puff the heavy Goldsmith's line,
> And hail his sentiment, though trite, divine.[18]

The literary instinct, the quickness at perceiving and utilizing the salient points in a theme, which astonish in the Rowley poems, can always be detected in these poor waifs and strays, though disguised in rancour, disdain, and despair. Even rare survivals, as it were, from a happier spirit of the past appear. Thus, we may note melody and fancy in the Elegy on Thomas Phillips:

> Nothing was Spring which Phillips did not draw,
> And every image of his Muse was May.[19]

Sometimes, when a touch of gold had diversified the leaden horizon, an actual gleam of boyish humour shoots from under the thunder-cloud. The Revenge—amid much of eighteenth-century stage coarseness—has streaks of excellent fun, and poetry also.[20] But everywhere I am amazed by a flow, a flood of intellect. It is intellect on a level, in the mass, though not for serene purity, with that which informs

Ælla itself. Any diversity is not in the man, or his mind. It is in the occasion of the poetry's birth.

Conceive the difference. See the boy among his precious parchments breathing of lovely Redcliffe Church. His whole being was bound up with them. Brooding over them in his Bristol den he forgot the mean surroundings, the charity school, the martinet attorney, the mocking citizens, the uncomprehending family. He had learnt, invented, a language, not of words alone, but of the heart. In it he and his Rowley, and their Canynge, talked and sang. For the publishers and editors of The Freeholder's Magazine, the Political Register, the Court and City Journal, the Middlesex Journal, he had to acquire a new tongue. He was for them a different being altogether, a changeling, a misanthrope, an Ishmael, resolved to conquer or die, with his hand against every man. It is absurd to charge that he would have fought for the opposite side if paid his price. His only conscience was a Rowley conscience. That he figures as a party-mercenary was the merest accident. I can but hope against hope that the mean cares and foggy squalor of the Town, with its miserable Whig and Tory feuds, lulled and lifted now and then to let him see the vision splendid of his Ællas and Goddwyns.

In the interest of Chatterton's reputation it was important to contradict a popular error that his poems in current English, which anybody is competent to estimate, are intellectually contemptible. The next step in the fallacy is a common inference that the archaic in form are unlikely, if not perhaps equally worthless, to repay at all events the certain trouble of translation. The Acknowledged Poems evince far more than enough poetical capacity to rebut any conclusion from them unfavourable to the others. It would, however, be preposterous to put them on the same level. As they are, they evince stormy power. With more experience of the Town and Affairs, and more personal interest in his work, the writer might have been a second Churchill. If so, he was, with all his miseries, happy in missing a career. With a sterner and loftier conscience, and more doggedness, he might possibly have risen to the volcanic, patriotic wrathfulness of Andrew Marvell. In their actual state, and for present reading, they have little or no attractiveness. Kew Gardens, the Consuliad, the Prophecy, the Whore of Babylon, have lost such vitality as they may once have possessed. Chatterton originally endowed them as slenderly as was prudent. They were fruits of the one money-making faculty he had; and he valued them on that account alone.

Nothing better measures the slightness of his regard than his habit of robbing one piece to eke out another. The Whore of Babylon has thus benefited. Every line of Rowley, on the contrary, bears witness to the author's loving treatment. Each separate poem there has an inviolable inspiration of its own. Lovers of poetry who are at such ordinary pains to interpret the text as they would devote, for instance, to Sordello, will speedily discover that they are being as richly compensated. They need take no account of Chatterton's youth, or of his manifold difficulties, as entitling him to allowances for deficiencies. In that respect, however, our point of view changes altogether when we regard, not so much the poems as the poet. As matter for added interest in the marvellous boy, the circumstances in which he wrote are of weight, every one. There are authors whom we read through their books, and books that we read through their authors. Chatterton belongs to the second order. I have tried, as I have been studying Ælla, to forget, as he would have had me forget, him in his counterfeit. In vain. He haunts the pages, as I turn them—the Solitary of St. Mary Redcliffe ; the Mad Boy of Bristol ; Johnson's Wonderful Whelp; born three centuries too late ; athirst for renown :

> Of all the warring passions in his breast
> Ambition still presided o'er the rest ; [21]

but with an ambition of a strange sort, centring round the towers and aisles of the great church his ancestors had served for generations ; preferring to rank as a manuscript scavenger for it to being acclaimed as a genius on his own account.

Pass from St. Mary's to Shoreditch, from Ælla to The Whore of Babylon—and still from every line will peer the Boy's haggard face ; the penniless adventurer in pitiless London ; with one burning resolve, never to be exposed alive to his mocking townsmen, to his easily deceived mother and sister, as again a failure. Not a word could I spare of those eight letters from London to the loving, believing women. Note the fond frauds, with but three words of truth in the whole : April 26, London, in 'high spirits' ; great encouragement from Dodsley—the son of Pope's publisher, who, six and twenty years earlier, had paid unknown Akenside £120 for the Pleasures of Imagination ! May 6, four guineas a month from one magazine, to be doubled by others, with occasional essays for the daily papers. Promises to country friends of overflow interest with London publishers. Wilkes's influence, to command ; quite familiar with 'all the geniuses' at the Chapter Coffee-house ; 'London ! Good God ! how superior to that despicable place Bristol !' 'What a glorious prospect !' May 14 ; friends Fell and Edwards, one in the King's Bench, the other in Newgate ; their 'misfortunes to me of no little service' ; Might have been travelling tutor to the young Duke of Northumberland ; ' but alas ! I spoke no tongue but my own ! '—and that, Rowley's and Canynge's ! Was to have conferred with the Duke of Bedford, but for ' his Grace's dangerous illness ' ; affectionate remembrances to Bristol young ladies, though in London there are so many beauties, ' that I have almost forgot myself.'

May 30 ; had been talking with Lord Mayor Beckford— ' as polite as a citizen could be '—on the subject of the Mayor's famous remonstrance to the King ; ' has learnt the art of bringing the booksellers of London to your own terms ', though unluckily ' patriots have no gratuities to spare ' ; ' if money flowed as fast upon me as honours,' would give his sister a portion of £5,000. July 11 and 20 ; articles by him in five magazines. ' I have an universal acquaintance ; my company is courted everywhere ' ; could have a choice of twenty places in Commerce ; ' but I must be among the great ; state matters suit me better than commercial.' Almost by every post presents are dispatched, to his grandmother British herb tobacco, to his mother and sister, china warranted in the fashion, patterns, a snuff-box ' right French ', fans, with the promise of a gown, as soon as an Oratorio is finished.

And all the time earnings at the rate of some twenty-five shillings a week, part of that pittance being in arrear ! The proud, brave, hawk-eyed boy's kind heart continually tasked to hide grinding penury from his people ! To me each lying letter home is a poem, tragically sweet and musical as the cries of beauteous Birtha to her war-bound Lord and Bridegroom !

I have never been able to appreciate, perhaps, pardon, the attitude of leaders of literary opinion in the past towards either Chatterton's attribution of his poems to a mythical Rowley, or his death by his own hand. I do not associate with the question Horace Walpole, who had no opportunity of judging of his correspondent's ability, except as a half-trained antiquary. My sole regret therein is for the delightful fribble himself, that he should have missed his one grand opportunity. My protest is in the first place against the high moral reprobation, as by Scott of all men, of the 'forgeries'. Chatterton's wonder-working fancy had manufactured Rowley; and to the end it breathed vitality into him. From some curious wrench in his nature his imagination burned more brightly when he masqueraded as another, than when he was his dreary eighteenth-century self. For him Rowley and Canynge actually existed. He insisted upon life for his creatures rather than on glory for himself. Had he survived to be old, I believe he would still never have consented to depose them that he might be himself enthroned. For the death, I like the usual compassionate acquittal on the ground of insanity as little as the condemnation for arrogance or moral cowardice. Think of the lad's plight on that twenty-fifth night of August, 1770. He ought, it is said, to have waited. He who had entered London in the mood of a conqueror, to wait, and for what? To die of hunger in his garret, or be carted thence to St. Andrew's workhouse! He had toiled valiantly; even with death in his heart had struggled for Resignation, and been beaten; a boy not eighteen, who had never left home till four months before! Read the letter to noble Edmund Burke from Crabbe, a grown man of twenty-seven; and see how near to suicide in despair at a fate scarcely so hard was another poet lost in London eleven years later!

The Poetical Works of Thomas Chatterton. Two vols. Cambridge, W. P. Grant, 1842.

[1] An Excelente Balade of Charitie, st. 12.
[2] The Tournament: Minstrelles, I-VIII.
[3] Elinoure and Juga.
[4] Goddwyn: A Tragedie,'by Thomas Rowlee; Prologue, by Maistre William Canynge. Chorus.
[5] Letter to the Dygne Mastre Canynge, st. 6.
[6] Ælla.   [7] Ibid.   [8] Ibid.
[9] Ibid., Minstrelles' Song, stanzas 1-4.
[10] Song to Ælla, Lorde of the Castel of Bristowe.
[11] Bristowe Tragedy; or, The Dethe of Syr Charles Bawdin, st. 85.
[12] Elegy on the Death of Mr. Phillips.
[13] Kew Gardens.   [14] The Prophecy, st. 13.
[15] Resignation.   [16] Ibid.
[17] The Whore of Babylon.
[18] The Art of Puffing; by a Bookseller's Journeyman.
[19] Elegy on the Death of Mr. Phillips.
[20] The Revenge: a Burletta.   [21] Resignation.

GEORGE CRABBE

1754—1832

I RANK Crabbe among great poets; and I am prepared for the double question: 'Why do you class him as great? Is he a poet at all?'

Doubtless he is not a poet after the usual and recognized fashion. He conforms to the standard neither in manner, nor in matter. Adopting the metre of Pope, as if he had no choice, he, in no spirit of independence, and from no theory, commonly misses the melody. The correctness of his versification points its general want of sweetness. He is not above tricks of poetic diction, and plays them awkwardly. Consciously or unconsciously, he follows and out-Cowpers Cowper, without being of his or any school. When inspired he often is not inspiring. He has no gift of discrimination or selection. Without intention he is diffuse, because such is his subject-matter. Though he deals mainly with the follies and vices of life, he is little or nothing of a satirist. From default of venom, rhetoric, and wit, though not humour—if sometimes unconscious—he has failed beyond all writers of his eminence to contribute to the language either aphorisms or sentiments.

The shortcomings are manifest, on the surface, and limited his popularity in his own time. In consequence of them he may almost be said to have ceased to have a public now. In excuse of the popular taste, or want of it, the defects must be admitted to be deep-seated. He has to be read thoroughly in order to be appreciated. Let him be studied, and then judged. The rule with poets is for them to pass facts through their own minds, and give them forth as mirrored there. The motives for the modifications, if any, for the mental reflections of the reflection, may be embodied in the verse or not. At all events that produces the reflection as the poet's nature has remodelled it. This is Wordsworth's way, and Scott's, and Byron's, alike. Crabbe delineated just what his bodily eyes saw, and his ears heard, of life's Dantesque Comedy. Never was there so scrupulous, so literal, a draughtsman. Not a detail is missing.

Had he gone no further, he must still have had his lodging in literature, though not exalted, scarcely perhaps in the porch of Poets' Corner. He is far from halting there. With no parade his pencil has Röntgen rays at its instinctive command. It figures to the life selfishness, passion, hope, joy, despair, agony. The thumbscrew is applied to every fact, compelling it to account for its existence. The whole is effected extraordinarily without egotism, without any apparent personal sense in the executioner of the torture in process. Crabbe, in the external circumstances of his narratives from preference, or from inability, availed himself of none of a poet's usual prerogatives of rejection, addition, reconstruction. The circumstances are before us as photographs. In penetrating beneath, his insight is impersonal still. He draws no fancy sketch of emotions. Very brain might be adjusting, balancing very heart as it pulsates. The exactness has operated against his fame. His own part in the composition has always been in danger of being underrated. For the average reader many of the features of the scene are crude, distasteful, or superfluous.

Distasteful, and crude, perhaps; none of them superfluous for their purpose. What a gallery it is of individualities, at once present and representative! All move in an atmosphere of harsh reality, generally dismal or sordid, sometimes deepening into despair or crime, sometimes grimly humorous. We have a sexton of eighty years welcoming the middle-aged successor of the

> Rectors five to one close vault conveyed,

and with a sly and pleasant glance at the sixth, praying:

> Heaven grant I lose no more!

We are introduced to an elderly Curate with an unsated passion for Greek, and a sickly wife; to rival attorneys, one surly and kind, the other crafty and grasping; to a learned schoolmaster; and the schoolmistress, whose whole fund of knowledge is

> with awe to look
> In every verse throughout one sacred book;

to a dissolute prodigal, and loose-living flirt, associates as almsman and almswoman now; to the wealthy farmer's daughter transported from her finishing academy to the kitchen meals, where, beside rough hinds, and father and brothers as coarse, she

> Minces the sanguine flesh in frustums fine,
> And wonders much to see the creatures dine;

to the solemn parish clerk, superior to all temptations of the world, the flesh, and the devil, till he succumbs to the ease of robbing the charity plate, and dies of the shame; to the deserted madwoman waiting in her lonely, turf-built hut on the desolate heath long years for her David, and fleeing from him as an evil spirit, when he returns to find her

> Turning her wheel, without its spindles, round,
> With household look of care, low singing to the sound;

and to fisher Grimes, companionless unless for hovering apparitions of the father he had cursed and beaten, and the three London workhouse apprentices he was rumoured to have murdered ; condemned by righteous opinion to his own haunted society :

> to live each day,
> To wait for certain hours the tide's delay,--
> At the same time the same dull views to see,
> The bounding marsh-bank, and the blighted tree,
> The water only, when the tides were high,
> When low, the mud half-cover'd and half-dry,
> The sun-burnt tar that blisters on the planks,
> And bank-side stakes in their uneven ranks,
> Heaps of entangled weeds that slowly float,
> As the tide rolls by the impeded boat.[1]

Lastly, we have the common village tragedies of maidens who loved not wisely but too well a hundred years ago. Never has the misery of the betrayed, where virtue survives lost honour, been burnt-in, without a pang spared, as, over and over again, and always with a fresh ache added, in The Tales of the Hall, the Borough, and the Parish. See, for example, Lucy, after her brief romance of a sailor's unlicensed love, as

> Throughout the lanes she glides, at evening's close,
> And softly lulls her infant to repose ;
> Then sits and gazes, but with viewless look,
> As gilds the moon the rippling of the brook,
> And sings her vespers, but in voice so low
> She hears their murmurs as the waters flow ;
> And she too murmurs, and begins to find
> The solemn wanderings of a wounded mind ;
> Visions of terror, views of woe succeed,
> The mind's impatience to the body's need ;
> By turns to that, by turns to this a prey,
> She knows what reason yields, and dreads what madness may.[2]

Follow Ruth, as distracted between her disgrace, grief for her undoer—captured by a press-gang, and slain in a sea-fight before he could return to wed her—and disgust at the ranting hypocrite her father was forcing her to marry, she wanders to the wild shore to die. Her mother repeats the tale as told to her :

> 'But oh ! what storm was in that mind ! what strife,
> That could compel her to lay down her life !
> For she was seen within the sea to wade
> By one at distance, when she first had pray'd ;
> Then to a rock within the hither shoal
> Softly and with a fearful step she stole ;
> Then, when she gain'd it, on the top she stood
> A moment still—and dropp'd into the flood ! ' [3]

Unhappy she ; yet unhappier, perhaps, Phoebe Dawson, once
> pride of Lammas Fair,
> The sweetest flower that ever blossom'd there,

wedded too late to her seducer, a captious tyrant, and a lazy sot.

The misery of it all is intensified rather than diminished by the apartness of the poet. The wofulness issues from the facts themselves. Comment is not added to heighten it. He might almost be thought to have found nothing excessively strange in the anguish upon anguish of another of the victims, Ellen Orford ; the perfidy to her of a rich lover, maltreatment by a bigoted husband, and his suicide, the death by the hangman of one son, the worse fate of two remaining children, culminating in her own blindness. Her original self-abandonment, and the man's perjuries do not appear to surprise, or greatly shock, the chronicler. Reprobation of womanly weakness and masculine faithlessness was, as may be gathered from Miss Austen's references to such faults, not extremely violent in the days of George III. Crabbe speaks by the mouth of a parent :

> 'They were as children, and they fell at length ;
> The trial doubtless is beyond their strength
> Whom grace supports not.' [4]

In Ellen's history the initial transgression counts simply as one of the trials she underwent, and blessed God for enabling her to survive.

But it is not all sorrow, disappointment, sin, privation, pettiness, in the Suffolk towns and villages. Mixed, if in unequal shares, there still, as actually seen, are some positive graces and lights. We are shown the widowed, childless merchant, grudging himself the poorest clothing, the meanest fare ; who slinks by night to cheer the wretched, and, walking home through the wintry darkness, is roused to anger at the thoughtfulness of his servants,

> When fire and rushlight met his troubled eyes ;

who finally spends on the creetion and endowment of an almshouse whatever wealth he could not otherwise distribute. He had his recognition. At his death there was mourning by many an orphan and widow who shed no tears over the grave of munificent Sir Denys Brand, reviver of the Races, and builder of the jail. Of a stamp yet rarer is the discovery by Burgess Charles, the prosperous Tory, that blood is thicker than water. Suddenly he hears that the ruin he had always predicted, and, as he fancied, desired, was befalling his visionary Radical brother, Burgess James :

> 'James a bankrupt ! Boy, my hat and cane.
> No ! he'll refuse my offers—let me think !
> So would I his ; here, give me pen and ink.
> There ! that will do.—What ! let my father's son,
> My brother, want, and I—Away, and run,

  Run as for life, and then return—but stay
  To take his message—Now, away, away!'
   . . . .
  And they too sleep! and, at their joint request,
  Within one tomb, beneath one stone, they rest! ⁵

A hallowed churchyard that, if only that there also lies the ' noble peasant ', Isaac Ashford:

  Noble he was, contemning all things mean,
  His truth unquestion'd, and his soul serene;
  Of no man's presence Isaac felt afraid;
  At no man's question Isaac look'd dismay'd;
  Shame knew him not, he dreaded no disgrace;
  Truth, simple truth, was written in his face;
  Yet while the serious thought his soul approv'd,
  Cheerful he seem'd, and gentleness he loved;
  A friend to virtue, his unclouded breast
  No envy stung, no jealousy distress'd—
  Bane of the poor! it wounds their weaker mind,
  To miss one favour, which their neighbours find—
  Yet far was he from stoic pride removed;
  He felt humanely, and he warmly loved;
  I mark'd his action, when his infant died,
  And his old neighbour for offence was tried;
  The still tears, stealing down that furrow'd cheek,
  Spoke pity, plainer than the tongue can speak.
  If pride were his, 'twas not their vulgar pride
  Who, in their base contempt, the great deride;
  Nor pride in learning—though my Clerk agreed,
  If fate should call him, Ashford might succeed;
  Nor pride in rustic skill, although we knew,
  None his superior, and his equals few;—
  But if that spirit in his soul had place,
  It was the jealous pride that shuns disgrace;
  A pride in honest fame by virtue gain'd,
  In sturdy boys to virtuous labours train'd;
  Pride in the power that guards his country's coast,
  And all that Englishmen enjoy and boast;

Pride in a life that slander's tongue defied,—
In fact, a noble passion, misnamed Pride.
 At length he found, when seventy years were run,
His strength departed, and his labour done ;
When he, save honest fame, retain'd no more,
But lost his wife, and saw his children poor ;
'Twas then a spark of—say not discontent—
Struck on his mind, and thus he gave it vent :—
 ' Kind are your laws—'tis not to be denied—
That in yon House, for ruin'd age, provide,
And they are just ; —when young, we give you all,
And for assistance in our weakness call,—
Why then this proud reluctance to be fed,
To join your poor, and eat the parish-bread ?
On some old master I could well depend ;
See him with joy and thank him as a friend ;
But ill on him, who doles the day's supply,
And counts our chances who at night may die ;
Yet help me, Heav'n ! and let me not complain
Of what I suffer, but my fate sustain.'
 Such were his thoughts, and so resign'd he grew ;
Daily he placed the Workhouse in his view !
But came not there, for sudden was his fate,
He dropp'd, expiring, at his cottage-gate.
 I feel his absence in the hours of prayer,
And view his seat, and sigh for Isaac there ;
I see no more those white locks thinly spread
Round the bald polish of that honour'd head ;
But he is blest, and I lament no more
A wise good man contented to be poor.[6]

Show me a worthier monument to warrior or statesman !

Modern English poetry can exhibit no range of portraits—breathing etchings—to equal The Borough, The Parish Register, The Tales, The Tales of the Hall. They have the directness, the stereoscopic palpableness of Chaucer's art. Had Crabbe but possessed his elder's gift of condensing and grouping, the same sense of colour, something of the same native sweetness, and mother-wit, literature might have been enriched with an eighteenth- or nineteenth-century renewal of the pageant of the Canterbury Pilgrimage. Alas for the difference in the atmosphere! But blackness of the tragic element does not explain why he has never been genuinely popular. It is not that he is saturnine; for in reality he is not. A main reason is the pervading, depressing tint of neutral grey. Cursory readers are apt to suspect that, because he is calm, he must be indifferent to the gloom of the drama he is representing. That is, however, an injustice. He is disposed to accept the general unkindliness of human existence as inevitable. Its aspect had been sombre to the poverty-stricken doctor, and continued to be sombre to the beneficed clergyman. One personal experience of life, when in the making, had been wellnigh fatal. A prophet always unhonoured at home, he must, but for the heart, the insight, of Edmund Burke, have perished in the wilderness of London by his own hand, or of hunger. His theory, deliberate or not, of literary duty itself disinclined him to much intermixture of moralizing with description. His primary obligation he considered, or acted as if he considered, was to report what he saw; and he saw for the most part impurity, dullness, and uncharitableness.

When he came upon generosity, dignity, repentance, self-restraint, mutual kindness among men, as sometimes, he gave them, as in Isaac Ashford, their noble due. He takes any opportunity of giving credit even for belated remorse; as in the terrible tale, when Isaac Fletcher, his wife's timid, mean tool, after repaying unstinted bounty as Regan and Goneril repaid Lear's, is conscience-stricken to find in the cheerless attic, untended, except by a pitying child:

    Oh God! my brother dead![7]

So with his scenery. He is a faithful painter of the rare cottage, sheltered but sunny, where, without, the woodbine climbs, and, within,

>Around the walls are heroes, lovers, kings,
>The print that shews them, and the verse that sings,

with, beside the cuckoo-clock, food for the mind; wonder-tales—Thumb the Great, Hickathrift the Strong, and Jack the Giant Killer—the Bible, bought by sixpence weekly saved, with prints and notes, the Pilgrim's Progress, Hermit Quarll, and the Wandering Jew: and, outside, the plot of garden-ground, rich in roots, and fruits, and pungent herbs, and glorious with blossoms—'all the cotter's own'—where

>on Sunday-eve, when service ends,
>Meet and rejoice a family of friends;
>There still the welcome and the words are old,
>And the same stories are for ever told;
>Yet theirs is joy that bursting from the heart,
>Prompts the glad tongue these nothings to impart;
>That talks or laughs or runs or shouts or plays,
>And speaks in all their looks and all their ways.[8]

His more habitual acquaintance was with the

>infected Row we term our street;

with the birthplace of the forsaken girl's nameless babe in the hovel:

>Where blinks through paper'd panes the setting sun; [9]

and with the wide, waste, level fen, and its marsh soured by salt springs:

>Beneath an ancient bridge, the straiten'd flood
>Rolls through its sloping banks of slimy mud;
>. Near it a sunken boat resists the tide;
>That frets and hurries to th' opposing side;
>The rushes sharp, that on the borders grow,
>Bend their brown flow'rets to the stream below;
>The few dull flowers that o'er the place are spread
>Partake the nature of their fenny bed;

> Here on its wiry stem, in rigid bloom,
> Grows the salt lavender that lacks perfume;
> Here the dwarf sallows creep, the septfoil harsh,
> And the soft slimy mallow of the marsh;
> Low on the ear the distant billows sound,
> And just in view appears their stony bound;
> No hedge nor tree conceals the glowing sun,
> Birds, save a wat'ry tribe, the district shun,
> Nor chirp among the reeds where bitter waters run.[10]

Melancholy and dreary themes were not of his selection, but the lot of his Muse; and he, being he, had to depict them.

I do not suppose he was of the stuff to have led a crusade; the prosaic hardnesses of his early years had worn down the edge of enthusiasm; it was a defect in him that he never rose to a consciousness that there was greatness in him; that he might be a power in the world. But his instincts were righteous, and he hated cruelty and unkindness. There was, if no impulsive tenderness, no sternness in the man. He never dissembled his indignation at injustice, whether the work of individuals, or of laws and institutions. He protests against the evil consequences of game-preserving, the brutalities of the press-gang, the workhouse,

> a prison with a milder name.

When, however, he was telling a tale, his business, he assumed, no longer was to protest, but to narrate; and he fulfilled that mandate with singleness of heart.

That his lines were cast thus in his receptive years amidst squalor and ugliness, and that the reflection of them through him is squalid and ugly, doubtless then is the cause why he no longer is largely read, if he ever were. Whether he will hereafter be I do not know. I am not certain that he could be expected to be. But I am sure that no student of literature who considers him dispassionately, having overcome the natural distaste for flat, boorish sadness and sin, will find any difficulty in replying to the queries I originally put, whether he were a poet, and of what rank. Let a reader mark the reality of the subject-matter with which this artist in black and white deals, the justness of proportion, the remorseless strength of the treatment, the natural subtlety; and he will wonder, like myself, how any one could ever have doubted. Both questions will be unhesitatingly answered as Byron and as Scott answered them : ' Yes ; a poet, and a great one ! '

The Poetical Works of the Rev. George Crabbe, edited by his Son. Eight vols. John Murray, 1834.
[1] The Poor (The Borough), Letter 22.
[2] Baptisms (The Parish Register, Part I).
[3] Ruth (Tales of the Hall, Book V). [4] Ibid.
[5] The Brother Burgesses (Posthumous Tales), Tale 12.
[6] Burials (The Parish Register, Part III).
[7] The Brothers, Tale 20.
[8] Introduction (The Parish Register, Part I).
[9] Baptisms (The Parish Register, Part I).
[10] The Lover's Journey (Tales), Tale 10.

WILLIAM BLAKE

1757—1827

A POET-PROPHET, who sang and prophesied for fifty years to a stone-deaf people. Mighty bards came into being and fame, when he had been singing and prophesying for a generation. Not a word from them, from Coleridge, Wordsworth, Byron, Shelley, Keats, Landor, is on record to show that any one of the number knew of his existence. When his name began to circulate, it was as that of an artist of ungoverned, almost hysterical, fancy. Then two or three short poems, phenomena, strange if beautiful, emerged into a half-light. They made their gradual way into anthologies; not he among the poets; scarcely even now into any recognized rank. Neither in diction, nor in imagery, is he faultless; yet, for what he attempted, for a combination of high thought, metrical music, passion, magic, within the narrow lines in which he worked, he had, and has, few equals, no superior.

With various moods, impulses, powers, he had one predominantly developed, the faculty of wonder. He wondered at everything; at life, its beginning, progress, end, and future; at fate and eternity; good and ill; infancy and age; man and beast; flower and weed; beauty and deformity, vice and virtue, Heaven and Hell. All surprised him; and he thirsted for clues to the legion of enigmas. The craving revealed to him that he possessed the gift of verse, and that it offered the natural medium for the expression of his astonishment. He versified from no covetousness of public admiration, from no wish to please others, or even himself. Many, not among the least lovely, of his poems have been disinterred from a notebook and memoranda accessible during his life to no eyes but his own. When by a spontaneous instinct he propounded a question in verse, he hoped for an answer from himself alone. Certainly his countrymen acted as if they so understood him. As if aware that he was not addressing them, they left him with his riddles to himself. If some of these are fascinatingly sweet and deliciously simple, it is not to be supposed that he had any thought of attracting thus popular attention. To him they were as curiously difficult as the most complex. In The Lamb he puts a question for a child to answer. Five years later, asking a second, in The Tiger, he intimates that on the reply hangs the balance of Heaven and Earth. The same theme has for him manifold phases. A song on it at one period plays as softly as a moonbeam; another on it becomes a lightning arrow flashing into the heart's recesses. The marvel is how the poetic spirit, while loyally striving to marshal and smooth out the inequalities of the universe, flutes on its pastoral pipe with the careless melody of a shepherd in Arcady.

In contradiction to that which might be supposed to be the natural order, art among poets often precedes passion. Accordingly Blake in the Poetical Sketches, written between the ages of eleven and twenty, though not printed till he was twenty-six, has caught admirably the early seventeenth-century manner; for instance:

> His face is fair as heaven
>   When springing buds unfold;
> Oh, why to him was 't given,
>   Whose heart is wintry cold?
> His breast is Love's all-worshipp'd tomb
> Where all Love's pilgrims come.

The beautiful song on Love's golden cage, of the same

period, with more glow, is still marked by the like rather artificial glitter.[1] A very different spirit permeates the Songs of Innocence, printed when their author was thirty-two. That to a Lamb gives warmth as well as light :

    Little Lamb, who made thee ?
    Dost thou know who made thee,
  Gave thee life, and bade thee feed
  By the stream, and o'er the mead ;
  Gave thee clothing of delight,
  Softest clothing, woolly, bright ;
  Gave thee such a tender voice,
  Making all the vales rejoice ?
    Little lamb, who made thee ?
    Dost thou know who made thee ?

    Little lamb, I'll tell thee ;
    Little lamb, I'll tell thee ;
  He is callèd by thy name,
  For He calls himself a Lamb.
  He is meek, and He is mild,
  He became a little child.
  I a child, and thou a lamb,
  We are callèd by His name.
    Little lamb, God bless thee !
    Little lamb, God bless thee ![2]

Infant Joy is a strayed sunbeam :

    ' I have no name ;
    I am but two days old.'
    What shall I call thee ?
    ' I happy am,
    Joy is my name.'
    Sweet joy befall thee !
    Pretty joy !
    Sweet joy, but two days old.
    Sweet joy I call thee :
    Thou dost smile,
    I sing the while ;
    Sweet joy befall thee ![3]

WILLIAM BLAKE

The exquisite first Cradle Song goes deeper, and perhaps rises higher:

> Sweet dreams, form a shade
> O'er my lovely infant's head!
> Sweet dreams of pleasant streams
> By happy, silent, moony beams!
> Sweet Sleep, with soft down
> Weave thy brows an infant crown!
> Sweet Sleep, angel mild,
> Hover o'er my happy child!
> Sweet smiles, in the night
> Hover over my delight!
> Sweet smiles, mother's smile,
> All the livelong night beguile.
> Sweet moans, dovelike sighs,
> Chase not slumber from thine eyes!
> Sweet moan, sweeter smile,
> All the dovelike moans beguile.
> Sleep, sleep, happy child!
> All creation slept and smiled.
> Sleep, sleep, happy sleep,
> While o'er thee doth mother weep.
> Sweet babe, in thy face
> Holy image I can trace;
> Sweet babe, once like thee
> Thy Maker lay, and wept for me:
> Wept for me, for thee, for all,
> When He was an infant small.
> Thou His image ever see,
> Heavenly face that smiles on thee! [4]

It is an earthly melody which Heaven might borrow; and that On Another's Sorrow one of which it must have been the birthplace:

> Can I see another's woe,
> And not be in sorrow too?
> Can I see another's grief,
> And not seek for kind relief?

Can I see a falling tear,
And not feel my sorrow's share?
Can a father see his child
Weep, nor be with sorrow filled?

Can a mother sit and hear
An infant groan, an infant fear?
No, no! never can it be!
Never, never can it be!

And can He who smiles on all
Hear the wren with sorrows small,
Hear the small bird's grief and care,
Hear the woes that infants bear—

And not sit beside the nest,
Pouring pity in their breast,
And not sit the cradle near,
Weeping tear on infant's tear?

He doth give His joy to all;
He becomes an infant small,
He becomes a man of woe,
He doth feel the sorrow too.

Think not thou canst sigh a sigh,
And thy Maker is not by;
Think not thou canst weep a tear,
And thy Maker is not near.

Oh He gives to us His joy,
That our grief He may destroy:
Till our grief is fled and gone
He doth sit by us and moan.[5]

The two companion pictures of The Little Boy Lost, and Found, show how much more may be conveyed by pathos than the merely pathetic:

'Father, father, where are you going?
  Oh do not walk so fast!
Speak, father, speak to your little boy,
  Or else I shall be lost.'

The night was dark, no father was there,
  The child was wet with dew;
The mire was deep, and the child did weep,
  And away the vapour flew.

The little boy lost in the lonely fen,
  Led by the wandering light,
Began to cry, but God, ever nigh,
  Appeared like his father, in white.
He kissed the child, and by the hand led,
  And to his mother brought,
Who in sorrow pale, through the lonely dale,
  The little boy weeping sought.[6]

As Blake advanced in years his verse is more given to putting questions than, as earlier, to answering them. Take for example that great, that august piece, The Tiger:

Tiger, Tiger, burning bright
In the forests of the night,
What immortal hand or eye
Framed thy fearful symmetry?

In what distant deeps or skies
Burned that fire within thine eyes?
On what wings dared he aspire?
What the hand dared seize the fire?

And what shoulder and what art
Could twist the sinews of thy heart?
When thy heart began to beat,
What dread hand formed thy dread feet?

What the hammer, what the chain,
Knit thy strength and forged thy brain?
What the anvil? What dread grasp
Dared thy deadly terrors clasp?

When the stars threw down their spears,
And watered heaven with their tears,
Did He smile His work to see?
Did He who made the lamb make thee?[7]

He grows more sombre, despairing :

>I saw a chapel all of gold
>   That none did dare to enter in,
>And many weeping stood without,
>   Weeping, mourning, worshipping.
>
>I saw a serpent rise between
>   The white pillars of the door,
>And he forced and forced and forced,
>   Till he the golden hinges tore ;
>
>And along the pavement sweet,
>   Set with pearls and rubies bright,
>All his shining length he drew,—
>   Till upon the altar white
>
>He vomited his poison out
>   On the bread and on the wine.
>So I turned into a sty,
>   And laid me down among the swine.[8]

Society and luxury, as he sees their results in his London, sicken him :

>In every cry of every man,
>   In every infant's cry of fear,
>In every voice, in every ban,
>   The mind-forged manacles I hear ;
>
>How the chimney-sweeper's cry
>   Every blackening church appals,
>And the hapless soldier's sigh
>   Runs in blood down palace walls ! [9]

And again :

>The harlot's cry from street to street
>Shall weave old England's winding-sheet ;
>The winner's shout, the loser's curse,
>Shall dance before dead England's hearse.[10]

He delights in proposing conundrums ; and the solutions, when they can be solved, have a bitter taste. Here are three of his riddles :

Never seek to tell thy love,
　　Love that never told can be ;
For the gentle wind doth move
　　Silently, invisibly.

I told my love, I told my love,
　　I told her all my heart ;
Trembling, cold, in ghastly fears,
　　Ah ! she did depart.

Soon after she was gone from me,
　　A traveller came by,
Silently, invisibly ;—
　　He took her with a sigh.[11]

　　I wandered in the forest
　　　　The green leaves among,
　　I heard a wild-flower
　　　　Singing a song :

　　' I slept in the earth
　　　　In the silent night ;
　　I murmured my thoughts,
　　　　And I felt delight.

　　' In the morning I went,
　　　　As rosy as morn,
　　To seek for new joy,
　　　　But I met with scorn.'[12]

I was angry with my friend ;
I told my wrath, my wrath did end.
I was angry with my foe ;
I told it not, my wrath did grow.

And I watered it in fears
Night and morning with my tears,
And I sunnèd it with smiles
And with soft deceitful wiles.

And it grew both day and night
Till it bore an apple bright,
And my foe beheld it shine,
And he knew that it was mine,—

> And into my garden stole
> When the night had veiled the pole;
> In the morning, glad, I see
> My foe outstretched beneath the tree.[13]

This last, by a concentration of irony, is entitled 'Christian Forbearance'!

Yet it was the same rich fancy, not yet arrived, the poet being barely fourteen, at years of sardonic discretion, which had indited:

> How sweet I roamed from field to field,
>   And tasted all the summer's pride,
> Till I the Prince of Love beheld
>   Who in the sunny beams did glide.
>
> He showed me lilies for my hair,
>   And blushing roses for my brow;
> He led me through his garden fair
>   Where all his golden pleasures grow.
>
> With sweet May-dews my wings were wet,
>   And Phoebus fired my vocal rage;
> He caught me in his silken net,
>   And shut me in his golden cage.
>
> He loves to sit and hear me sing,
>   Then, laughing, sports and plays with me;
> Then stretches out my golden wing,
>   And mocks my loss of liberty.[14]

Little wonder that a soul thus naturally attuned to sweetness, even gaiety, as its eyes opened wider and wider to the wretchedness, coarseness, unkindness, of a supposed civilization, its carelessness of things high, and immersement in the low, should make the child, roused from happy visions, complain:

> 'What do we here,
> In this land of unbelief and fear?
> The land of dreams is better far,
> Above the light of the morning star!'[15]

I have endeavoured to demonstrate my right to admire, and wish space had permitted even ampler proof. Where so much is great, it is as painful as invidious to omit. Their task whose duty it was to select from Blake's manuscripts must have been harder still. Think of a museum of jewels, like the grand, dark riddles of Broken Love,[16] the Angel's and Devil's duel of blessing and cursing,[17] the forked lightnings of the Defiled Sanctuary, the puzzles at once and gems of the Wild Flower's Song, and Love's Secret, the mysteries of the Crystal Cabinet,[18] and Smile and Frown,[19] the longing regretfulness of The Land of Dreams, and that treasure-house of warnings and rules—many celestial—Auguries of Innocence,[20] having been left to the chances and hazards of resurrection from a graveyard of chaotic scrawls!

Real poetry is always so far the result of a species of ecstasy that the writer cannot seem even to himself, at the moment of composition, to be the actual 'maker'. This is the rule of the most artificial as of the most natural verse—wherever there is greatness. It is true of Gray no less than of Herrick. But the poets are few who, in going out of themselves when possessed by the poetic flame, have not locked up something personal in a corner apart. Blake, with the poet-prophet's mantle upon him, had no reservations. After the first flush of Elizabethan inspiration, he was, while he sang, nothing but seer-singer. He is continually and wholly in a rapture. It may be easier or harder for readers to follow upwards in his train. It is easier, for example, when God personates the father to the boy lost in the lonely fen; harder, when a kingly lion houses another strayed child in his palace, and thither guides the despairing parents.[21] For Blake, with Heaven in his soul, and Hell without, there were no degrees in a world of enigmas. Fortunately for his other Art, as well as for Poetry, his habitual mood was

> To see a world in a grain of sand,
>   And a Heaven in a wild flower;
> Hold Infinity in the palm of your hand,
>   And Eternity in an hour.[22]

The temper does not exclude indignation against cruelty to man, or bird, or beast:

> A skylark wounded on the wing
> Doth make a cherub cease to sing; [23]

against profanity, and against scepticism:

> He who mocks the infant's faith
> Shall be mocked in age and death;
> If the sun and moon should doubt,
> They'd immediately die out.[24]

But the spirit is most in its element when meditating in rapt amazement on God's goodness to all His creatures; even to a mother-worm nursing its little ones beneath a clod with a fond and grateful cry:

> 'My bosom of itself is cold, and of itself is dark;
> But He that loves the lowly pours His oil upon my head,
> And kisses me, and binds His nuptial bands around my breast,
> And says: "Thou mother of my children, I have loved thee,
> And I have given thee a crown that none can take away."
> But how this is I know not, and I cannot know;
> I ponder, and I cannot ponder; yet I live and love!' [25]

Perhaps, in this habit of abstraction into a Seventh Heaven of enthusiasm the clue may be found to the popular inability to regard Blake's poetry as more than an aesthetic curiosity. The public is timid of poets in the ordinary habit of ranging among the stars. If indeed a condition for enjoyment of Blake's songs were capacity or liking for the interpretation of intricate, though melodious, mysteries, such as Broken Love, the Agony of Faith, or The Mental Traveller, the world's diffidence would be justifiable. But the charm of the Singer is that, lark-like, while the wings aspire, heart and eye are with the nest upon the dewy ground. Never did poetry succeed better in uniting loftiest aspirations with a bewitching simplicity. In Blake it is sublime for a philosopher, and a lullaby for a child.

The Poetical Works of William Blake, edited by W. M. Rossetti. George Bell & Sons, 1891.
[1] Songs (Poetical Sketches), stanzas 2 and 43.
[2] The Lamb (Songs of Innocence). [3] Infant Joy (ibid.).
[4] A Cradle Song (ibid.). [5] On Another's Sorrow (ibid.).
[6] The Little Boy Lost (ibid.), The Little Boy Found (ibid.).
[7] The Tiger, Second Version.
[8] The Defiled Sanctuary (From Jerusalem).
[9] London (Songs of Experience), stanzas 2 and 3.
[10] Auguries of Innocence (From Jerusalem), vv. 71-4.
[11] Love ; Secret. [12] The Wild-Flower's Song.
[13] Christian Forbearance (Songs of Experience).
[14] Song—How Sweet, &c. (Poetical Sketches).
[15] The Land of Dreams. [16] Broken Love.
[17] The Two Songs. [18] The Crystal Cabinet.
[19] Smile and Frown. [20] Auguries of Innocence.
[21] The Little Girl, Lost and Found (Songs of Experience).
[22] Auguries of Innocence, vv. 1-4. [23] Ibid., vv. 19-20.
[24] Ibid., vv. 79-80 and 103-4. [25] The Book of Thel.

SAMUEL ROGERS

1763—1855

A DELIGHTFUL example of a class, which might have been expected to be the largest, and is all but the smallest, in the commonwealth of poets. In these days the readers of Rogers are, I fear, few. Anybody, not already among them, in repairing the neglect will have only one regret, that he had deferred the enjoyment. A single indispensable condition is that he shall require no raptures. Rogers had and has no special message to deliver. The emotions to which he appeals, the ideas he suggests, may easily be considered to be commonplace and antiquated. He has no remarkable personality in himself to reveal. He was never 'possessed', as were some of his contemporaries. Simply and solely he saw, admired, was pleased, occasionally sorrowed, and allows it to be seen that he was moved, and how. A natural function of the poet is to feel poetical possibilities wherever they may be, and then concentrate them into melody. His intuition operates as the instinct of the miner who has guessed at a vein, before he labours with his pick. If Rogers did not mine, he had at least the poet's instinct for recognizing where precious ore was likely to be found, and keen enough appreciation to gather the grains, genuine if few, from the river's bank.

The parading of glittering pebbles as if they were bullion,

is the danger besetting writers of his order. A mere charge of triteness itself does not alarm me. Allusions to natural emotions are never to be decried as trite, unless a writer enunciate them with an air of publishing novelties. As a term of reproach it can be so easily flung. From some points of view it might be applied to Goldsmith's Deserted Village; even to Gray's Elegy. We may be grateful to Rogers, whose verse often reminds of Goldsmith, that he was not scared by the possibility of the imputation from dwelling on scenes

> When nature pleased, for life itself was new,
> And the heart promised what the fancy drew.[1]

If, as in the tedious tale of Florio and Julia, he slips into actual triteness, it is because he has become melodramatic under an apprehension that his public might weary of feelings and thoughts scattered by the wayside. On his own ground, whatever the themes, whether the lights and shades of Memory, those of the more mature and satisfying, if less popular, diorama of statecraft, literature, and humours, in Human Life, or of a dead world-empire, his pen goes far towards harmonizing them, so long as he is content to let them play about it.

Without apparent effort of his, picturesque images are constantly passing through his verse, as reflections from the unquiet stir outside over the Lady of Shalott's mirror. It may be she,

> most gentle, most unfortunate,
> Crowned but to die—who in her chamber sate
> Musing with Plato;[2]

or the

> sweet Saint who sate by Russell's side
> Under the Judgment-seat.[3]

It may be Grattan,

> When the sweet limes, so full of bees in June,
> Led us to meet beneath their boughs at noon;
> And thou didst say which of the Great and Wise,
> Could they but hear and at thy bidding rise,
> Thou wouldst call up and question.[4]

Fox himself we see, in his garden at St. Anne's:

> so soon of Care beguiled,
> Playful, sincere, and artless as a child!
> Thee, who wouldst watch a bird's nest on the spray,
> Through the green leaves exploring, day by day.
> How oft, from grove to grove, from seat to seat,
> With thee conversing in thy loved retreat,
> I saw the sun go down!—Ah, then 'twas thine
> Ne'er to forget some volume half divine,
> Shakespeare's or Dryden's—thro' the chequered shade
> Borne in thy hand behind thee as we strayed;
> And where we sat—and many a halt we made—
> To read there with a fervour all thy own,
> And in thy grand and melancholy tone,
> Some splendid passage not to thee unknown.[5]

Then Italy, the Italy of history and romance, of love and war, art and nature, opens her rich gallery to him—every picture framed in a glory of its own. In the glowing light of his grateful sympathy we view the home of blind old Dandolo, the Foscari, and the Falieri:

> a glorious city in the sea,
> ... an exhalation from the deep;
> A scene of light and glory, a dominion,
> That has endured the longest among men;
> ... where in monstrous league
> Two phantom-shapes were sitting, side by side,
> Or up, and, as in sport, chasing each other;
> Horror and Mirth;[6]

her sister republic, as royal by land as herself by water :

> Of all the fairest cities of the Earth
> None is so fair as Florence. 'Tis a gem
> Of purest ray ; and what a light broke forth
> When it emerged from darkness ! Search within,
> Without ; all is enchantment ;—

from its miracles of art, such as the gates of the Baptistery :

> so marvellously wrought,
> That they might serve to be the gates of Heaven ; [7]

to the Gardens of the Hundred Tales,

> where many a syren voice
> Sung down the stars ; [8]

and ever-Imperial Rome, where

> The very dust we tread stirs as with life ;
> And not a breath but from the ground sends up
> Something of human grandeur. [9]

Rogers works in silver-grey tints, while his friend, and for a brief space his travelling companion,

> a star that thro' the firmament
> Shot and was lost,[10]

paints much the same scenes in fire. Yet I am not sure that the black and white may not be as lasting. Under the spell of Childe Harold one is tempted to regard the Italy of Rogers as a versified guide-book. Study it, and you will find it possesses a witchery of its own. Its author is a pilgrim like the Childe, and with more of faith in the motives for his pilgrimage. With his youth cast in a time when the Continent was a sealed chamber, he had longed for Italy as fairyland, and now he has at last discovered it. We can feel him continually comparing facts with fancy, and rejoicing to recognize his dream-children in a material reality equally adorable. As he identifies he worships, and he wonders. His own ingenuous surprise is as captivating as the surprises other poets engineer for their readers. The experience is, in the nature of things, not of a kind for us to repeat for ourselves; and it is precious.

At its highest and best it becomes within the three gaunt, hollow-eyed, majestic skeletons of the temples of Paestum, a vision, marvellous for mystery and atmosphere, of thirty centuries of history. Into it the poet gathers up his whole soul. It is a sufficient reply to any who have ever questioned his title to the name. During more than fifty years since I discovered the lines in the volume he gave my father, I have read them over and over again with unceasing admiration. I turn the pages now, and am as sensible of the magic as ever:

> They stand between the mountains and the sea;
> Awful memorials, but of whom we know not!
> The seaman, passing, gazes from the deck,
> The buffalo-driver, in his shaggy cloak,
> Points to the work of magic, and moves on.
>   How many centuries did the sun go round
> From Mount Alburnus to the Tyrrhene sea,
> While, by some spell rendered invisible,
> Or, if approached, approached by him alone
> Who saw as though he saw not, they remained
> As in the darkness of a sepulchre,
> Waiting the appointed time! All, all within
> Proclaims that Nature had resumed her right,
> And taken to herself what man renounced.
>   The air is sweet with violets, running wild
> Mid broken friezes and fallen capitals;
> Sweet as when Tully, writing down his thoughts,
> Those thoughts so precious, and so lately lost,
> Sailed slowly by, two thousand years ago,
> For Athens; when a ship, if north-east winds
> Blew from the Paestan gardens, slacked her course.

On as he moved along the level shore,
Those temples, in their splendour eminent
Mid arcs and obelisks, and domes, and towers,
Reflecting back the radiance of the west,
Well might he dream of Glory!—Now, coiled up,
The serpent sleeps within them. Nothing stirs
Save the shrill-voiced cicala flitting round,
Or the green lizard rustling through the grass.
 In such an hour he came, who saw and told,
Led by the mighty Genius of the Place.
 Walls of some capital city first appeared,
Half razed, half sunk, or scattered as in scorn.
—And what within them? What but in the midst
These Three in more than their original grandeur,
And, round about, no stone upon another;
As if the spoiler had fallen back in fear,
And, turning, left them to the elements!
 'Tis said a stranger in the days of old—
Some say a Dorian, some a Sybarite—
Traced out the site; and Posidonia rose,
Severely great, Neptune the tutelar God;
A Homer's language murmuring in her streets,
And in her haven many a mast from Tyre.
Then came another, an unbidden guest.
He knocked and entered with a train in arms;
And all was changed, her very name and language!
The Tyrian merchant, shipping at his door
Ivory and gold, and silk, and frankincense,
Sailed as before, but, sailing, cried 'For Paestum!'
And now a Virgil, now an Ovid sung
Paestum's twice-blowing roses; while, within,
Parents and children mourned—and every year—
'Twas on the day of some old festival—
Met to give way to tears, and once again
Talk in the ancient tongue of things gone by.
 At length an Arab climbed the battlements,
Slaying the sleepers in the dead of night;
And from all eyes the glorious vision fled!
Leaving a place lonely and dangerous,

> Where whom the robber spares, a deadlier foe
> Strikes at unseen.
>   But what are These still standing in the midst?
> The Earth has rocked beneath! the Thunder-stone
> Passed thro' and thro', and left its traces there;
> Yet still they stand as by some Unknown Charter!
> Oh, they are Nature's own! and, as allied
> To the vast Mountains and the eternal Sea,
> They want no written history; theirs a voice
> For ever speaking to the heart of Man![11]

Descriptions like this prove that the author's reason for chronicling was not because he was incapable of creating. Doubtless he could, if he pleased, have produced more of the same texture. Had he elected for plain living and high thinking, he might even have soared higher, and penetrated deeper. But he would have had to sacrifice a life he loved, and to suppress instincts in his blood. He could not well then have played Mecaenas for the lettered fraternity, the fine gentleman, the finer that he was born in a counting-house. When the business sense conflicted with fancy, he must have risked the delirium of inspiration. He chose a middle course. He remained a banker, if not very diligent at the desk, yet to the continual advantage of genius in want of a home and wise kindness.

Popularly he bore the reputation of cynicism. He made no effort to contradict the legend founded on words, not acts. Neither, on the other hand, did he endeavour to suppress poetical impulses as they rose. The childless bachelor could see the beauty of mother and infant's mutual love:

> As with soft accents round her neck he clings,
> And cheek to cheek her lulling song she sings,
> How blest to feel the beatings of his heart,
> Breathe his sweet breath, and kiss for kiss impart.[12]

The man of the world could reverence unworldliness :

> When by a good man's grave I muse alone,
> Methinks an Angel sits upon the stone.[13]

He analyses a tear with a dexterity Waller could not have excelled :

> That very law which moulds a tear,
> And bids it trickle from its source,
> That law preserves the earth a sphere,
> And guides the planets in their course ;[14]

and he mourns a redbreast with a tenderness Waller could not have equalled :

> Tread lightly here, for here, 'tis said,
> When piping winds are hushed around,
> A small note wakes from underground,
> Where now his tiny bones are laid.
> No more in lone and leafless groves,
> With ruffled wing and faded breast,
> His friendless, homeless spirit roves ;
> —Gone to the world where birds are blest !
> Where never cat glides o'er the green,
> Or school-boy's giant form is seen ;
> But Love, and Joy, and smiling Spring
> Inspire their little souls to sing ![15]

The eyes glance instinctively to the bottom of the page, in expectation of a reference to a Latin original of Vincent Bourne's, rendered into English by Cowper.

He used no trickery, no rhetoric ; or such only as distilled from the occasion itself. His process was little else than a liberating from casual excrescences, a selecting of essential graces. The art is not that of the Elegy, which might have imposed upon Nature herself ; nor that of the Deserted Village, which was Nature glassed in a heart. It is true nevertheless, and of a gentle refinement which will charm and soothe, when grandeur and sublimity bewilder and tire.

Poems by Samuel Rogers, 1834. Italy: a Poem by Samuel Rogers, 1830. R. Cadell and E. Moxon.
[1] The Pleasures of Memory (The Poems).
[2] Human Life (ibid.).   [3] Ibid. (ibid.).   [4] Ibid. (ibid.).
[5] Ibid. (ibid.).   [6] Venice (Italy).   [7] Florence (ibid.).
[8] The Campagna of Florence (ibid.).   [9] Rome (ibid.).
[10] Bologna (ibid.).   [11] Paestum (ibid.).
[12] Human Life (Poems).   [13] Ibid. (ibid.).   [14] On a Tear (ibid.), st. 6.
[15] An Epitaph on a Robin-Redbreast (ibid

THOMAS CAMPBELL
1777—1844

Some poets by a sort of chance have identified themselves with the national life. Public opinion finds itself unconsciously thinking along the lines their verse has traced. They are of very various degrees of merit. Writers superior to many among them do not belong to the number. Campbell, from his first appearance as a poet, vindicated his right to be included. Throughout he had the gift of crystallizing speech into proverbs and watchwords. From time to time he made himself the voice of a people.

He had started on his course by storming public admiration with the Pleasures of Hope. The poem is full of passages stored once in every cultivated mind. The noble protest against the iniquitous massacre of Polish independence has never ceased to echo :

> Oh, bloodiest picture in the book of Time,
> Sarmatia fell, unwept, without a crime ;
> Found not a generous friend, a pitying foe,
> Strength in her arms, nor mercy in her woe !
> Dropp'd from her nerveless grasp the shattered spear,
> Closed her bright eye, and curb'd her high career ;—
> Hope, for a season, bade the world farewell,
> And Freedom shriek'd—as Kosciusko fell ! [1]

Again and again he repeated his triumph ; and on fresh ground, and with new weapons.

That is the special feature of his career. His first production doubtless was written in emulation of The Pleasures of Memory ; and the two have been popularly bracketed. The works have little similarity of spirit. They have, however, an affinity in belonging in manner to the school of Pope. Rogers never altogether quitted it, though he infused the sweetness of Goldsmith. Campbell changed with his generation which had adopted a new style or styles. He gave up being Georgian, without either establishing a sect of his own, or affiliating himself to one of the many revolutionary fraternities in poetry. It would be difficult to trace in his multiform verse any predominant contemporary influence, whether of Wordsworth, Scott, Byron, Shelley, or Keats. He neither kept to his first fashion, nor frankly adopted another. Yet never in his changes did he lose touch with the popular taste.

At intervals he gave to the world poems of some length. The world invariably read and applauded; and, on the whole, none can say that the praise was undeserved. In Gertrude a Garden of Eden was painted, as by Watteau:

> Delightful Wyoming! beneath thy skies,
> The happy shepherd swains had nought to do
> But feed their flocks on green declivities,
> Or skim perchance thy lake with light canoe,
> From morn till evening's sweeter pastime grew,
> With timbrel, when beneath the forests brown,
> The lovely maidens would the dance renew;
> And aye those sunny mountains half-way down
> Would echo flagelet from some romantic town.[2]

The tale

> Why wanders she a huntress wild—
> O'Connor's pale and lovely child,[3]

was acknowledged to be as full of melody as of sadness. A noble picture of devotion and supernatural deliverance was presented in the legend of the Norseman's raid upon holy Iona, with its chastisement, and the fate of the bride of the chief of the dark-robed Culdees, Reullura,

> Star of the morn and eve![4]

Generally grace of character-and-landscape-drawing abounds; and its charm was recognized. Even Theodric— an admitted failure as a whole—had its eulogists—and not without good cause—for lines such as :
> Her fingers witched the chords they passed along,
> And her lips seem'd to kiss the soul in song.[5]

Probably inferior work occasionally was accepted from him in expectation of better to come. At all events, he was never deposed from the rank he had gained.

It is very different now from when, whatever keys he struck, and at whatever length, he was sure of an audience. The present age unkindly discriminates. His longer pieces are remembered principally by their titles. The cruel doom of happy Wyoming, its gentle villagers, and fairest Gertrude, with the flitting, stately shadow of the Indian warrior,
> A stoic of the woods—a man without a tear,[6]

no longer interests. Reullura is forgotten, and even the Pleasures of Hope, unless for lines here and there. Happily that has not been the fate of the lyrics. For the most part they survive to us, if, some, with the strange, mummy-like fragrance hanging round them of imprisoned rose-petals. Though the poet after his original fortunate venture shook off the formal tradition of Pope, he frequently recurred in tone of sentiment to the period from which he had emerged. We feel the eighteenth-century element in his address to The Rainbow :
> Triumphal arch, that fill'st the sky
> When storms prepare to part,
> I ask not proud Philosophy
> To teach me what thou art—
> Still seem, as to my childhood's sight,
> A midway station given
> For happy spirits to alight
> Betwixt the Earth and Heaven.[7]

When the south wind obeys the summons to gather all his wild wood's sweets about the name of Caroline, and, in her service,

> Where'er thy morning breath has played,
> Whatever isles of ocean fanned,
> Come to my blossom-woven shade,
> Thou wandering wind of fairy-land,[8]

it is as if on its way the kindly breeze had strayed about ancient bookshelves on which Shenstone and his fellows repose.

The same well-preserved old-world flavour is perceptible alike in the gay frolicking with Love's fickleness:

> Bind the sea to slumber stilly,
> Bind its odour to the lily,
> Bind the aspen ne'er to quiver,
> Then bind Love to last for ever;[9]

in the melancholy grace of the beech-tree's petition:

> Though bush or floweret never grow
> My dark unwarming shade below,
> Nor summer bud perfume the dew
> Of rosy blush, or yellow hue;
> Yet leave this barren spot to me;
> Spare, woodman, spare the beechen tree![10]

and in the mannered simplicity of the lines to the

> Star that bringest home the bee,
> And sett'st the weary labourer free![11]

Old-fashioned, again, though not after the Pope or Shenstone type, are Exiles of Erin, Wounded Hussars, Field Flowers—'little wildings of June'—possibly, too, the vigorous ballad, Lord Ullin's Daughter, and—though it surprises even myself to add the name—The Last Man.

I recollect days when The Last Man blazed in the front of lyrics. It was an inspired anthem; deemed worthy

THOMAS CAMPBELL

to rank for loftiness of thought with Intimations of Immortality, and judged to possess twice the fire. Certainly it has its sublime lines, which must live :

> The Sun's eye had a sickly glare,
>   The Earth with age was wan,
> The skeletons of nations were
>   Around that lonely man !
> Some had expired in fight—the brands
> Still rusted in their bony hands ;
>   In plague and famine some !
> Earth's cities had no sound nor tread ;
> And ships were drifting with the dead
>   To shores where all was dumb ![12]

The meagre proportion of the leading idea to the splendour of diction puts it irretrievably out of date. A combination of reflection and fancy in modern inspiration, British and American, has made the present age intolerant of English verse in which a just balance is, as here, not kept.

Perhaps something of the same charge might be brought against the majesty of Lochiel's Warning, though, for myself, I cannot consent to part from its ringing melody :

> Ha ! laugh'st thou, Lochiel, my vision to scorn ?
> Proud bird of the mountain, thy plume shall be torn !
> Say, rush'd the bold eagle exultingly forth,
> From his home, in the dark rolling clouds of the north ?
> Lo ! the death-shot of foemen outspeeding, he rode
> Companionless, bearing destruction abroad ;
> But down let him stoop from his havoc on high !
> Ah ! home let him speed,—for the spoiler is nigh.
> Why flames the far summit ? Why shoot to the blast
> Those embers, like stars from the firmament cast ?
> 'Tis the fire-shower of ruin, all dreadfully driven
> From his eyrie, that beacons the darkness of heaven.
> Oh, crested Lochiel ! the peerless in might,
> Whose banners arise on the battlements' height,

> Heaven's fire is around thee, to blast and to burn;
> Return to thy dwelling! all lonely return!
> For the blackness of ashes shall mark where it stood,
> And a wild mother scream o'er her famishing brood.[13]

At all events, so far as I have for the present surveyed an illustrious life's work, the sum is disappointing, as judged by modern standards. The bulk of Campbell's verse has fallen upon evil days since its publication, when each successive piece was hailed with enthusiasm. He founded no school, and left no disciples interested in the maintenance of his fame. His poems themselves have little of the unity of spirit which might have rendered them mutually supporting and enlightening. While I have directed attention to qualities which ensure literary benevolence, the prospect of that, and nothing more, would have been mortifying indeed to a once popular idol. But I have left to the last exceptions to the chill which has replaced the former promiscuous admiration.

His spirit must be hungrier for posthumous fame than even a bard's has a prescriptive right to be, if it be not content with the praise four pieces have never missed. And they deserve it. Hohenlinden, the pair of Naval songs, and The Soldier's Dream—in which even Tennyson could complain only of three consecutive sibilants—have earned a wreath which would adorn any singer's brow. The materials are of the simplest, approaching meagreness in the famous battle-songs; the effect was, and is, direct, unmistakable, and overwhelming. In an age remarkable for the gulf between the cultivated and the uncultivated, the merit of these was allowed by the highest intelligence; the meanest perfectly appreciated them. From the moment they were launched on the world they became national possessions, and have never ceased to be.

A hundred years of insular security have not muffled the double peal of defiance hurled by Campbell at a hostile Europe when Britain was still in the throes of a struggle for national existence :

> Ye Mariners of England !
> That guard our native seas ;
> Whose flag has braved, a thousand years,
> The battle and the breeze !
> Your glorious standard launch again
> To match another foe !
> And sweep through the deep,
> While the stormy winds do blow ;
> While the battle rages loud and long,
> And the stormy winds do blow.[14]

Little does it matter to the twin tribute to Nelson's 'glorious day', that, for entire sympathy with it, some sturdy insensibility to the niceties of international jurisprudence is needed. At all events it is—condoling mermaid and all—a noble beat to arms and dirge in one :

> Now joy, Old England, raise !
> For the tidings of thy might,
> By the festal cities' blaze,
> Whilst the wine-cup shines in light ;
> And yet amidst that joy and uproar,
> Let us think of them that sleep,
> Full many a fathom deep,
> By thy wild and stormy steep,
> Elsinore ![15]

To gauge the grandeur of such songs we have only to glance at Campbell's own drudging attempt to exalt the untoward victory of Navarino.[16]

And then there is a third martial lyric—Hohenlinden :

> On Linden, when the sun was low,
> All bloodless lay th' untrodden snow,
> And dark as winter was the flow
> Of Iser, rolling rapidly.

> But Linden saw another sight,
> When the drum beat, at dead of night,
> Commanding fires of death to light
> The darkness of her scenery.
>
> Few, few, shall part where many meet!
> The snow shall be their winding-sheet,
> And every turf beneath their feet
> Shall be a soldier's sepulchre.[17]

At first sight an ill-assorted paean this, over a bloody French triumph, to be associated with a pair of heroic British odes! But the air of Campbell's prime was surcharged with battle-steam. Also, it may well have been that to his fancy Moreau's overthrow of Austria was a victory of light over darkness. At any rate, poetically, the outburst ranks in perfection of simplicity with the two. It is not the mere 'drum and trumpet thing' decried by himself. Yet I should like to think that his habitual temper towards the murderous miseries of the Europe of his early manhood was more characteristically reflected in the music lingering long on the inner ear—music with a soul in it—of The Soldier's Dream:

> Our bugles sang truce—for the night-cloud had lowered,
>   And the sentinel stars set their watch in the sky;
> And thousands had sunk on the ground overpowered,
>   The weary to sleep, and the wounded to die.
>
> When reposing that night on my pallet of straw,
>   By the wolf-scaring faggot that guarded the slain;
> At the dead of the night a sweet vision I saw,
>   And thrice ere the morning I dreamt it again.
>
> Methought from the battle-field's dreadful array,
>   Far, far I had roam'd on a desolate track;
> 'Twas Autumn—and sunshine arose on the way
>   To the home of my fathers, that welcomed me back.

I flew to the pleasant fields traversed so oft
  In life's morning march, when my bosom was young;
I heard my own mountain-goats bleating aloft,
  And knew the sweet strain that the corn-reapers sung.

Then pledged we the wine-cup, and fondly I swore,
  From my home and my weeping friends never to part;
My little ones kissed me a thousand times o'er,
  And my wife sobbed aloud in her fullness of heart.

Stay, stay with us—rest, thou art weary and worn;
  And fain was their war-broken soldier to stay;—
But sorrow returned with the dawning of morn;
  And the voice in my dreaming ear melted away.[18]

One is tempted to discover a relation among the four; and certainly they insist upon withdrawing together from the miscellany of their author's work. They form a group apart. But the single intrinsic common quality they possess is negative: it is that we find it almost impossible to realize how and whence one and all emanated. Of their spiritual birth from Campbell in particular I see no trace. Not that, as I have shown, he could otherwise have been regarded as incapable of poetry of a high order. But the excellence itself of his more ordinary verse, as fixing his legitimate level, heightens the difficulty of accounting for the peculiar ascendancy of the sister Four. Kinship between them and verses to Caroline there is none. They are bolts from the blue; and this is the point of view from which contemporaries regarded them. I am not claiming for them that they are of the first rank. For that three of them at any rate want the indefinable something represented to my mind by 'atmosphere'. Their distinction is in a sense they produce of positive completeness which satisfies the judgement. To this is joined the more personal feeling of surprise. Such as they are, they are immortal; it is impossible to think of them as doomed to oblivion.

The soil of poetry is indeed so variously constituted that abnormal growths may without warning be discovered in it at any moment. The strange thing is that Campbell's nature should have fostered them. I admire him, and do not think that he receives his proper share of educated applause at present. At the same time he does not give me the impression of capability for the unexpected. I should have supposed he knew what he could do, and undertook that, and nothing else ; that his mind had always in advance a clear perception of practicable effects before he set to work at realizing them. His habit is to say outright what he has to say. He does not leave his readers to interpret his thought. Even in his moments of loftiest inspiration he is objective, not subjective. It is, however, I dare say, not necessarily inconsistent with this that, perhaps, after all, throughout his career he was always groping after his true poetic mission, without ever actually finding it. Therein may lie a clue, as well to the multifariousness of the forms his poetical impulses took, as to occasional flights, apparently unpremeditated. Equally it may explain his sudden folding, from time to time, of wings meant to bear him to the skies, which Scott attributed to 'fear of the shadow his own fame cast before him'.[19] Thus the issue of his aspirations might be a great patriotic hymn, or a Domestic Tale. It might be a song worthy of Byron, or one too feeble for Thomas Haynes Bayly. He was ever feeling his way, and, I am afraid, never, to his own contentment, hit the direct track, before I, as a child—though not too young to have glowed with indignant pity for Sarmatia, fallen,

<blockquote>unwept, without a crime,—</blockquote>

watched the long pomp of leaders in statesmanship and letters escorting his dead body to its grave in the Abbey.

A poet-soul harnessed to do work which any literary hack could have done as well—spending besides on the foundation of a University for the Empire, of which Brougham appropriated the credit, genius sufficient to have trebled the number of his imperishable lyrics—that is Thomas Campbell! An imperfect, in some respects, a foundered, career, but with precious salvage!

The Poetical Works of Thomas Campbell. Edward Moxon, 1837.
[1] The Pleasures of Hope.
[2] Gertrude of Wyoming, Part i, st. 2.
[3] O'Connor's child; or, The Flower of Love lies Bleeding, st. 2.
[4] Reullura.   [5] Theodric: a Domestic Tale, vv. 30-1.
[6] Gertrude of Wyoming, Part i, st. 23.
[7] To the Rainbow.   [8] Caroline, Part i, st. 5.
[9] Song, st. 4.   [10] The Beech-tree's Petition, vv. 3-6 and 11-12.
[11] To the Evening Star, vv. 1-2.   [12] The Last Man, st. 2.
[13] Lochiel's Warning, vv. 23-40.
[14] Ye Mariners of England: a Naval Ode, st. 1.
[15] Battle of the Baltic, st. 7.
[16] Stanzas on the Battle of Navarino.
[17] Hohenlinden, stanzas 1, 2, and 8.   [18] The Soldier's Dream.
[19] Scott in Conversation with Washington Irving, 1817. Lockhart's Life.

ROBERT BURNS

1759—1796

LITERARY achievements far below those of Burns would have been miraculous in an English labourer, or even small farmer. In a Scottish peasant they are just comprehensible. Young minds in Scotland were put at the parish school in a way of thinking after a fashion unintelligible to an Englishman of the same rank. The Sabbath catechizing and sermonizing continued and developed the training. Knotty problems, terrestrial and celestial, were familiarly handled beside every cottage hearth. So far as literature is concerned, both in what of education was given, and what was withheld, fortune could not have dealt a more fatal blow than had she used her bounty to endow Robert Burns with a Snell Exhibition, and sent him to Balliol. In a Lowland parish the powers of intellect, and fancy as well, were evenly developed. Besides that the whole grand Hebrew literature was a child's inalienable inheritance, an abyss separated weird Scottish from matter-of-fact English ballad-and-folk-lore in the days of Burns. Sentiment, no less than Latin and theology, was thus cultivated among low as among high. At the same time that abundant nutriment was supplied to the mental faculties, another phase altogether of imaginative exuberance existed in rural Scottish life to which similar tendencies in Burns were by no means strange. By the side of Calvinistic despotism there has always risen in recognized, rank rebellion a temper of whimsical revelry and licence, to which, for good or ill, the grossness of English bucolic morals is no counterpart.

So far the circumstances were not unfavourable, as south

of the Tweed they would have been, to the apparition of a genuine poet in a cotter family. A generation later another, if of inferior quality, grew up in Ettrick Forest. The wonder with Burns is in the degree. In his case the character of the results is so extraordinary that it ought to be superfluous to consider whether he owed much or little to the accidents of country, period, or surroundings; to regard anything but, as with Shakespeare, the actual work. In any common case, even when the local advantages enjoyed by an Ayrshire ploughman were set in full against the general impediments to the emergence of rustic genius from its clay, allowance would still have to be made in favour of the parvenu. Such an act of grace would be an insult to Burns. At any moment he may be beheld soaring where he needs none. It cannot matter whether he were peer or peasant who wrote To a Mountain Daisy, The Cotter's Saturday Night, Bannockburn, For A' That and A' That, John Barleycorn, Mary in Heaven, Auld Lang Syne, and fifty other miracles of melody.

Love, Pity, Indignation at despotism and arrogance, ecclesiastical or social, and a sparkling humour—all by turns, and sometimes one or more in combination—could always wake the poet in Burns. Love took the first place. It might be general admiration, which a passing vision of beauty would stir into a flame recognized as equally transient:

> O saw ye bonnie Lesley
>   As she gaed o'er the border?
> She's gane, like Alexander,
>   To spread her conquests farther.
>
> To see her is to love her,
>   And love but her for ever;
> For Nature made her what she is,
>   And ne'er made sic anither!

Thou art a queen, fair Lesley,
　　Thy subjects we, before thee ;
Thou art divine, fair Lesley,
　　The hearts o' men adore thee.

The Deil he couldna scaith thee,
　　Or aught that wad belang thee ;
He'd look into thy bonnie face,
　　And say, ' I canna wrang thee ' !

The Powers aboon will tent thee ;
　　Misfortune sha'na steer thee ;
Thou'rt like themselves sae lovely,
　　That ill they'll ne'er let near thee.

Return again, fair Lesley,
　　Return to Caledonie !
That we may brag, we hae a lass
　　There 's nane again sae bonnie.[1]

For the moment more usually it concentrated itself upon a particular object ;—once in a way, lawfully, as, during his honeymoon, upon his bride :

Of a' the airts the wind can blaw,
　　I dearly like the west,
For there the bonnie lassie lives,
　　The lassie I lo'e best :
There wild woods grow, and rivers row,
　　And monie a hill between ;
But day and night my fancy's flight
　　Is ever wi' my Jean.

I see her in the dewy flowers,
　　I see her sweet and fair ;
I hear her in the tunefu' birds,
　　I hear her charm the air ;
There 's not a bonnie flower that springs
　　By fountain, shaw, or green ;
There 's not a bonnie bird that sings,
　　But minds me o' my Jean.[2]

More often it wandered, now to a Highland Mary, still on earth, and of

> form sae fair and faultless;

or now to Nancy, severed from him to their mutual despair:

> Had we never lov'd sae kindly,
> Had we never lov'd sae blindly,
> Never met—or never parted,
> We had ne'er been broken-hearted.³—

A heart-break readily healed if it were his; less easily, as I should be glad to infer from his own verse that he too felt, when it was hers:

> Ye banks and braes o' bonnie Doon,
>   How can ye bloom sae fresh and fair!
> How can ye chant, ye little birds,
>   And I sae weary, fu' o' care!
> Thou'lt break my heart, thou warbling bird,
>   That wantons thro' the flowering thorn;
> Thou minds me o' departed joys,
>   Departed—never to return.
>
> Aft hae I rov'd by bonnie Doon,
>   To see the rose and woodbine twine;
> And ilka bird sang o' its luve,
>   And fondly sae did I o' mine.
> Wi' lightsome heart I pu'd a rose,
>   Fu' sweet upon its thorny tree;
> And my fause luver stole the rose,
>   But ah! he left the thorn wi' me.⁴

In any case, and however fleeting, the pity, it may be pleaded for the singer, was real whenever it came, and whoever the object, whether a lover, or a Prince, an outlaw in the realm his natural patrimony:

> Where the wild beasts find shelter, but I can find none;⁵

or a captive Queen :

>   Now blooms the lily by the bank,
>   The primrose down the brae :
>   The hawthorn's budding in the glen,
>   And milk-white is the slae ;
>   The meanest hind in fair Scotland
>   May rove their sweets amang ;
>   But I, the Queen of a' Scotland,
>   Maun lie in prison strang.
>   Oh ! soon, to me, may summer-suns
>   Nae mair light up the morn !
>   Nae mair, to me, the autumn winds
>   Wave o'er the yellow corn !
>   And in the narrow house o' death
>   Let winter round me rave ;
>   And the next flow'rs that deck the spring
>   Bloom on my peaceful grave ! [6]

Each eddy of sympathy—or it might be antipathy—flowed straight from the poet's heart. It continued to flow so long as he sang. Therein is the secret of his charm; that, in song, the man and the poet were one. Inspiration, when it descended upon him, entered into possession of every faculty, gift, instinct, of his humanity, and used the whole for its present purpose. In all circumstances he joyed in singing. Thanks to it, life grew for him ' a' enchanted fairy land '. Let but his wonted visitors, cauld poverty and cankert care, grant him a short reprieve, and ' Wi' a rime or sang he lasht em, and thought it sport '. A jest, a sob, a cry of revelry, perhaps a little far gone, occasionally a local spite, as in grim Death and Dr. Hornbook, a curse, a blessing, as it issued from him, melted, smiled, or flamed, into verse. Listen how, without an effort, the Dedication to rich and beneficent Gavin Hamilton rises, in its last score of lines, into a region where man approaches the angelic without ceasing to be human :

Whilst your wishes and endeavours
Are blest with Fortune's smiles and favours,
I am, dear Sir, with zeal most fervent,
Your much indebted, humble servant.
But if—which pow'rs above prevent!—
That iron-hearted carl, Want,
Attended, in his grim advances,
By sad mistakes, and black mischances,
While hopes, and joys, and pleasures fly him,
Make you as poor a dog as I am,
Your 'humble servant' then no more;
For who would humbly serve the poor!
But, by a poor man's hopes in Heav'n!
While recollection's pow'r is giv'n,
If, in the vale of humble life,
The victim sad of fortune's strife,
I, thro' the tender gushing tear,
Should recognize my Master dear,
If friendless, low, we meet together,
Then, Sir, your hand—my Friend and Brother! [7]

Nothing in fancy was beyond his powers; but transcendent among them is the sense of humour, blending with pathos, in a multitude of varying shades. It plays about the plough-evicted mouse:

Wee, sleekit, cow'rin, tim'rous beastie,
O, what a panic 's in thy breastie!
Thou needna start awa sae hasty,
  Wi' bickering brattle!
I wad be laith to rin an' chase thee,
  Wi' murdering prattle!

I'm truly sorry man's dominion
Has broken Nature's social union,
An' justifies that ill opinion
  Which makes thee startle
At me, thy poor earth-born companion,
  An' fellow-mortal!

> Thy wee bit housie, too, in ruin !
> Its silly wa's the win's are strewin !
> An' naething, now, to big a new ane,
>   O' foggage green !
> An' bleak December's winds ensuin,
>   Baith snell an' keen !
>
> Thou saw the fields laid bare an' waste,
> An' weary winter comin fast,
> An' cozie here, beneath the blast,
>   Thou thought to dwell,
> Till crash ! the cruel coulter past
>   Out-thro' thy cell.
>
> But, Mousie, thou art no thy lane,
> In proving foresight may be vain ;
> The best-laid schemes o' mice an' men
>   Gang aft a-gley,
> An' lea'e us nought but grief and pain,
>   For promis'd joy.[8]

I confess to a little surprise—almost disappointment—at failing to find a similar touch, a smile, mingled with the lovely eagerness of apology to the Mountain Daisy, a later victim of that remorseful plough :

> Wee, modest, crimson-tipped flow'r,
> Thou 's met me in an evil hour ;
> For I maun crush amang the stoure
>   Thy slender stem ;
> To spare thee now is past my pow'r,
>   Thou bonnie gem.
>
> Alas ! it 's no thy neebor sweet,
> The bonnie Lark, companion meet !
> Bending thee 'mang the dewy weet !
>   Wi' spreckled breast,
> When upward springing, blythe, to greet
>   The purpling east.
>
> Cauld blew the bitter-biting north
> Upon thy early, humble birth ;

> Yet cheerfully thou glinted forth
>   Amid the storm,
> Scarce rear'd above the parent earth
>   Thy tender form.
> There, in thy scanty mantle clad,
> Thy snawy bosom sun-ward spread,
> Thou lifts thy unassuming head
>   In humble guise;
> But now the share uptears thy bed,
>   And low thou lies! [9]

Humour enlivens, however, abundantly the homely tenderness of the old farmer's New Year's greeting to his auld mare Maggie:

> A guid New Year I wish thee, Maggie!
> Hae, there's a ripp to thy auld baggie;
> Tho' thou's howe-backit, now, an' knaggie,
>   I've seen the day,
> Thou could hae gane like onie staggie
>   Out-owre the lay.
>
> When thou an' I were young and skeigh,
> An' stable-meals at fairs were dreigh,
> How thou wad prance, an' snore, and skreigh
>   An' tak the road;
> Town's bodies ran, an' stood abeigh,
>   An' ca't thee mad.
>
> When thou was corn't, an' I was mellow,
> We took the road aye like a swallow;
> At Brooses thou had ne'er a fellow
>   For pith an' speed;
> But every tail thou paid them hollow,
>   Whare'er thou gaed.
>
> Monie a sair daurk we twa hae wrought,
> An' wi' the weary warl' hae fought!
> An' monie an anxious day, I thought
>   We wad be beat!
> Yet here to crazy age we're brought,
>   Wi' something yet.

390   FIVE CENTURIES OF ENGLISH VERSE

> We've worn to crazy years thegither;
> We'll toyte about wi' ane anither;
> Wi' tentie care I'll flit thy tether
>   To some hain'd rig,
> Whare ye may nobly rax your leather,
>   Wi' sma' fatigue.[10]

When encouraged to enjoy itself, yet with a poet's taste in command still, and prepared to curb excess, the spirit of fun revels. Thus, though never slipping in, even in the audacious mocking of the Address to the Deil, it skirts, as almost necessarily with such a theme, the edge of profanity:

> Hear me, auld Hangie, for a wee,
> An' let poor damned bodies be;
> I'm sure sma' pleasure it can gie,
>   E'en to a deil,
> To skelp and scaud poor dogs like me,
>   An' hear us squeel![11]

In Tam O'Shanter it rises into an exulting frolic of melody, unparalleled in British—perhaps, in the world's poetry,—inimitable!

The night is a wild one when, after drinking at the inn till

> glorious,
> O'er a' the ills of life victorious,

Tam begins his long ride homewards on his grey mare Meg. The storm he does not mind a 'whistle', yet is not so sure about the spirit world as to neglect any practicable precautions against being caught 'by bogles unawares'; for

> Kirk-Alloway was drawing nigh,
> Whare ghaists and houlets nightly cry—
> By this time he was cross the ford,
> Whare in the snaw the chapman smoor'd;
> And past the birks and meikle stane,
> Whare drunken Charlie brak's neck-bane;

And thro' the wins, and by the cairn,
Whare hunters fand the murder'd bairn ;
And near the thorn, aboon the well,
Whare Mungo's mither hang'd hersel.—
Before him Doon pours all her floods ;
The doubling storm roars thro' the woods ;
The lightnings flash from pole to pole ;
Near and more near the thunders roll ;
When glimmering thro' the groaning trees,
Kirk-Alloway seem'd in a bleeze ;
Thro' ilka bore the beams were glancing ;
And loud resounded mirth and dancing.—

Maggie stood right sair astonish'd,
Till, by the heel and hand admonish'd,
She ventured forward on the light ;
And, vow ! Tam saw an unco sight !
Warlocks and witches in a dance.
A winnock-bunker in the east,
There sat auld Nick, in shape o' beast ;
A towzie tyke, black, grim, and large ;
To gie them music was his charge ;
He screw'd the pipes, and gart them skirl,
Till roof and rafters a' did dirl.—
Coffins stood round like open presses,
That shaw'd the dead in their last dresses ;
And by some devilish cantrip slight,
Each in its cauld hand held a light,—
By which heroic Tam was able
To note upon the haly table,
A murderer's banes in gibbet airns ;
Twa span-lang, wee, unchristen'd bairns ;
A garter, which a babe had strangled ;
A knife, a father's throat had mangled,
Wi' mair o' horrible and awfu',
Which e'en to name wad be unlawfu'.

As Tammie glowr'd, amaz'd, and curious,
The mirth and fun grew fast and furious ;
The piper loud and louder blew ;
The dancers quick and quicker flew ;

They reel'd, they set, they cross'd, they cleekit,
Till ilka carlin swat and reekit,
And coost her duddies to the wark,
And linket at it in her sark!

There was ae winsome wench and walie,
That night inlisted in the core,
(Lang after kenn'd on Carrick shore!)
Her cutty sark, o' Paisley-harn,
That while a lassie she had worn,
In longitude tho' sorely scanty,
It was her best, and she was vauntie.—
Ah! little kenn'd thy rev'rend grannie,
That sark she coft for her wee Nannie
Wi' twa pund Scotch ('twas a' her riches),
Wad ever grac'd a dance o' witches!

But here my muse her wing maun cour;
Sic flights are far beyond her pow'r;
To sing how Nannie lap and flang,
(A souple jade she was and strang)
Till first ae caper, syne anither,
Tam tint his reason a'thegither,
And roars out, 'Weel done, Cutty-sark!'
And in an instant all was dark;
And scarcely had he Maggie rallied,
When out the hellish legion sallied.
So Maggie runs, the witches follow,
Wi' monie an eldritch skreech and hollow.

Ah, Tam! ah, Tam! thou'll get thy fairin!
In hell they'll roast thee like a herrin!
Now, do thy speedy utmost, Meg,
And win the key-stane o' the brig:
There at them thou thy tail may toss,
A running stream they darena cross.

But ere the key-stane she could make,
The fient a tail she had to shake!
For Nannie, far before the rest,
Hard upon noble Maggie prest,

> And flew at Tam wi' furious ettle ;
> But little wist she Maggie's mettle,
> Ae spring brought aff her master hale,—
> But left behind her ain grey tail ! [12]

Posterity might have cared to recollect only the enchantment of the singing. It might not have troubled to recall the sins, joys, and woes of the singer. He himself has rendered it impossible to forget ; he would have it to be impossible ; for he himself could not, would not, forget. A mutineer, a fighter, in poetry as in life, he is always challenging criticism of his feelings and his acts. His aberrations are never removed more than one thrill, one heart-beat, from his ethereal inspirations. He insists on exposing his passions, his penitences, and his relapses, as if his inner being were a skeleton clock. The pathos of his vow to cherish and shield ' my sweet wee lady ', his illegitimate child, as ever ' dear and near my heart ', [13] is spoilt by reminiscences of the merry amour which has brought the hapless mother to disgrace. While he is withering with the pitiless satire of the Holy Fair, the Ordination, and Holy Willie's Prayer, the 'eldritch squeel and gestures', the merciless orthodoxy, and secret vices, of ruling clergy and elders, he scarcely dissembles the extent to which he is avenging himself for his own well-deserved tribulation on the stool of shame. He broke women's hearts and honour as lightly as if he were an instrument of blind chance. Knowing that duty to weans and wife is ' the true pathos and sublime of human life ', he regularly repented in dust and ashes, in the intervals between his outbursts, as contritely as King David. He invited the whole world to listen to the tale of his delinquencies and their sad consequences, with no more active sense of responsibility than if he had been a harp touched into music, whether gay or mournful, by emotional gusts with which he had no personal concern. On occasions when indulgence of a passion compromised, or wrecked, another's good name, or peace of mind, he would act as if what had been a crime, a cruelty, in an ordinary man, became in an inspired minstrel just a licensed, even useful and inevitable, professional experience. The relation between himself and his transgressions was much the same for him as between noble operatic music and an imbecile libretto.

For his own sake, as well as in compassion for hearts which came in his way, not to speak of morals, one wishes he had been gifted with self-restraint ; that his emotions had been less ardent, or he had been exposed to fewer temptations. I am afraid the gain to virtue would have been a loss to literature. Taken as he is, composite of earth very earthy, and spirit often almost heavenly, he fills a space which would be blank indeed without him as he was. Not that he produced nothing but a casket of jewels, like Gray, or a mine of perfect crystals, like Pope. He was apt to forget when to leave off. At his best he would be beguiled from ideas into rhetoric. Indignation would degenerate into scurrility. He could mistake coarseness for manly humour, rudeness for independence, and indecency for wit. Even he could be dull, and sometimes at once dull and angry. But when the poet awoke in him, it was a poet with wings ; it might have been the discoverer of the art of verse ; the first poet that ever sang. The shadow of earlier poetic fancies—even of his own—never frighted him off a beautiful thought or image with the bugbear of plagiarism. He takes for his uses big words and little, Latin and Saxon, just as they suit, with no theory but the duty of charm. Fancies shot from his pen as free, fast, and piercing as pebbles of the brook from the shepherd boy's sling. He was incapable of using a natural image falsely. He could do anything with verse, beg a guinea, turn a greasy haggis into a being honest, sonsie, of moral beauty, glorious to sight and taste, glad to be immolated for the nourishment of auld Scotland's champions. The marvel, besides, of the quick changes! Tears and sighs, even tempests, will have been brooding about his lyre. Then, in a moment, the clouds disperse; there are sunshine, gaiety, innocent affectionateness. With the absolute nature in every phase! Never in Great Britain, since Robin Herrick, had a poet arisen with so much of a lark's, a nightingale's, necessity of singing in him as in Robert Burns! Never in that quality has he had a successor to match him!

The Poetical Works of Robert Burns (Aldine Edition of the British Poets). William Pickering.
(Also, The Complete Poetical Works of Robert Burns (Kilmarnock Popular Edition), ed. by W. Scott Douglas. Kilmarnock: J. M'Kie, 1871.)

[1] Bonnie Lesley.   [2] I love my Jean.
[3] Farewell to Nancy, st. 2.   [4] The Banks of Doon.
[5] The Chevalier's Lament, v. 12.
[6] Lament of Mary Queen of Scots, on the Approach of Spring, stanzas 3 and 7.
[7] A Dedication to Gavin Hamilton, Esq.
[8] To a Mouse; on turning her up in her Nest, stanzas 1, 2, 4, 5, and 7, vol. i.
[9] To a Mountain Daisy; on turning one down with the Plough, stanzas 1, 2, 3, and 5.
[10] The Auld Farmer's New Year Morning Salutation to his Auld Mare Maggie, stanzas 1, 8, 9, 16, and 18.
[11] Address to the Deil, st. 2.   [12] Tam O'Shanter: A Tale.
[13] The Poet's Welcome to his Illegitimate Child, st. 1.

INDEX OF FIRST WORDS

	PAGE
A blackening train Of clamorous rooks	261
Abra was ready ere I called her name	221
Adieu, goodman drivel	45
A fool at forty is a fool indeed	256
Again deceives him, and again	158
A genius for all stations fit	229
A glorious city in the sea	364
A God all mercy is a God unjust	254
A golden chain let down from heaven	60
A good man was ther of religioun	15
A guid New Year I wish thee, Maggie!	389
A health to the Nut-brown Lasse	164
Ah, Dorcas, Dorcas! now adieu!	144
Ah me! the blooming pride of May	225
Ah, my deare God! though I am clean forgot	84
Ah, poore Love, whi dost thou live	23
Ah, yet, ere I descend to th' grave	189
A kind of knack at rhyme	230
A knuckle of veal—You may buy it, or steal	248
Alas, 'tis true I have gone here and there	53
All are but parts of one stupendous whole	235
All in the Downs the fleet was moor'd	250
All love, all liking, all delight	137
All men think all men mortal but themselves	256
All one desert, desolate and grey	264
All that sweetness, all that youth	133
All worldly joyes go lesse	91
Along the brooks the crimson-spotted fry	265
Along the milky way by many a star	134

INDEX OF FIRST WORDS

	PAGE
A man he was to all the country dear	298
A manly man, to been an abbot able	15
A man severe he was, and stern to view	297
A mead a wanton river dresses	129
A mere mechanic art	243
A mind so pure, so perfect fine	59
A mistress moderately fair	189
Amoret, as sweet and good	158
A name Which bids defiance to all sense of shame	331
And art thou grieved, sweet and sacred Dove	85
And ever as they mount, like larks they sing	87
And glittering temples of the hostile gods	214
And scatters day	174
And what Timotheus was is Dryden now	213
And yet—as if some deep hate and dissent	106
And you, brave Cobham! to the latest breath	241
An ecstasy too big to be suppressed	313
Another Savage to be starved in me	330
An undevout astronomer is mad	256
A pleasing land of drowsy head it was	265
A prison with a milder name	348
A pure seed-pearl of infant dew	137
A ringlet of her hair	139
A rosebud born in snow	112
Around the steel no tortur'd worm shall twine	246
Around the walls are heroes, lovers, kings	347
A salmon's belly, Helluo, was thy fate	239
A silver stream shall roll his waters near	188
Ask with painful shyness, and refused	307
A skylark wounded on the wing	360
A star that thro' the firmament	365
A stoic of the woods—a man without a tear	373
A summer's day	51
A sweet disorder in the dress	138
As with soft accents round her neck he clings	368
A tender shepherdess, whose hair	199

INDEX OF FIRST WORDS 399

	PAGE
At every turn she made a little stand	217
At heart's desire	223
At the close of the day, when the hamlet is still	319
Beauty clear and fair	69
Before that sinne turn'd flesh to stone	86
Behold the child, by Nature's kindly law	238
Beneath an ancient bridge, the straiten'd flood	347
Be thine own palace, or the world's thy gaol	77
Bid me to live, and I will live	145
Bind the sea to slumber stilly	374
Bless'd be the great! for those they take away	242
Blest place of my nativity	136
Blubb'ring her sable tears lets fall	129
Brave Hector went to see	215
Bright Scolopendraes arm'd with silver scales	32
But all our praises why should lords engross?	241
But oh! what storm was in that mind! what strife	342
But who the melodies of morn can tell?	318
By cutting off all kisses	170
By night an atheist half believes a God	256
By the full Kingdom of that final kiss	96
Call, and I'll come; say Thou the when and where	141
Can a woman's tender care	309
Can draw you to her with a single hair	216
Can I see another's woe	353
Careless and unthoughtful, lying	188
Cast the feather'd hook	247
Catching the sense at two removes	83
Caught and caged, and starved to death	308
Cease, eager Muse; peace, pen; for my sake stay	27
Chaste as th' air whither she's fled	176
Cheer up, my mates, the wind does fairly blow	184
Cherry-ripe, ripe, ripe, I cry	139
Christ's gallant humbleness	77

INDEX OF FIRST WORDS

	PAGE
Clever Tom Clinch, while the rabble was bawling	229
Come thou, who art the wine and wit	141
Come unto these yellow sands	44
Comming to kisse her lyps—such grace I found	36
Dare The toilette's sacred mysteries declare	247
Dear love, for nothing less than thee	76
Dear Night! this world's defeat	106
Death, be not proud, though some have called thee	77
Delightful Wyoming! beneath thy skies	372
Denied the charity of dust, to spread	255
Difficult is the penance, yet I'll strive	327
Divinest Spenser, heav'n-bred, happy Muse!	128
Doth by Huntingdon and Cambridge flit	40
Doth she chide thee? 'Tis to shew it	23
Doubt wisely; in strange way	80
Down on the deck he laid himself, and died	203
Drink on't even till we weep	197
Drink to me, only with thine eyes	57
Each seem'd to act that part he came to see	193
Earth-born, bloodless, undecaying	308
E'en in the spring and playtime of the year	312
Emelye, that fairer was to sene	12
Endless pillows rose to prop the head	266
Entertains a lovely guest	67
Eurus waves his murky wings	290
Even undemanded by a sign or sound	265
Every truant knew	299
Extremes beyond extremity	48
Facit indignatio versus	230
Fair daffodils, we weep to see	146
Fairest, when I am gone, as now the glass	131
Fair pledges of a fruitful tree	146
Fair sweet goddess, queen of loves	68

INDEX OF FIRST WORDS

	PAGE
Far'd as dauncing in delight	33
Farwel my studie, as lasting that sesoun!	19
Father, father, where are you going?	354
Fayre is my Love, when her fayre golden haires	35
Feminyne creature	10
Few are the pleasures Chatterton e'er knew	330
First Fear his hand, its skill to try	280
Fool not; for all may have	90
For a little, little pleasure	68
For a quart of ale is a dish for a king	45
For her gait, if she be walking	131
For Lucrece thought he blush'd to see her shame	49
Form sae fair and faultless	385
For now against himself he sounds this doom	48
For to be Cromwell was a greater thing	203
For we were nursed upon the self-same hill	118
For yesterday the Court of Heaven with Jove	215
Fresh and green as Flora	137
Friend to my life, which did not you prolong	243
From loveless youth to unrespected age	238
From out thy sweet abode	280
From whose celestiall ray	36
Ful faste imagining	12
Full fifteen thousand lusty fellows	222
Full many a glorious morning have I seen	51
Ful simple and coy	14
Future ages shall adore	304
Gallantly crown'd with large sky-kissing trees	134
Gather ye rose-buds, while ye may	139
Gay and glad	86
Gazing back upon the skies	199
Gentle Spring, ethereal Mildness	267
Give me a look, give me a face	56
Glorious, O'er a' the ills of life victorious	390
God loved he best with al his hole herte	17

VOL. I   C C

INDEX OF FIRST WORDS

	PAGE
God the first garden made, and the first city Cain	188
Go, lovely Rose!	160
Go now, her happy parents, and be sad	61
Go seek thy peace in war	60
Go, Soul, out of thyself, and seek for more	96
Graybeard corrupter of our listening youth	306
Great and good	213
Great Anna, whom three realms obey	236
Great cannon oaths, and shot	170
Great relick! thou too, in this port of ease	185
Grecian ghosts, that in battle were slain	213
Had almost forgot his poetry	165
Had we never lov'd sae kindly	385
Hail, holy Light! Thee I revisit safe	125
Hail thou my native soil! thou blessed plot	130
Ha! laugh'st thou, Lochiel, my vision to scorn?	375
Happy those early days, when I	107
Hard favour'd tyrant, ugly, meagre, lean	48
Hark! hark! the lark at heaven's gate sings	44
Haste, light the tapers, urge the fire	290
Hast thou courageous fire to thaw the ice	79
Hast thou ever weigh'd a sigh	259
Hast thou seen the down i' the air	167
Have you seen but a bright lily grow	61
Having this day my horse, my hand, my launce	26
Hearken then awhile to me	132
Hear me, auld Hangie, for a wee	390
Heaven grant I lose no more!	340
He many a creature did anatomize	288
Hence, all you vain delights	67
He nothing common did, or mean	202
Here, a little child, I stand	143
Here a pretty baby lies	140
Her eyes the glow-worm lend thee	138
Her feet beneath her petticoat	168

INDEX OF FIRST WORDS

	PAGE
Her fingers witched the chords they passed along	373
Her sorrows through the night; and on the bough	262
Her supple breast thrills out	98
He that believes himself doth never lie	77
He that will to bed go sober	69
He who lov'd best, and them defended best	173
He who mocks the infant's faith	360
Him that yon soars on golden wing	115
His being was in her alone	24
His face is fair as heaven	351
His river hemmes	39
His shepherd's lay, yet equaliz'd of none	128
Hither thou com'st; the busy wind all night	106
How courteous it ascends	197
How fresh, O Lord, how sweet and clean	88
How happy could I be with either	248
How oft I saw her dead, while yet in smiles!	256
How shin'd the soul, unconquer'd, in the Tower!	242
How sweet I roamed from field to field	358
I do believe the good, and I	142
If aught of oaten stop, or pastoral song	283
If manly sense, if Nature link'd with Art	303
If thou be'est born to strange sights	74
I had much rather be myself the slave	307
I, hapless soul, that never knew a friend	133
I have no name	352
I little thought before	182
I'll undo The world by dying	75
I love thee, all unlovely as thou seemst	313
I may not here abide	327
In all my wanderings round this world of care	299
In all the labour'd artifice of speech	302
Indeed, poor Solomon in rhyme	221
In early days did to my wondering sense	291
In every cry of every man	356

INDEX OF FIRST WORDS

	PAGE
Infected Row we term our street	347
Infinite wings! till all the plume-dark air	261
In his mistress' flame, playing like a fly	62
In Nature's fairest forms, is aught so fair	289
Insignificance of face	331
In the gardin, at the sonne up-riste	217
In the joly tyme of May	19
In the world look out and see	68
In the worst inn's worst room with mat half hung	239
Into his tender system took	263
In whose gentle spright	9
I prythee send me back my heart	167
I saw a chapel all of gold	356
I saw him dead: a leaden slumber lies	204
I serve the fairy queen	43
It is not growing like a tree	61
It is the law	62
I walk'd the other day, to spend my hour	111
I walk to find a true love: and I see	74
I wandered in the forest	357
I was angry with my friend	357
I will through the wave and foam	79
I wonder any man alive will ever rear a daughter	248
James a bankrupt! Boy, my hat and cane	343
Jocund his verse was, but his life was chaste	142
Kirk-Alloway was drawing nigh	390
Knew no shrill alarming bell	266
Large Euclid's strict epitome	177
Lay a garland on my hearse	66
Layde the whol world a falldstole att thie feete	326
Lest she should see him go to bed	197
Let him have time to tear his curled hair	49

INDEX OF FIRST WORDS

	PAGE
Let one poor sprig of bay around my head	305
Let the toast pass!	164
Life of my life, take not so soon thy flight	140
Life's a debtor to the grave	259
Life's a name	184
Ligurge him-self, the grete king of Trace	11
Like Love in arms; he wrote but five	175
Like Moses, led us forth at last	183
Like snails did creep	139
Like the morning star	194
Like the nymphs, their pleasing themes	102
Little Lamb, who made thee?	352
Lord Chancellor of both their laws	183
Love in her eyes sits playing	249
Love in her sunny eyes does basking play	185
Lowly do I bend my knee	67
Made at the Sun	136
Makes her silk-worms beds	224
Man by his own strength to Heaven would soar	208
Man wants but little, nor that little long	256
Many a poet	62
March, march—quoth I—the word straight give	171
Margarita first possest	186
May! Be thou never graced with birds that sing	134
May his pretty dukeship grow	143
Merry London, my most kyndly nurse	39
Methought I saw my late espoused saint	126
Mighty poets in their misery dead	278
Minces the sanguine flesh in frustums fine	340
More fat than bard beseems	267
Mortality, behold, and fear	71
Most gentle, most unfortunate	363
Most gentle spirite breathed from above	40
Most glorious Lord of lyfe! that, on this day	37
Mourning-weeds for hearts forlorn	166

INDEX OF FIRST WORDS

	PAGE
Music can soften pain to ease	235
Must live by Courts, or starve	207
My best civility	74
My bosom of itself is cold, and of itself is dark	360
My country waits my march : I must away	326
My God, when I walk in those groves	106
My lyre I tune, my voice I raise	223
My noble, lovely, little Peggy	224
My soul, there is a country	108
My Starre, because a sugred kisse	27
Nature is the glass reflecting God	256
Near the pavilions where we slept, still ran	266
Neglect the heart to compliment the head	302
Never seek to tell thy love	357
Nine months Thy hands are fashioning us	105
Noble he was, contemning all things mean	344
No, no, your King's not yet to seek	95
No palace to the clouds did swell	175
Nor second He, that rode sublime	271
Nor stoops to take the staff, nor lays it down	229
Nor think the kindred muses thy disgrace	218
Nothing was Spring which Phillips did not draw	331
Now blooms the lily by the bank	386
Now fades the glimmering landscape on the sight	275
Now great Hyperion left his golden throne	130
Now I in you without a bodie move	87
Now in circling troops they meet	271
Now joy, Old England, raise !	377
Now the bright morning-star, Day's harbinger	116
O Ælla, friend, and lord	327
O be a man, and thou shalt be a God	259
O blessed bodie ! Whither art thou thrown ?	84
O could I flow like thee, and make thy stream	195

INDEX OF FIRST WORDS

	PAGE
O Day most calm, most bright	86
O'er the smooth enamelled green	116
O faire! O swete! when I do look on thee	22
Of alle the floures in the mede	19
Of all the fairest cities of the Earth	365
Of all the tyrannies on human kind	209
Of all the warring passions in his breast	334
Of a' the airts the wind can blaw	384
Of my first love the fatall band	24
Of my love's conquest, peerless beauties prise	37
O for a law to noose the villain's neck!	307
Oft have I musde, but now at length I finde	28
Of these the false Achitophel was first	211
Oft, on a plat of rising ground	115
O happie Thames, that didst my Stella beare	27
Oh, bloodiest picture in the book of Time	371
Oh for a lodge in some vast wilderness	307
Oh God! my brother dead!	346
Oh! lyre divine, what daring spirit	270
O, how much more doth beauty beauteous seem	51
Oh! the turn'd neck, and smooth white skin	249
On bokes for to rede I me delyte	19
One band of friends unconquerable	264
One king, one faith, one language, and one isle	203
One little world or two	96
One spirit, His Who wore the platted thorns	312
On her white breast a sparkling cross she wore	237
O Nightingale, that on yon bloomy spray	119
On Isis' banks	134
On Linden, when the sun was low	377
On Sunday-eve, when service ends	347
On the breast of Thames	134
O ruddier than the cherry!	249
O saw ye bonnie Lesley	383
O! sing unto my roundelay	327
O souls, in whom no heavenly fire is found	216

	PAGE
O, that I now could write as well as then!	155
Our bugles sang truce—for the night-cloud had lowered	378
Our ladies and our men now speak more wit	206
Out upon it, I have loved	166
O! what an endlesse work have I in hand!	32
Plucked, the fairest, sweetest flower	193
Poets near our princes sleep	194
Poor Pope will grieve a month, and Gay	230
Possessed his soul before he died	54
Pride of Lammas Fair	342
Princes we are if we prevail	193
Procrastination is the Thief of Time	256
Pure and eloquent blood	79
Putte he nat his wyf in greet assay	13
Pygmies are pygmies still, tho' percht on alps	256
Queen and huntress, chaste and fair	58
Rectors five to one close vault conveyed	340
Remembering still its former height	199
Remembrance oft shall haunt the shore	279
Remote, unfriended, melancholy, slow	295
Rich, attir'd With golden hands	33
Rise up, my fair, my spotless one	95
Rise, ye debtors, then, and fall	141
Robed in the sable garb of woe	272
Sabrina fair	117
Sacharissa's beauty's wine	158
Sacred to the household gods	262
Saw the obsequious Seraphim	95
Say, for you saw us, ye immortal lights	181
Scolle of locusts caste oppe bie the sea	326

INDEX OF FIRST WORDS

	PAGE
Scorn'd the trifling rules of art	281
Scorn no man's love, though of a mean degree	91
See! rosy is her bower	175
See the green space; on either hand	287
See! what a clouded majesty! and eyes	176
Self-proclaim'd in a gazette	306
Sergeant of the Lawe, war and wys	15
Shadwell alone, of all my sons, is he	209
She, she is dead, she's dead; when thou know'st this	79
Shines in all climates like a star	229
Sigh no more, ladies, sigh no more	43
Since His will is that to posterity	79
Sir Plume, of amber snuff-box justly vain	237
Sleep-soothing groves, and quiet lawns between	265
Slow time with woollen feet make thy soft pace	177
So barren of new pride	52
So good, so lovely, and so young	158
So long as men can breathe, or eyes can see	54
So marvellously wrought	365
Some asked me where the rubies grew	138
Some natural tears they dropped, but wiped them soon	125
Some royal mastiff panting at their heels	306
Son and Mother Discourse alternate wounds	96
Sorrow can make a verse without a muse	70
So soon of Care beguiled	364
Soul of the age!	63
Spare diet is the cause love lasts	165
Spend his life's declining part	230
Spite of all the criticizing elves	302
Splendid wit Entangled in the cobwebs of the schools	185
Star of the morn and eve!	372
Star that bringest home the bee	374
Stay O sweet, and do not rise	75
Still as I did the leaves inspire	159
Stricken deer, that left the herd	314
Such health and gaiety of heart enjoy	313

INDEX OF FIRST WORDS

	PAGE
Sweet day, so cool, so calm, so bright	88
Sweet dreams, form a shade	353
Sweet harmonist! and beautiful as sweet!	255
Sweet Saint who sate by Russell's side	363
Sweet, smiling village, loveliest of the lawn	299
Sweet was the sound, when oft at evening's close	296
Taint the Stage for some small snip of grain	207
Take, O take those lips away	44
Take starres for money; starres not to be told	90
Take thy way; for sure thy way is best	86
Tarts and custards, creams and cakes	137
Taught to join The varying verse	242
Teach me, my God and King	87
Teach me thy love to know	87
Tell me, dearest, what is love?	69
Tell me not, sweet, I am unkind	178
Th' adorning thee with so much art	186
That eagle's fate and mine are one	158
That every wight, in his degree	13
That fro the tyme that he first bigan	14
That han left hir song	19
That keep'st us chaste and free	68
That paint the voice, and silent speak to sight	263
That so He might be weak enough	77
That stubborn crew	151
That things of greatest, so of meanest worth	147
That very law which moulds a tear	369
That wear this world out to the ending doom	49
That which her slender waist confin'd	159
The broke heart of a nightingale	137
The cooly shade	40
The curfew tolls the knell of parting day	277
The curl'd drops, soft and slow	95
The fairest garden in her looks	189
The folk hire folwe wepinge in hir weye	13

INDEX OF FIRST WORDS

	PAGE
The friend of man, assign'd	280
The grete Emetraeus, the king of Inde	11
The guilty goddess of my harmful deeds	53
The harlot's cry from street to street	356
The heart when half wounded is changing	248
The huge dusk, gradual, swallows up the plain	261
Theie moved gentle oere the dewie meeds	324
The King of Terrors is the Prince of Peace	259
The lark begins his flight	114
The lonely mountains o'er	118
The meanest floweret of the vale	274
The mounting lark, day's herald, got on wing	129
Then hate me when thou wilt	52
Then let us like Horace and Lydia agree	224
The nursery of charms	247
The passing bell doth toll	141
The ploughman, near at hand	114
The poplars are fell'd	309
The redbreast oft, at evening hours	279
There is in love a sweetnesse readie penn'd	85
There never yet was woman made	170
The rosy hand that wear thee	62
The scar'd owl on pinions gray	320
The Shape—If shape it might be called	124
The soul, that drop, that ray	199
The still ruins of dejected Rome	264
The Sun's eye had a sickly glare	375
The sweets of love are mix'd with tears	140
The sweets of sense	287
The things which these proud men despise, and call	182
The thirsty earth soaks up the rain	190
The traveller thus, that o'er the midnight waste	319
The triumph o'er the timid hare	262
The twentieth year is well nigh past	310
The very dust we tread stirs as with life	365
The wall command	247

412 INDEX OF FIRST WORDS

	PAGE
The winds to blow the tedious night away	141
The wondrous softness of his heart	204
The world shall in its atoms end	231
They are all gone into the world of light!	109
They puff the heavy Goldsmith's line	331
They rake the green-appearing ground	260
They stand between the mountains and the sea	366
They were as children, and they fell at length	343
Think thee laid on thy death-bed, loose and slack	76
This small wind, which so sweete is	25
This thing call'd pain	150
Those heavenly attracts of yours, your eyes	149
Thou first shalt sigh, and say shee's fair	166
Though bush or floweret never grow	374
Though the sun be far	112
Thoughts that breathe, and words that burn	277
Though you be absent here, I needs must say	189
Thou most virtuous and most blessed	65
Thou, Scythian-like, dost round thy lands above	183
Thou so full of pity art—	110
Thou vermin slander, bred in abject mind	169
Through still silence of the night	68
Throughout the lanes she glides, at evening's close	341
Thy anger I could kiss, and will	104
Thy bosom is endeared with all hearts	50
Thy friend put in thy bosome; wear his eies	90
Thy joyous birdes shrouded in chearefull shade	38
Thy pictures look a voice	210
Thy pictures think, and we divine their thought	213
Tiger, Tiger, burning bright	355
'Tis merry in hall when beards wag all	45
'Tis surer much they brought thee there; and they	182
To all the country dear	299
To bed they creep	114
To help me through this long disease my life!	243
To hym that soe much dreaded dethe	329

INDEX OF FIRST WORDS

	PAGE
To live each day	341
Toll for the brave!	309
To measure all those wild diversities	98
Too low they build who build beneath the stars	259
To prevent The course of justice	303
To say, she lived a virgin chaste	198
To see a world in a grain of sand	360
To swell the riot of the autumnal feast	263
To the ocean now I fly	117
To this sad shrine, whoe'er thou art, draw near	241
Towered cities please us then	114
Tread lightly here, for here, 'tis said	369
Tread through the valleys, dance about the streams	131
Triumphal arch, that fill'st the sky	373
Truth is the trial of itself	57
Truths which, at Church, you might have heard in prose	253
Turning her wheel, without its spindles, round	340
Underneath this sable herse	59
Underneath this stone doth lie	58
Underneath this stone there lies	133
Under the greenwood tree	44
Unknown to fame—the passion of the groves	261
Unwept, without a crime	380
Vearse maie be goode, botte poesie wantes more	325
Wait on her to the park and play	224
Wake now, my Love, awake; for it is time	36
Waller, longs	289
Warm'd, while it lasts, by labour, all day long	311
We are Goddes stewards all, nete of oure owne we bare	324
Weave the warp, and weave the woof	272
Wee, modest, crimson-tipped flow'r	388
Weep no more, nor sigh, nor groan	66
Weep with me, all ye that read	58

INDEX OF FIRST WORDS

	PAGE
Wee, sleekit, cow'rin, tim'rous beastie	387
Wel loved he by the morwe a sop in wyn	15
Were there one whose fires	234
What can atone, oh, ever injured shade!	240
What do we here	358
Whate'er he did was done with so much ease	209
What is Hell?	259
What of Elysium's missing	177
What shall I do to be for ever known	191
What things have we seen	70
What wondrous life is this I lead?	201
When by a good man's grave I muse alone	369
When Dacia's sons, whose hair of blood-red hue	328
When fire and rushlight met his troubled eyes	343
When first thy sire to send on earth	273
When Freedom, dressed in blood-stained vest	324
When I am laid to rest hard by thy streams	102
When I see her, my sinewes shake for feare	24
When love with unconfinèd wings	178
When nature pleased, for life itself was new	363
When on my sickly couch I lay	231
When she ceas'd, we sighing saw	174
When the sweet limes, so full of bees in June	364
When to the sessions of sweet silent thought	50
When, twining subtle fears with hope	202
When you entombed in men's eyes shall lie	54
Where birds from heat or weather	134
Where blinks through paper'd panes the setting sun	347
Where'er the goddess roves	271
Where'er thy morning breath has played	374
Where first it sprang in beams	112
Where many a syren voice	365
Where may I find my shepherdess?	137
Where nut-brown draughts inspir'd	297
Where the bee sucks, there suck I	44
Where the Northern ocean, in vast whirls	261

INDEX OF FIRST WORDS

	PAGE
Where the remote Bermudas ride	200
Where the wild beasts find shelter, but I can find none	385
Where was inwoven many a gentle tale	266
Whether allured with my pipes delight	40
Which to bright science blooming fancy bore	263
While greasy Joan doth keel the pot	45
While, not dreaming ill	262
While wavering woods, and villages, and streams	260
Whilst your wishes and endeavours	387
Whistled as he went, for want of thought	216
Who can hope his line should long	155
Who charms us with his spleen	242
Whoe'er she be	99
Who ever saw a noble sight	210
Who, in times Dark and untaught	288
Who is Silvia? What is she	43
Whose arrows they would gladly stain!	156
Whose good grace was to open the scene	222
Whose lightning pierc'd th' Iberian lines	242
Whose purple blush the day foreshews	194
Whose subtle art invisibly can wreathe	199
Who stalks his round, an hideous form	279
Why do ye weep, sweet babes? Can tears	142
Why so pale and wan, fond Lover?	164, 167
Why wanders she a huntress wild	372
Wide o'er the fields of glory bear	207
Winter's voice, that storms around	290
With assuming pace, Cocks his broad hat	247
With a strong, and yet a gentle hand	156
With awe to look	340
With empty purse, and aching head	229
With his handkerchief of light	174
With how sad steps, O Moone, thou clim'st the skies!	26
Without the bed her other fair hand was	48
With sweetest milk and sugar first	198
Worn with cares and age	211

INDEX OF FIRST WORDS

	PAGE
Ye banks and braes o' bonnie Doon	385
Ye horrid towers, the abode of broken hearts	306
Ye Mariners of England!	377
Yet can I music too; but such	177
Yet do thy worst, old Time; despite thy wrong	54
Yet more pure, sweet, straight, and fair	197
You read with all the malice of a friend	256

END OF VOL. I

Oxford: Horace Hart, Printer to the University

CPSIA information can be obtained
at www.ICGtesting.com
Printed in the USA
BVHW090738220421
605543BV00001B/45

9 781010 139454